HARRAP'S

COMPUTERS
& THE INTERNET

DICTIONARY · DICCIONARIO
English-Spanish · Español-Inglés

HARRAP

First published in Great Britain in 2003
by Chambers Harrap Publishers Ltd.
7 Hopetoun Crescent
Edinburgh EH7 4AY
www.harrap.co.uk

Publicado en España por
SPES EDITORIAL, S.L
Aribau, 197-199, 3ª planta
08021 Barcelona
www.harraps.com

ISBN 0245 60712 9 (UK)
ISBN 84-8332-417-2 (España)

Depósito legal: B. 16.725-2003

Designed and typeset by Chambers Harrap Publishers Ltd, Edinburgh
Printed in Spain by A&M GRAFIC, S.L.

Contents
Índice

Editor/Redactor
José A. Gálvez

with/con
Teresa Álvarez
Joaquín Blasco
Amalia Jauri Gamba
Dileri Johnston
Óscar Ramírez Molina

Publishing Manager/Dirección editorial
Patrick White

Prepress/Preimpresión
David Reid

Preface

Computers have come to dominate both business and everyday life. This new dictionary covers the whole range of IT terminology, from business and personal computing to the Internet, desktop publishing (DTP), and telecommunications.

The Internet is becoming more and more a part of modern business life, as e-commerce revolutionizes the way business is conducted at the beginning of the 21st century. Users of this dictionary will find all the key terms in the dictionary itself, and will also find practical help in a guide on writing e-mails.

Because so many new terms are being invented in this area, it is difficult to know with certainty which terms and which usages will become accepted. Advice on usage is given in panels, with the heading FAQ, at certain entries.

Illustrative panels have been included throughout the text on the journey of an e-mail, printers, the Internet, networks, a multimedia computer and the Spanish and English keyboards, in order to give the reader further context.

Prefacio

La tecnología de la información ha pasado a dominar tanto el mundo de los negocios como la vida cotidiana. Este nuevo diccionario cubre todos los campos de la terminología informática, desde la informática personal y de negocios hasta la autoedición, pasando por las telecomunicaciones.

Internet es cada vez más una parte integral de la vida de las empresas modernas y el comercio electrónico está revolucionando la forma en la que se llevan a cabo los negocios en este comienzo del siglo XXI. Además del vocabulario sobre Internet que aparece en el texto del diccionario, en el suplemento aportamos consejos útiles sobre cómo redactar mensajes de correo electrónico.

En el área de la tecnología informática se están inventando nuevos términos constantemente, por lo que resulta difícil saber con certeza qué términos y qué usos van a perdurar a largo plazo. Acompañan al texto recuadros con explicaciones sobre el uso de algunos términos.

El lector encontrará información adicional en los paneles ilustrativos intercalados en el texto, que versan sobre el viaje de un mensaje de correo electrónico, impresoras, Internet, redes, el ordenador multimedia, y los teclados inglés y español.

Abbreviations and Labels
Abreviaturas y marcas

gloss [introduces an explanation]	=	glosa [introduce una explicación]
cultural equivalent [introduces a translation which has a roughly equivalent status in the target language]	≃	equivalente cultural [introduce un equivalente que tiene función similar en la lengua de destino]
abbreviation	*abbr, abrev*	abreviatura
adjective	*adj*	adjetivo
adverb	*adv*	adverbio
Latin American Spanish	*Am*	español de América
Andean Spanish	*Andes*	español andino
desktop publishing	*Autoedición*	autoedición
British English	*Br*	inglés británico
desktop publishing	*DTP*	autoedición
Peninsular Spanish	*Esp*	español peninsular
feminine	*f*	femenino
familiar	*Fam*	familiar
Internet-related term	*Internet*	término relacionado con Internet
Mexican Spanish	*Méx*	español de México
masculine and feminine noun [same form for both genders]	*mf*	nombre masculino y femenino [formas idénticas]
masculine and feminine noun [different form in the feminine]	*m,f*	nombre masculino y femenino [forma femenina diferente]
noun	*n*	nombre
feminine noun	*nf*	nombre femenino
feminine plural noun	*nfpl*	nombre femenino plural
masculine noun	*nm*	nombre masculino
masculine and feminine noun [same form for both genders]	*nmf*	nombre masculino y femenino [formas idénticas]
masculine and feminine noun [different form in the feminine]	*nm,f*	nombre masculino y femenino [forma diferente en el femenino]
masculine plural noun	*nmpl*	nombre masculino plural

plural	*pl*	plural
Argentinian, Uruguayan and Paraguayan Spanish	*RP*	español del Río de la Plata
telecommunications	*Tel*	telecomunicaciones
North American English	*US*	inglés americano
Venezuelan Spanish	*Ven*	español de Venezuela
intransitive verb	*vi*	verbo intransitivo
reflexive verb	*vpr*	verbo pronominal
transitive verb	*vt*	verbo transitivo
inseparable transitive verb [phrasal verb where the verb and the adverb or preposition cannot be separated, eg **go into**; he **went into** the program]	*vt insep*	verbo transitivo con partícula inseparable [por ejemplo, "**go into**" (entrar en); he **went into the program** (entró en el programa)]
separable transitive verb [phrasal verb where the verb and the adverb or preposition can be separated, eg **shut down**; 'he **shut** the computer **down** ' or '**he shut down** the computer']	*vt sep*	verbo transitivo con partícula separable [por ejemplo, "**shut down**" (apagar); "he **shut** the computer **down**"o "he **shut down** the computer" (apagó la computadora)]

abandon *vt (file, routine)* cancelar

abort 1 *n (of program)* cancelación *f*
2 *vt (program)* cancelar

.ac *Internet* = en las direcciones de Internet, abreviatura que designa las páginas de universidades y entidades educativas británicas

accelerate *vt (computer)* acelerar

acceleration *n* aceleración *f*

accelerator *n* acelerador *m*

◇ *accelerator board* placa *f* aceleradora

◇ *accelerator card* tarjeta *f* aceleradora

accent *n* acento *m*

Acceptable Use Policy *n Internet* = código de conducta definido por un proveedor de acceso a Internet

access 1 *n* acceso *m*; **to have access to the Internet** tener acceso a Internet; *Internet* **up to 56K access** conexión hasta 56k
2 *vt (data)* acceder a

◇ *access authorization* autorización *f* de acceso

◇ *access code* código *m* de acceso

◇ *access control* control *m* de acceso

◇ *access level (in network)* nivel *m* de acceso

◇ *Internet access number (to ISP)* número *m* de acceso

◇ *access privileges* privilegios *mpl* de acceso

◇ *Internet access provider* proveedor *m* de acceso

◇ *access speed* velocidad *f* de acceso

◇ *access time* tiempo *m* de acceso

account *n (with Internet service provider)* cuenta *f* (**with** con); **to set up an account with sb** abrir una cuenta con alguien

accounting program *n* programa *m* de contabilidad

accumulator *n* acumulador *m*

acknowledgement, *US* **acknowledgment** *n Internet* acuse *m* de recibo

ACL *n (abbr* **access control list)** lista *f* de control de accesos

acronym *n* siglas *fpl*, acrónimo *m*

activate *vt* activar

active *adj* activo(a)

◊ *active desktop (in Windows)* escritorio *m* activo

◊ *active file* archivo *m* activo

◊ *active matrix* matriz *f* activa

◊ *active matrix screen* pantalla *f* de matriz activa

◊ *active program* programa *m* activo

◊ *active window* ventana *f* activa

acute accent *n* acento *m* agudo

adapter, adaptor *n* adaptador *m*

◊ *adapter card* tarjeta *f* adaptadora

additive colour, *US* **additive color** *n DTP* color *m* aditivo

add-on *n* extra *m*, suplemento *m*

address 1 *n* dirección *f*
2 *vt* (**a**) *(message)* dirigir, direccionar (**b**) *(memory)* direccionar

◊ *address book (in e-mail program)* agenda *f*, libreta *f* de direcciones

◊ *address bus* bus *m* de direccionamiento *or* direcciones

◊ *address file* archivo *m* de direcciones

ADF *n* (*abbr* **automatic document feeder**) alimentador *m* automático de documentos

ADP *n* (*abbr* **automatic data processing**) proceso *m* or procesamiento *m* automático de datos

ADSL *n* (*abbr* **asymmetrical digital subscriber line**) ADSL *m*

◊ *ADSL line* línea *f* ADSL

advertising banner *n Internet (on web page)* banner *m* publicitario

adware *n Internet* software *m* espía

agent *n (software)* agente *m*

AGP *n* (*abbr* **accelerated graphics port**) puerto *m* de gráficos acelerado

AI *n* (*abbr* **artificial intelligence**) inteligencia *f* artificial

AIFF *n* (*abbr* **audio interchange file format**) AIFF

◊ *AIFF file* archivo *m* AIFF

airtime *n Tel* tiempo *m* de antena

◊ *airtime provider* proveedor *m* de telefonía móvil

alert box *n* mensaje *m* de alerta

ALGOL *n* (*abbr* **Algorithmic Oriented Language**) ALGOL *m*

algorithm *n* algoritmo *m*

algorithmic *adj* algorítmico(a)

alias *n* (**a**) *(in e-mail)* alias *m inv* (**b**) *(on desktop)* alias *m inv*

aliasing *n DTP* dientes *mpl* de sierra, dentado *m*

align *vt (characters, graphics)* alinear

alignment *n (of characters, graphics)* alineación *f*

allocate *vt (memory)* asignar

allocation *n (of memory)* asignación *f*

alphanumeric *adj* alfanumérico(a)

◇ *alphanumeric code* código *m* alfanumérico

◇ *alphanumeric field* campo *m* alfanumérico

◇ *alphanumeric keypad* teclado *m* alfanumérico

alphasort 1 *n* ordenación *f* alfabética; **to do an alphasort on sth** ordenar algo alfabéticamente

2 *vt* ordenar alfabéticamente

alpha version *n (of program)* versión *f* alfa

alt *n* **e acute is alt 130** para la e con acento hay que presionar alt 130

◇ *alt key* tecla *f* alt

.alt *Internet (abbr* **alternative)** *(in newsgroups)* = abreviatura que designa a los foros de discusión abiertos a temas alternativos

ALU *n (abbr* **Arithmetic Logic Unit)** UAL *f*

always-on *adj Internet* permanente

amazon *vt Internet* **to be amazoned** perder cuota de negocio ante un competidor electrónico

ampersand *n* signo *m* et, *Am* ampersand *m*

AMPS *n Tel (abbr* **Advanced Mobile Phone Standard)** AMPS *m*

analog(ue) *adj* analógico(a)

anchor *n Internet* anclaje *m*

animate *vt* animar

animated GIF *n Internet* GIF *m* animado

animation *n* animación *f*

anonymous FTP *n Internet* FTP *m* anónimo

ANSI *n (abbr* **American National Standards Institute)** = instituto estadounidense de normalización, *Esp* ≃ AENOR *m*

answering *adj*

◇ *answering machine* contestador *m* (automático)

◇ *answering service* servicio *m* de atención de llamadas *or Am* llamados, servicio *m* contestador

answer mode *n (of modem)* modo *m* de recepción (de llamadas)

answerphone *n Tel* contestador *m* (automático)

anti-aliasing *n DTP* suavizado *m* de contornos, antidentado *m*

anti-glare *adj*

◇ *anti-glare filter* filtro *m* de pantalla

◇ *anti-glare screen* filtro *m* de pantalla

anti-static *adj* antiestático(a)

antivirus *n* antivirus *m inv*

◇ *antivirus program* programa *m* antivirus

◇ *antivirus check* comprobación *f* antivirus

aperture priority *n DTP* prioridad *f* a la abertura

apostrophe *n* apóstrofo *m*

append *vt (list, document)* adjuntar; **to append a document**

to a file adjuntar un documento a un archivo

Apple menu *n (on Macintosh)* menú *m* Apple

applet *n Internet* applet *m*, pequeño programa *m*

application *n* aplicación *f*, programa *m*

◊ *application program* programa *m* de aplicación

◊ *application programming interface* interface *m or f* de programación de aplicaciones

◊ *application software* software *m* de aplicación

Archie *n Internet* Archie

architecture *n* arquitectura *f*

archive 1 *n* archivo *m*; **archive (copy)** copia *f* de archivo **2** *vt* archivar

◊ *Internet* **archive site** sitio *m* de archivos

area code *n US Tel* prefijo *m*, *Am* característica *f*

arithmetic logic unit *n* unidad *f* aritmético-lógica

array *n* matriz *f*, *Am* array *f*

arrow *n* flecha *f*

◊ *arrow key* tecla *f* de dirección *or* de movimiento del cursor

article *n Internet (in newsgroups)* artículo *m*

artificial intelligence *n* inteligencia *f* artificial

artwork *n DTP* ilustraciones *fpl*

ascending *adj* ascendente

◊ *ascending order* orden *m* ascendente

◊ *ascending sort* clasificación *f* por orden ascendente

ASCII *n (abbr* **American Standard Code for Information Interchange)** ASCII *m*

◊ *ASCII art* ilustraciones *fpl* en ASCII

◊ *ASCII code* código *m* ASCII

◊ *ASCII file* archivo *m* ASCII

◊ *ASCII text* texto *m* en ASCII

◊ *ASCII value* valor *m* ASCII

assembler *n (program)* ensamblador *m*, *Am* assembler *m*

assembly language *n* lenguaje *m* ensamblador, *Am* lenguaje *m* assembler

◊ *assembly language program* programa *m* en lenguaje ensamblador, *Am* programa *m* en lenguaje assembler

assistant *n (program)* asistente *m*

asterisk *n* asterisco *m*

asynchronous *adj* asíncrono(a)

◊ *asynchronous transfer mode* modo *m* asíncrono de transferencia

at *prep (in e-mail address)* arroba *f*; **"gwilson at transex, dot, co, dot, uk"** gwilson, arroba transex, punto, co, punto, uk

◊ *at sign* arroba *f*

ATM *n (abbr* **asynchronous transfer mode)** ATM *m*, modo *m* asíncrono de transferencia

attach *vt (file)* adjuntar (**to** a); **to attach a file to an e-mail**

adjuntar un archivo a un correo electrónico; **please find attached...** se adjunta...

attachment n (of e-mail) archivo m adjunto, anexo m

attribute n atributo m

audit trail n registro m de actividad

AUP n Internet (abbr **Acceptable Use Policy**) = código de conducta definido por un proveedor de acceso a Internet

authenticate vt autenticar

authentication n autenticación f

◇ **authentication certificate** certificado m de autenticación

◇ **authentication key** llave f de autenticación

authoring n

◇ **authoring language** lenguaje m de autor

◇ **authoring software** software m de autor

◇ **authoring tool** herramienta f de autor

authorization n autorización f

autocorrect vt corregir automáticamente

autocropping n DTP autorrecorte m

autodiagnosis n autodiagnóstico m

autoexec.bat n autoexec.bat m

autoflow n salto m automático de línea

automatic adj automático(a)

◇ **automatic data processing** proceso m or procesamiento m automático de datos

◇ Tel **automatic dialling** marcado m automático, marcación f automática, Andes, RP discado m automático

◇ **automatic document feeder** alimentador m automático de documentos

◇ **automatic feed** carga f automática

◇ **automatic pagination** paginación f automática

automation n automatización f

autoredial n Tel remarcado m automático, Andes, RP rediscado m automático

autoresponder n Internet generador m automático de respuestas

autosave 1 n autoguardado m **2** vt guardar automáticamente

autostart n autoarranque m, arranque m automático

available adj disponible; **available on CD-ROM** disponible en CD-ROM; **available on DVD, available in DVD format** disponible en DVD, disponible en formato DVD; **available for the Mac/PC** disponible para (el) Mac/PC; **available to download from our web site** puede ser descargado desde nuestro sitio web

◇ **available memory** memoria f disponible

avatar n Internet avatar m

B2B *adj* (*abbr* **business to business**) B2B, entre empresas

B2C *adj* (*abbr* **business to consumer**) B2C, de empresa a consumidor

back *adj*

◇ *Internet* **back button** botón *m* atrás

◇ *back end* (*of computer*) parte *f* trasera

▸ **back up 1** *vt sep* (*data, file*) hacer una copia de seguridad de (**to** en)
2 *vi* hacer una copia de seguridad (**to** en); **this medium is excellent for backing up** este sistema es excelente para hacer copias de seguridad

backbone *n Internet* red *f* troncal

background *n* (**a**) (*of program*) segundo plano *m*; **the program works in the background** el programa se ejecuta en segundo plano
(**b**) *DTP* fondo *m*

◇ *background job* tarea *f* en segundo plano

◇ *background (mode) printing* impresión *f* subordinada *or* en segundo plano

◇ *background task* tarea *f*

en segundo plano

backlight *n* (*of screen*) retroiluminación *f*

backlit *adj* (*screen*) retroiluminado(a)

backslash *n* barra *f* invertida

backspace *n* retroceso *m*

◇ *backspace key* tecla *f* de retroceso

backup *n* (*of data*) copia *f* de seguridad; **to do the backup** hacer la copia de seguridad; **the backup has failed** ha fallado la copia de seguridad

◇ *backup copy* copia *f* de seguridad

◇ *backup device* dispositivo *m* para copias de seguridad

◇ *backup drive* unidad *f* para copias de seguridad

◇ *backup file* copia *f* de seguridad

◇ *backup system* (*for doing the backup*) sistema *m* de copias de seguridad; (*auxiliary system*) sistema *m* auxiliar

backward-compatible *adj* compatible con versiones anteriores

backward search *n* búsqueda *f* hacia atrás

bad *adj* (*in error messages*)

◇ **bad command** comando *m* erróneo

◇ **bad file name** nombre *m* de archivo incorrecto

◇ **bad sector** sector *m* dañado

balloon help *n* globos *mpl* de ayuda

bandwidth *n* ancho *m* de banda

banner *n* Internet *(on web page)* banner *m*, pancarta *f* publicitaria

◇ **banner ad** banner *m* publicitario

bar *n (menu bar)* barra *f*

◇ **bar chart** gráfico *m* de barras

barebones system *n* sistema *m* básico

baseline *n* DTP línea *f* de base

BASIC *n* BASIC *m*

batch *n* lote *m*

◇ **batch file** fichero *m* por lotes

◇ **batch processing** proceso *m* por lotes

◇ **batch scanning** escaneo *m* por lotes

battery *n* batería *f*

◇ **battery pack** batería *f*

baud *n* baudio *m*; **at 58,600 baud** a 58.600 baudios

◇ **baud rate** velocidad *f* de transmisión

bay *n (for disk drive)* hueco *m*, bahía *f*

BBS *n* Internet *(abbr* **bulletin board system***)* BBS *f*

Bcc Internet *(abbr* **blind carbon copy***)* Cco

beeper *n (pager)* buscapersonas *m inv*, *Esp* busca *m*, *Méx* localizador *m*, *RP* radiomensaje *m*

benchmark *n* punto *m* de referencia

Bernoulli® *n*

◇ **Bernoulli® disk** disco *m* Bernoulli®

◇ **Bernoulli® drive** unidad *f* Bernoulli®

beta version *n (of program)* versión *f* beta

Bézier curve *n* DTP curva *f* de Bézier

bidirectional *adj* bidireccional

Big Blue *n* = nombre por el que se conoce a IBM

binary *adj* binario(a)

◇ **binary code** código *m* binario

◇ **binary digit** dígito *m* binario

◇ **binary file** archivo *m* binario

◇ **binary search** búsqueda *f* binaria

BinHex *(abbr* **Binary Hexadecimal***)* BinHex

BIOS *n (abbr* **Basic Input/Output System***)* BIOS *m or f*

bisync, bisynchronous *adj* bisíncrono(a)

bit *n* bit *m*; **bits per second** bits por segundo; **24-bit** de 24 bits

◇ **bit command** comando *m* binario

◇ **bit depth** *(of scanner, digital camera)* profundidad *f* de bits

bitmap **1** *n* mapa *m* de bits **2** *adj (image, font)* en mapa de bits

bit-mapped, bitmapped *adj (image, font)* en mapa de bits

blank *adj (screen)* en blanco; *(disk)* virgen; **blank unformatted disk** disco virgen sin formatear

blanking plate *n* tapa *f* posterior

bleed *n DTP* sangrado *m*

blend *n DTP* degradado *m*

blink rate *n (of cursor)* velocidad *f* de parpadeo

block **1** *n (of text)* bloque *m* **2** *vt (text)* seleccionar; **to block text** seleccionar un bloque de texto; **to block and copy** seleccionar y copiar

blocking software *n Internet* software *m* de control

Bluetooth *n Tel* Bluetooth *m*

BMP *(abbr bitmap)* BMP

board *n* placa *f*; **on board** instalado(a)

body *n (of letter, document, e-mail)* cuerpo *m*

bold **1** *n* negrita *f*; **in bold** en negrita **2** *adj* negrita; **bold face** *or* **type** letra negrita; **bold italics** cursiva en negrita

bolted-on *adj (software, function)* añadido(a)

bookmark **1** *n (for web page)* marcador *m*, favorito *m* **2** *vt* **to bookmark a page** añadir una página a la lista de marcadores; **don't forget to bookmark this page** no te olvides de añadir esta página a tu lista de marcadores

◇ **bookmark list** lista *f* de marcadores

Boolean *adj* booleano(a)

◇ **Boolean operator** operador *m* booleano

◇ **Boolean search** búsqueda *f* booleana

boot *vt (computer)* arrancar

◇ **boot disk** disco *m* de arranque

◇ **boot sector** sector *m* de arranque

▸ **boot up** **1** *vt sep (computer)* arrancar **2** *vi (of computer)* arrancar

bootable *adj (disk)* de arranque

border *n (of paragraph, cell)* borde *m*

borderless printing *n DTP* impresión *f* a sangre

bot *n Internet* robot *m*

bounce *Internet* **1** *n* **bounce(d) message** mensaje rebotado **2** *vi* rebotar

box *n* (**a**) *(for graphic)* caja *f* (**b**) *(computer)* caja *f*

bpi *n (abbr* **bits per inch***)* bpp

bps *n (abbr* **bits per second***)* bps

bracket *n* paréntesis *m inv*; **angle brackets** paréntesis angulares

branch *n (of network)* ramificación *m*, bifurcación *f*

break *n*

◇ **break character** carácter *m* de interrupción

◊ *break key* tecla *f* de interrupción

bricks and clicks company *n Internet* empresa *f* con presencia física y en Internet

bridge *n (in network)* puente *m*

brightness *n* brillo *m*

broadband *Tel* **1** *n* banda *f* ancha
2 *adj* de banda ancha

broadcast 1 *n* difusión *f*
2 *vt* emitir

broken link *n Internet* enlace *m* roto

browse 1 *vt* to browse the Net / Web navegar por Internet/la Web; to browse the contents of a hard disk navegar por los contenidos de un disco duro
2 *vi (on Internet)* navegar

▸ **browse through** *vt insep* navegar por

browser *n Internet* navegador *m*

browsing *n Internet* navegación *f*; fast/secure browsing navegación rápida/segura

BSI *n (abbr British Standards Institute)* = instituto británico de normalización, *Esp* ≃ AENOR *m*

bubble-jet printer *n* impresora *f* de inyección

bubble memory *n* memoria *f* de burbuja

buffer *n* buffer *m*, búfer *m*; buffer underrun *(message)*

saturación del buffer

◊ *buffer memory* memoria *f* buffer

bug *n* error *m*

bug-free *adj (program)* sin errores

bug-ridden *adj (program)* plagado(a) de errores

built-in *adj (incorporated)* incorporado(a)

built-to-order *adj* construido(a) a medida, construido(a) a la carta

bullet *n (symbol)* topo *m*, viñeta *f*

bulleted list *n* lista *f* con topos *or* viñetas

bulletin board service *n Internet* tablón *m* de anuncios electrónico

bundle 1 *n* paquete *m*, kit *m*
2 *vt (software)* it comes bundled with over \$2,000 worth of software viene acompañado de software valorado en más de 2.000 dólares

burn *vt (CD-ROM)* tostar, grabar

BURN-Proof® *adj* BURN-Proof®

bus *n* bus *m inv*

◊ *bus controller* controlador *m* del bus

business *n*

◊ *business computing* informática *f* de gestión *or Am* comercial

◊ *business graphics* gráficos *mpl* para presentaciones

busy *adj* (**a**) *US (telephone)* **the line** *or* **number is busy** (el teléfono) da ocupado, *Esp* (el teléfono) está comunicando; **I got the busy signal** daba ocupado, *Esp* comunicaba
(**b**) *(printer)* ocupado(a)

button *n (on mouse, screen)* botón *m*

buy wizard *n Internet* asistente *m* de compras

byte *n* byte *m*; (**eight-bit**) **byte** byte *m*

C++ *n (programming language)* C++ *m*

CA *n Internet (abbr* **certification authority**) autoridad *f* de certificación

cable modem *n* módem *m* cable

cabling *n* cableado *m*

cache 1 *n* caché *f*; **cache (memory)** (memoria *f*) caché *f*
2 *vt (data)* meter en la caché

CAD *n (abbr* **computer-assisted design**) CAD *m*

CAD/CAM *n (abbr* **computer-assisted design/computer-assisted manufacture**) CAD/CAM *m*

CAE *n (abbr* **computer-aided engineering**) ingeniería *f* asistida por *Esp* ordenador *or Am* computadora

CAI *n (abbr* **computer-aided instruction**) enseñanza *f* asistida por *Esp* ordenador *or Am* computadora

CAL *n (abbr* **computer-aided learning**) enseñanza *f* asistida por *Esp* ordenador *or Am* computadora

calculator *n* calculadora *f*

call 1 *n* llamada *f*, *Am* llamado *m*; **to take a call** contestar a una llamada *or Am* llamado; **to receive a call** recibir una llamada *or Am* llamado; **there was a call for you** te llamaron; *US* **to call collect** llamar a cobro revertido
2 *vt* **to call sb** llamar a alguien
3 *vi* llamar; **to call long-distance** *Esp* poner una conferencia, *Am* hacer un llamado de larga distancia

◇ *call barring* bloqueo *m or* restricción *f* de llamadas
◇ *call connection* establecimiento *m* de la conexión
◇ *call credit voucher* tarjeta *f* de prepago
◇ *call diversion* desvío *m* de llamada
◇ *call forwarding* desvío *m* de llamada
◇ *call forwarding service* servicio *m* de desvío de llamada
◇ *call screening* filtrado *m* de llamadas
◇ *call transfer* transferencia *f* de llamadas
◇ *call waiting service* servicio *m* de llamada en espera

▸**call up** *vt sep* (**a**) *(on telephone)* llamar (**b**) *(help screen, file)* visualizar

caller *n Tel*

◇ *caller display* identificador *m* de llamada

◇ *caller ID* identificador *m* de llamada

CAM *n* (*abbr* **computer-assisted manufacture**) CAM *f*

camera-ready copy *n* DTP copia *f* lista para ser filmada

cancel 1 *vt* cancelar; **cancel button** botón de cancelar
2 *vi* cancelar; **press 'esc' to cancel** presione 'esc' para cancelar; **cancel entry** (*command*) cancelar entrada

caps *npl* (*abbr* **capital letters**) (letras *fpl*) mayúsculas *fpl*

◇ *caps lock* mayúsculas *fpl* fijas

◇ *caps lock key* tecla *f* de mayúsculas fijas

capture 1 *n* (*of data*) captura *f*
2 *vt* (*data*) capturar

card *n* (*circuit board*) tarjeta *f*

◇ *card slot* ranura *f* para tarjeta

caret *n* signo *m* de intercalación

carpal tunnel syndrome *n* síndrome *m* del túnel carpiano

carriage return *n* retorno *m* de carro

carrier *n* (*for signal*) portadora *f*; **no carrier** (*message*) no hay portadora

◇ *carrier (detect) signal* señal *f* de portadora

◇ *carrier tone* tono *m* de portadora

cartridge *n* (*disk*) cartucho *m*; **ink/toner cartridge** cartucho de tinta/tóner

cascade style sheet *n* Internet hoja *f* de estilo en cascada

cascading menu *n* menú *m* en cascada

CASE *n* (*abbr* **computer-aided software engineering**) ingeniería *f* de sistemas asistida por *Esp* ordenador *or* Am computadora

case-insensitive *adj* que no distingue entre mayúsculas y minúsculas; **this URL is case-insensitive** esta URL no distingue entre mayúsculas y minúsculas

case-sensitive *adj* que distingue entre mayúsculas y minúsculas; **this e-mail address is case-sensitive** esta dirección de correo distingue entre mayúsculas y minúsculas, hay que respetar las mayúsculas y las minúsculas al escribir esta dirección de correo

casing *n* carcasa *f*

CASM *n* (*abbr* **computer-aided sales and marketing**) ventas *fpl* y márketing asistidos por *Esp* ordenador *or* Am computadora

cathode ray tube *n* tubo *m* de rayos catódicos

◇ *cathode ray tube monitor* monitor *m* con tubo de rayos catódicos

Cc Internet (*abbr* **carbon copy**) cc, copias a

CCD *n* (*abbr* **charge-coupled device**) CCD (**chip**) (chip *m*) CCD *m*

CD n (abbr **compact disc**) CD m

◇ **CD burner** tostadora f de CD

◇ **CD rewriter** regrabadora f de CD

◇ **CD writer** grabadora f de CD

CD-I, CDI n (abbr **compact disc interactive**) CD-I m

CD-R n (a) (abbr **compact disc recorder**) CD-R m (b) (abbr **compact disc recordable**) CD-R m

CD-ROM n (abbr **compact disc-read only memory**) CD-ROM m

◇ **CD-ROM burner** estampadora f de CD-ROM

◇ **CD-ROM drive** unidad f de CD-ROM

◇ **CD-ROM newspaper** periódico m en CD-ROM

◇ **CD-ROM reader** lector m de CD-ROM

◇ **CD-ROM recorder** grabadora f de CD-ROM

◇ **CD-ROM rewriter** regrabadora f de CD-ROM

◇ **CD-ROM writer** grabadora f de CD-ROM

CD-RW n (abbr **compact disc rewritable**) CD-RW m

◇ **CD-RW drive** unidad f de CD-RW

cedilla n cedilla f

cell n (a) (on spreadsheet) celda f (b) US (cellular phone) móvil m, Am celular m

cellphone, cellular phone n teléfono m móvil, Am teléfono m celular

central processing unit n unidad f central de proceso

centre, US **center** vt (text) centrar

certification authority n Internet autoridad f de certificación

CGA n (abbr **colour graphics adaptor**) CGA m

CGI n (a) Internet (abbr **common gateway interface**) CGI m, interfaz f común de pasarela (b) (abbr **computer-generated images**) imágenes fpl generadas por Esp ordenador or Am computadora

channel n (of communication, data flow, for IRC) canal m

character n carácter m; **characters per inch** caracteres por pulgada; **characters per second** caracteres por segundo

◇ **character code** código m de carácter

◇ **character generator** generador m de caracteres

◇ **character insert** inserción f de carácter

◇ **character map** mapa m de caracteres

◇ **character mode** modo m carácter

◇ **character recognition** reconocimiento m de caracteres

◇ **character set** juego m de caracteres

◇ **character smoothing** suavizado m de caracteres

◇ **character space** espacio m

◇ **character spacing** espaciado m de caracteres

◇ **character string** cadena f de caracteres

chart n gráfico m

chat *Internet* **1** *n* charla *f*, chat *m*

2 *vi* charlar, chatear

◇ *chat room* sala *f* de conversación *or* chat

◇ *chat software* software *m* de charla *or* chat

chatiquette *n Internet* chatiqueta *f*

check box *n* casilla *f* de verificación

checksum *n* suma *f* de comprobación *or* control

chip *n* chip *m*

chipset *n* chipset *m*

chooser *n* selector *m*

circuit *n* circuito *m*

◇ *circuit board* placa *f* de circuitos

circuitry *n* circuitería *f*

circular reference *n* referencia *f* circular

circumflex accent *n* acento *m* circunflejo

CISC *n* (*abbr* **complex instruction set computer**) CISC *m*

clamshell *n* (*type of mobile phone*) móvil *m or Am* celular *m* con tapa desplegable

clear *vt* borrar; **to clear the screen** borrar la pantalla

click 1 *n* clic *m*

2 *vt* hacer clic en, pinchar

3 *vi* hacer clic, pinchar (**on** en); **to click and drag** hacer clic y arrastrar, pinchar y arrastrar

clickable image *n Internet* imagen *f* interactiva

◇ *clickable image map* mapa *m* interactivo

click-and-mortar store *n Internet* tienda *f* con presencia física y en Internet

clickstream *n Internet* rastro *m* de clics

click-through *n Internet* clic *m* en un banner

◇ *click-through rate* número *m* de clics en banner

client *n* (*part of network*) cliente *m*

client-server *adj* cliente/servidor

◇ *client-server database* base *f* de datos cliente/servidor

◇ *client-server model* modelo *m* cliente/servidor

clip art *n* clip *m* art, imágenes *fpl* prediseñadas

clipboard *n* (*for cut text*) portapapeles *m inv*

clock *n* reloj *m*

◇ *clock speed* velocidad *f* del reloj

◇ *clock speed doubler* doblador *m* de la velocidad del reloj

clone *n* clónico *m, Am* clon *m*

close box *n* cuadro *m* de cierre

closing tag *n* etiqueta *f* de cierre

cluster *n* cluster *m*; (*of terminals*) agrupamiento *m*

CMYK *DTP* (*abbr* **cyan, magenta, yellow, black**) CMYK

.co *Internet* = en las direcciones

de Internet, abreviatura que utilizan las empresas británicas

coated paper n papel m couché or cuché

co-ax(ial) cable n cable m coaxial

COBOL n (abbr **Common Business-Oriented Language**) COBOL m

code 1 n código m; Tel (**dialling**) **code** prefijo m, Am característica f
2 vt codificar

codec n (abbr **compressor/decompressor**) compresor m descompresor

coded adj codificado(a)

coding n (a) (providing codes) codificación f (b) (system of codes) códigos mpl
◇ **coding error** error m de codificación

cold adj
◇ **cold boot** arranque m en frío, Am carga f fría
◇ **cold start** arranque m en frío, Am carga f fría

collapse vt (subdirectories) contraer

collate vt (documents, data) recopilar

collect call n US Tel llamada f or Am llamado m a cobro revertido

colon n (punctuation mark) dos puntos mpl

colour, US **color** n color m
◇ DTP **colour depth** profundidad f de color

◇ **colour display** monitor m en color, Am monitor m color
◇ **colour graphics** gráficos mpl en color
◇ **colour monitor** monitor m en color, Am monitor m color
◇ **colour printer** impresora f en color, Am impresora f color
◇ **colour printing** impresión m en color
◇ DTP **colour separation** separación f de colores
◇ DTP **colour temperature** temperatura f del color

column n (in table, spreadsheet) columna f
◇ **column graph** gráfico m de columnas

.com Internet = en las direcciones de Internet, abreviatura que utilizan las empresas

▶**come out** vi (exit) salir; **to come out of a document** salir de un documento

comma n coma f

command n comando m
◇ **command code** código m de comando
◇ **command file** archivo m de comandos
◇ **command interpreter** intérprete m de comandos
◇ **command key** tecla f de comando
◇ **command language** lenguaje m comando, lenguaje m de comandos
◇ **command line** línea f de comando
◇ **command processor** intérprete m de procesos

◇ *command sequence* secuencia *f* de comandos

commerce server *n Internet* servidor *m* de comercio electrónico

common gateway interface *n Internet* interfaz *m or f* común de pasarela

comms *n* comunicaciones *fpl*

◇ *comms package* paquete *m* de comunicaciones

◇ *comms port* puerto *m* de comunicaciones

communication *n*

◇ *communication network* red *f* de comunicaciones

◇ *communication protocol* protocolo *m* de comunicaciones

◇ *communications software* software *m* de comunicaciones

.comp *Internet* (*abbr* **computers**) (*in newsgroups*) = abreviatura que designa a los foros de discusión que versan sobre temas informáticos

compact 1 *n* **compact disc** disco *m* compacto
2 *vt (file)* compactar

◇ *compact disc interactive* disco *m* compacto interactivo

◇ *compact disc player* reproductor *m* de discos compactos

◇ *compact disc reader* lector *m* de discos compactos

◇ *compact disc recordable* disco *m* compacto grabable

◇ *compact disc recorder* grabadora *f* de discos compactos

◇ *compact disc rewritable* disco *m* compacto regrabable

◇ *compact disc rewriter* regrabadora *f* de discos compactos

◇ *compact disc writer* grabadora *f* de discos compactos

CompactFlash® card *n* tarjeta *f* CompactFlash®

compacting *n (of file)* compactación *f*

compatibility *n* compatibilidad *f*

compatible *adj* compatible (**with** con); **IBM-compatible** compatible IBM

◇ *compatible computer Esp* ordenador *m or Am* computadora *f* compatible

compile *vt* compilar

compiler *n* compilador *m*

compliant *adj* conforme (**with** a); **year 2000 compliant** adaptado al *or* a prueba del efecto 2000, *Am* año 2000 compatible

component *n* componente *m*

compose *vt (e-mail)* redactar

compress *vt (file)* comprimir

compressed *adj (file)* comprimido(a)

compression *n (of file)* compresión *f*

◇ *compression ratio* índice *m* de compresión

compressor/decompressor *n* compresor descompresor *m*

computer *n Esp* ordenador *m*, *Am* computadora *f*, *Am* computador *m*; **he works in computers** es informático; **to have sth on computer** tener algo en *Esp* el ordenador *or Am* la computadora; **to put sth on computer** meter algo en *Esp* el ordenador *or Am* la computadora

⋄ **computer analyst** analista *mf* informático(a)

⋄ **computer animation** animación *f* por *Esp* ordenador *or Am* computadora

⋄ **computer** *Br* **centre** *or US* **center** centro *m* de cálculo, *Am* centro *m* de cómputos

⋄ **computer department** departamento *m* de informática

⋄ **computer engineer** ingeniero(a) *m,f* informático(a)

⋄ **computer equipment** equipo *m* informático

⋄ **computer expert** experto(a) *m,f* informático(a)

⋄ **computer game** juego *m* de *Esp* ordenador *or Am* computadora

⋄ *Fam* **computer geek** fanático(a) *m,f* de la informática

⋄ **computer graphics** gráficos *mpl* informáticos; *(technique)* infografía *f*

⋄ **computer literacy** conocimientos *mpl* de informática

⋄ **computer network** red *f* informática

⋄ **computer operator** operador(ora) *m,f* de *Esp* ordenadores *or Am* computadoras

⋄ **computer printout** copia *f* impresa

⋄ **computer program** programa *m* informático

⋄ **computer programmer** programador(ora) *m,f* informático(a)

⋄ **computer programming** programación *f* (de *Esp* ordenadores *or Am* computadoras)

⋄ **computer rage** violencia *f* contra el equipamiento informático

⋄ **computer science** informática *f*

⋄ **computer scientist** informático(a) *m,f*

⋄ **computer simulation** simulación *f* por *Esp* ordenador *or Am* computadora

⋄ **computer system** sistema *m* informático

⋄ **computer technician** técnico(a) *m,f* informático(a)

⋄ **computer terminal** terminal *m* de *Esp* ordenador *or Am* computadora

⋄ **computer virus** virus *m inv* informático

computer-aided, computer-assisted *adj* asistido(a) por *Esp* ordenador *or Am* computadora

⋄ **computer-aided design** diseño *m* asistido por *Esp* ordenador *or Am* computadora

⋄ **computer-aided engineering** ingeniería *f* asistida por *Esp* ordenador *or Am* computadora

⋄ **computer-aided learning** enseñanza *f* asistida por *Esp* ordenador *or Am* computadora

⋄ **computer-aided manufacturing** fabricación *f* asistida por *Esp* ordenador *or Am* computadora

◇ *computer-aided presentation* presentación *f* asistida por *Esp* ordenador or *Am* computadora

◇ *computer-aided sales and marketing* ventas *fpl* y márketing asistidos por *Esp* ordenador or *Am* computadora

◇ *computer-aided translation* traducción *f* asistida por *Esp* ordenador or *Am* computadora

computer-based training *n* formación *f* asistida por *Esp* ordenador or *Am* computadora

computer-enhanced *adj* retocado(a) por *Esp* ordenador or *Am* computadora

computer-generated *adj* generado(a) por *Esp* ordenador or *Am* computadora

computer-integrated manufacturing *n* fabricación *f* asistida por *Esp* ordenador or *Am* computadora

computerization *n* (of organization, records etc) informatización *f*, *Am* computarización *f*, *Am* computadorización *f*

computerize *vt* (organization, filing system etc) informatizar, *Am* computarizar, *Am* computadorizar

computerized *adj* (system, records, information) informatizado(a), *Am* computarizado(a), *Am* computadorizado(a)

computer-literate *adj* to be computer-literate tener conocimientos de informática

computing *n* informática *f*, *Am* computación *f*; **she works in computing** trabaja en informática or *Am* computación

◇ *computing* *Br* **centre** or *US* **center** centro *m* de cálculo, *Am* centro *m* de cómputos

◇ *computing course* curso *m* de informática

◇ *computing skills* conocimientos *mpl* de informática

concatenated *adj* concatenado(a)

concatenation *n* concatenación *f*

condensed *adj* DTP (font, print) condensado(a)

conference *n* Internet (in newsgroup) conferencia *f*

◇ *Tel* **conference call** multiconferencia *f*

config.sys *n* config.sys *m*

configurable *adj* configurable

configuration *n* configuración *f*

configure *vt* configurar

confirm *vt* confirmar

conflict *n* conflicto *m*

congestion *n* congestión *f*

connect 1 *n* conexión *f*
2 *vt* (component, cable) conectar (**to** a)
3 *vi* (**a**) (component, cable) conectarse (**to** a) (**b**) (to Internet) conectarse (**to** a)

◇ *connect time* tiempo *m* de conexión

▸ **connect up** *vi* (to Internet) conectarse

connection n (a) *(of two components)* conexión f
(b) *Tel* conexión f; **we had a very bad connection** teníamos una conexión muy mala
(c) *(to Internet)* conexión f; **to establish a connection** establecer una conexión, conectarse; **to have a fast/slow connection** tener una conexión rápida/lenta

◇ *connection kit* kit m de conexión

connectivity n conectividad f

connector n conector m

console n (a) *(for gaming)* consola f (b) *Internet (advertising banner)* consola f

consumables npl consumibles mpl

content n *Internet* contenido m

◇ *content management system* sistema m de gestión de contenidos

◇ *content provider* proveedor m de contenidos

context-sensitive help n ayuda f contextual

continuous adj continuo(a)

◇ *continuous mode* modo m continuo

◇ *continuous paper or stationery* papel m continuo

◇ *DTP continuous tone* tono m continuo

contrast n contraste m

control n *(key)* (tecla f de) control m

◇ *control character* carácter m de control

◇ *control key* tecla f de control

◇ *control panel* panel m de control

controller n controlador(ora) m,f

conventional memory n memoria f convencional

conversational adj *(mode)* conversacional

conversion n conversión f

◇ *conversion program* programa f de conversión

◇ *conversion software* software m de conversión

convert vt *(file, document)* convertir (**to/into** en)

cookie n *Internet* cookie m or f

◇ *cookie file* archivo m cookie

co-processor, coprocessor n coprocesador m

copy n *(of document, letter)* copia f; **to make a copy of sth** hacer una copia de algo
2 vt (a) *(document, letter)* copiar (b) *(computer file, text)* copiar; **to copy sth to disk** copiar algo a un disco; **to copy and paste sth** copiar y pegar algo
3 vi **to copy and paste** copiar y pegar

◇ *copy and paste* copiar y pegar m

◇ *copy block* copia f de bloque

◇ *copy disk* disco m de copia

◇ *copy protection* protección f contra copia

copy-protect vt proteger contra copia

copy-protected adj protegido(a) contra copia

cordless *adj* inalámbrico(a)

◇ **cordless keyboard** teclado *m* inalámbrico

◇ **cordless mouse** *Esp* ratón *m* inalámbrico, *Am* mouse *m* inalámbrico

◇ **cordless telephone** teléfono *m* inalámbrico

corrupt 1 *adj (disk, file)* dañado(a)
2 *vt (disk, file)* dañar

corruption *n (of disk, file)* corrupción *f*

counter *n (on web page)* contador *m*

country code *n (on web address)* código *m* de país

courseware *n* software *m* didáctico

coverage *n Tel* cobertura *f* por habitante

cover page, cover sheet *n (of fax)* página *f* de portada

cpi *(abbr* **characters per inch)** cpp

CPM *n Internet (abbr* **cost per thousand)** costo *m or Esp* coste *m* por mil

◇ **CPM rate** tarifa *f* por mil impresiones

cps *(abbr* **characters per second)** cps

CPU *n (abbr* **central processing unit)** CPU *f*, UCP *f*

crack 1 *n (program)* crack *m*, = programa utilizado para desproteger otro programa
2 *vt* desproteger

cracker *n* cracker *mf*, pirata *mf* informático(a)

cracking *n* pirateo *m*

cradle *n (for telephone receiver)* soporte *m*, base *f*

crash 1 *n (of computer)* bloqueo *m*, caída *f*; *(of system)* caída *f*
2 *vi (computer network, system)* bloquearse, caerse; *(computer)* colgarse

crawler *n Internet* rastreador *m*

CRC *n DTP (abbr* **camera-ready copy)** copia *f* lista para ser filmada

crop *vt DTP (graphic)* recortar

◇ **crop mark** marca *f* de (re)corte

cross-platform *adj* multiplataforma *inv*

cross-post *vt Internet* hacer un envío masivo de

crossposting *n Internet* = envío masivo de mensajes por correo electrónico a diferentes foros

cross-refer *vt* remitir

cross-reference *n* remisión *f*, *Am* referencia *f* cruzada

CRT *n (abbr* **cathode ray tube)** TRC *m*, tubo *m* de rayos catódicos

crunch *vt (numbers, data)* devorar

cryptographic key *n Internet* llave *f* criptográfica

cryptography *n* criptografía *f*

CSP *n Internet (abbr* **commerce services provider)** servidor *m* de servicios de comercio electrónico

CTR *n Internet (abbr* **Click-Through Rate)** número *m* de clics en banner

curly quotes *n* comillas *fpl* tipográficas

cursor *n* cursor *m* ; **to move the cursor to the right/left** mover el cursor a la derecha/izquierda ; **the word where the cursor is** la palabra en la que se encuentra el cursor

◇ *cursor blink rate* velocidad *f* de parpadeo del cursor

◇ *cursor control* control *m* del cursor

◇ *cursor key* tecla *f* de cursor

◇ *cursor movement* movimiento *m* de cursor

◇ *cursor position* posición *f* de cursor

CU-See Me *n Internet* programa *m* de videoconferencias CU-See Me

customizable *adj (menu, program)* personalizable

customize *vt (menu, program)* personalizar

cut 1 *vt* cortar; **to cut and paste sth** cortar y pegar algo
2 *vi* **to cut and paste** cortar y pegar

◇ *cut sheet feed* alimentación *f* hoja a hoja

◇ *cut sheet feeder* alimentador *m* hoja a hoja

cyberbanking *n* banca *f* electrónica

cybercafe *n* cibercafé *m*

cybercrime *n* cibercrimen *m*

cyberculture *n* cibercultura *f*

cybermall *n* centro *m* comercial electrónico

cybermoney *n* ciberdinero *m*

cybernaut *n* cibernauta *mf*

cybernetic *adj* cibernético(a)

cybernetics *n* cibernética *f*

cyberporn *n* ciberporno *m*

cyberpunk *n* ciberpunk *m*

cybersex *n* cibersexo *m*

cyberspace *n* ciberespacio *m* ; **in cyberspace** en el ciberespacio

cybersquatter *n* = persona que ocupa ilegalmente un dominio, *Esp* ciberokupa *mf*

cybersquatting *n* ocupación *f* ilegal de dominios, *Esp* ciberokupación *f*

cycle *n* ciclo *m*

daisy-chain *vt* conectar en bucle

daisy-chaining *n* conexión *f* en bucle

daisy-wheel printer *n* impresora *f* de margarita

dash *n (symbol)* guión *m*; *DTP* **em-dash** guión *m* m, raya *f*; *DTP* **en-dash** guión *m* n, signo *m* menos

DAT *n (abbr digital audio tape)* cinta *f* digital de audio, DAT *f*

◇ **DAT cartridge** cartucho *m* DAT

◇ **DAT drive** unidad *f* DAT

data *n* datos *mpl*; **an item of data** un dato; **to collect data on sb/sth** reunir datos sobre alguien/algo

◇ **data acquisition** recogida *f* de datos

◇ **data analysis** análisis *m inv* de datos

◇ **data bank** banco *m* de datos

◇ **data bus** bus *m* de datos

◇ **data capture** recogida *f* de datos

◇ **data collection** recogida *f* de datos

◇ **data communications** transmisión *f* (electrónica) de datos

◇ **data compression** compresión *f* de datos

◇ **data encryption** encriptación *f* de datos

◇ **data entry** introducción *f* de datos

◇ **data exchange** intercambio *m* de datos

◇ **data input** entrada *f* de datos

◇ **data link** enlace *m* para transmisión de datos

◇ **data loss** pérdida *f* de datos

◇ **data management** gestión *f* de datos

◇ **data mining** minería *f* de datos

◇ **data path** ruta *f* de acceso a los datos

◇ **data privacy** confidencialidad *f* de los datos

◇ **data processing** proceso *m* *or* procesamiento *m* de datos

◇ **data processor** procesador *m* de datos

◇ **data protection** protección *f* de datos

◇ **Data Protection Agency** Agencia *f* de Protección de Datos

◇ **data recovery** recuperación *f* de datos

◇ **data security** seguridad *f* de los datos

◇ **data set** conjunto *m* de datos

◇ **data storage** almacenamiento *m* de datos

◇ **data traffic** tráfico *m* de datos

◇ **data transfer** transferencia *f* de datos

◇ **data transfer rate** velocidad *f* de transferencia de datos

◇ **data warehouse** almacén *m* de datos

databank *n* banco *m* de datos

database *n* base *f* de datos; **to enter sth into a database** introducir algo en una base de datos

◇ **database administrator** administrador *m* de bases de datos

◇ **database integration** integración *f* de bases de datos

◇ **database management** gestión *f* de bases de datos

◇ **database management system** sistema *m* de gestión de bases de datos

datacomms *n* transmisión *f* de datos

◇ **datacomms software** software *m* de transmisión de datos

dataglove *n* guante *m* de datos

datagram *n* *Internet* datagrama *m*

dbase *n* (*abbr* **database**) base *f* de datos

DBMS *n* (*abbr* **database management system**) sistema *f* de gestión de bases de datos

DD *n* (*abbr* **double density**) doble densidad *f*

DDE *n* (*abbr* **dynamic data exchange**) intercambio *m* dinámico de datos

DDR RAM *n* (*abbr* **double data-rate random access memory**) RAM *f* DDR

dead *adj* (*not working*) **the phone/line is dead** no hay línea, *RP* da muerto

debugger *n* (*program*) depurador *m*, *Am* debugger *m*

debugging *n* (*of program*) depuración *f*, *Am* debugging *m*

decode *vt* descodificar, decodificar; **the file is automatically decoded when it is received** el archivo se descodifica *or* decodifica automáticamente al recibirse

decoder *n* descodificador *m*, decodificador *m*

decoding *n* descodificación *f*, decodificación *f*

decompress *vt* (*file*) descomprimir

decompressed *adj* (*file*) descomprimido(a)

decrypt *vt* descifrar, desencriptar

decryption *n* descifrado *m*, desencriptado *m*

dedicated *adj* (*terminal*) dedicado(a)

◇ **dedicated line** línea *f* dedicada

◇ **dedicated word processor** procesador *m* de textos

default 1 *n* **by default** por defecto, predeterminado(a)
2 *vi* **to default to sth** seleccionar algo por defecto

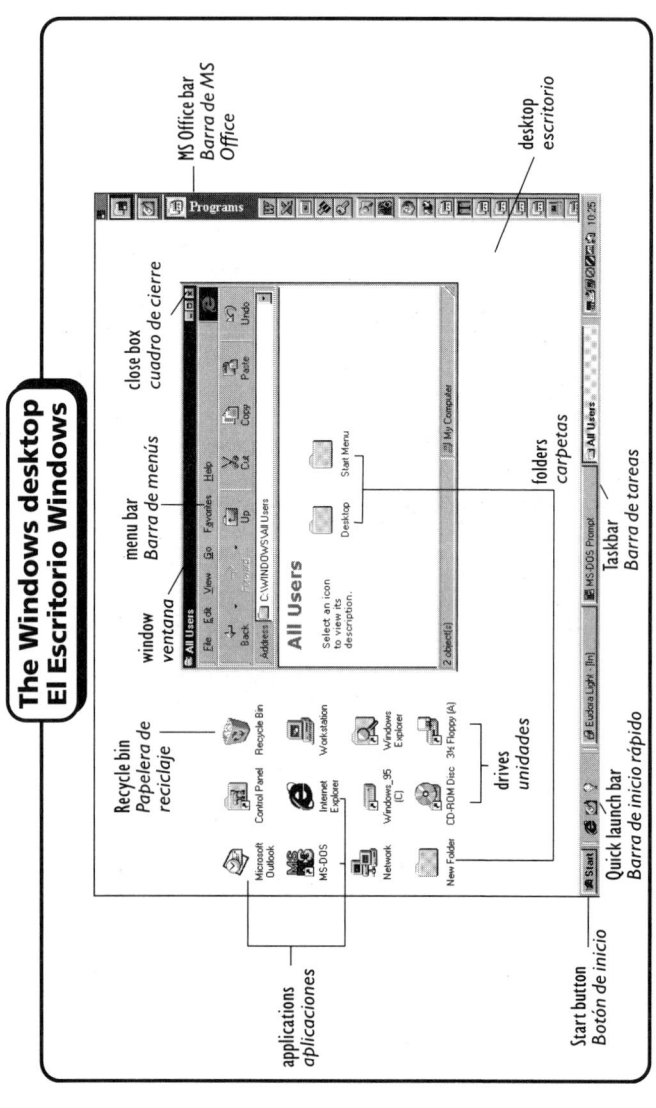

The Windows desktop
El Escritorio Windows

MS Office bar
Barra de MS Office

desktop
escritorio

close box
cuadro de cierre

menu bar
Barra de menús

window
ventana

folders
carpetas

Taskbar
Barra de tareas

Recycle bin
Papelera de reciclaje

drives
unidades

Quick launch bar
Barra de inicio rápido

Start button
Botón de inicio

applications
aplicaciones

All Users

Select an icon to view its description.

Desktop   Start Menu

◇ *default drive* unidad *f* (de disco) por defecto *or* predeterminada

◇ *default font* fuente *f* por defecto *or* predeterminada

◇ *default setting* valor *m* por defecto *or* predeterminado

◇ *default value* valor *m* por defecto *or* predeterminado

define *vt (value)* definir

definition *n* definición *f*

defragment *vt* desfragmentar

defragmentation *n* desfragmentación *f*

defragmenter *n* desfragmentador *m*

degaussing *n* desmagnetización *f*

deinstall *vt* desinstalar

deinstallation *n* desinstalación *f*

deinstaller *n* desinstalador *m*

delete 1 *vt* borrar
2 *vi* borrar

◇ *delete key* tecla *f* de suprimir *m*

deletion *n* borrado *m*

del key *n* tecla *f* de suprimir

delimit *vt (field)* delimitar

delimiter *n (of field)* delimitador *m*

demo *n (abbr* demonstration) demo *f*; **we have received a demo of the new software** hemos recibido una versión demo *or* de demostración del nuevo software

◇ *demo disk* disco *m* demo *or* de demostración

◇ *demo version* versión *f* demo *or* de demostración

demodulator *n* demodulador *m*

density *n* densidad *f*

depth of field *n DTP* profundidad *f* de campo

descending *adj* descendente

◇ *descending order* orden *m* descendente

◇ *descending sort* clasificación *f* por orden descendente

descriptor *n* descriptor *m*

deselect *vt* deseleccionar

desk accessory *n* accesorio *m* de escritorio

desktop *n (screen area)* escritorio *m*; **you will find the icon on your desktop** el icono aparece en el escritorio

◇ *desktop calculator* calculadora *f* de escritorio

◇ *desktop computer or PC Esp* ordenador *m* de sobremesa, *Am* computadora *f* de sobremesa

◇ *desktop publishing* autoedición *f*

◇ *desktop publishing operator* autoeditor(ora) *m,f*

◇ *desktop publishing package* programa *m* de autoedición

destination *n* destino *m*

◇ *destination disk* disco *m* de destino

◇ *destination drive* unidad *f* (de disco) de destino

develop *vt* desarrollar

developer n desarrollador(ora) m,f

device n (peripheral) dispositivo m, periférico m

◇ **device driver** controlador m de dispositivos or periféricos

◇ **device manager** administrador m de dispositivos or periféricos

DHCP n Internet (abbr **Dynamic Host Configuration Protocol**) protocolo m de configuración de anfitriones dinámicos

diagnostic n diagnóstico m

◇ **diagnostic disk** disco m de diagnóstico

◇ **diagnostic program** programa m de diagnóstico

dial vt (telephone number) marcar, Andes, RP discar; **to dial a number** marcar or Andes, RP discar un número; **the number you have** Br **dialled** or US **dialed has not been recognized** el número marcado no existe

◇ Br **dial code** prefijo m (telefónico), Am característica f

◇ US **dial tone** tono m (de marcar)

dialling n Tel

◇ **dialling code** prefijo m (telefónico), Am característica f

◇ Br **dialling tone** prefijo m telefónico), Am característica f

dialogue, US **dialog** n diálogo m

◇ **dialogue box** cuadro m de diálogo

◇ **dialogue mode** modo m diálogo

dial-up n Internet

◇ **dial-up access** acceso m telefónico or por línea conmutada

◇ **dial-up account** cuenta f telefónica or por línea conmutada

◇ **dial-up connection** conexión f telefónica or por línea conmutada

Dictaphone® n dictáfono m

digest n Internet (of newsgroup, mailing list) resumen m

digicash n dinero m electrónico

digit n dígito m

digital adj digital

◇ **digital analog(ue) converter** convertidor m analógico digital

◇ **digital audio tape** cinta f digital de audio

◇ **digital camera** cámara f digital

◇ Internet **digital cash** dinero m digital

◇ Internet **digital certificate** certificado m digital

◇ **digital display** monitor m digital

◇ **digital imaging** fotografía f digital

◇ **digital photography** fotografía f digital

◇ **digital signal** señal f digital

◇ **digital signal processing** procesado m digital de señales

◇ **digital signal processor** procesador m digital de señales

◇ Internet **digital signature** firma f electrónica

◇ **digital tape** cinta f digital

◇ *digital versatile disk* disco m versátil digital

◇ *digital video* Esp vídeo m or Am video digital

◇ *digital video camera* cámara f de Esp vídeo or Am video digital

◇ *digital video disk* disco m de Esp vídeo or Am video digital

◇ Internet *digital wallet* billetera f digital

◇ *digital zoom* zoom m digital

digitally adv digitalmente

digitize vt (data) digitalizar

digitizer n digitalizador m

DIMM n (abbr **dual in-line memory module**) DIMM m

dingbat n (carácter m) dingbat m

DIP switch n interruptor m DIP or basculante

dir n (abbr **directory**) directorio m

direct line n Tel línea f directa

directory n (a) (of files) directorio m (b) (of telephone numbers) guía f (telefónica), listín m (de teléfonos), Am directorio m de teléfonos

◇ US *directory assistance* (servicio m de) información f telefónica

◇ Br *directory enquiries* (servicio m de) información f telefónica

◇ *directory structure* estructura f de directorio

◇ *directory tree* árbol m de directorios

disable vt (option) desactivar

disabled adj (option) desactivado(a)

disconnect vt (machine) desconectar

discussion n Internet discusión f

◇ *discussion group* grupo m de discusión

◇ *discussion list* lista f de discusión

disintermediation n Internet eliminación f de intermediarios

disk n disco m; (floppy) disco m, disquete m; **to get sth on disk** poner algo en un disco

◇ *disk access time* tiempo m de acceso al disco

◇ *disk box* caja f en forma de disco

◇ *disk capacity* capacidad f del disco

◇ *disk controller* controlador m del disco

◇ *disk controller card* tarjeta f controladora del disco

◇ *disk drive* unidad f de disco, disquetera f

◇ *disk fragmentation* fragmentación f del disco

◇ *disk mailer* sobre m para el envío de discos

◇ *disk memory* memoria f de disco

◇ *disk operating system* sistema m operativo de disco

◇ *disk space* espacio m en disco

diskette n disquete m; **on diskette** en disquete

◇ *diskette box* caja f de disquetes

disk-to-disk copy n copia f de disco a disco

display 1 n (screen) pantalla f **2** vt visualizar

◇ *display area* área f de visualización

◇ *display card* tarjeta f de monitor

◇ *display unit* monitor m

distributed database n base f de datos distribuida

distribution list n Internet lista f de distribución

dithering n DTP difuminado m

DLL n (abbr **dynamic link library**) DLL f

◇ *DLL file* archivo m DLL

DNS n Internet (abbr **Domain Name System**) DNS m, sistema m de nombres de dominio

◇ *DNS parking* reserva f de nombres de dominio

docking station n (for notebook) estación f base

document n documento m

◇ *document file* documento m

◇ *document reader* digitalizador m, lector m de documentos

documentation n documentación f

dollar sign n símbolo m or signo m del dólar

domain n Internet dominio m

◇ *domain hosting* alojamiento m de dominios

◇ *domain name* nombre m de dominio

◇ *Domain Name System* Sistema m de Nombres de Dominio

dongle n llave f de hardware, mochila f

DOS n (abbr **disk operating system**) DOS m

◇ *DOS command* comando m DOS

◇ *DOS prompt* indicador m or señal f de DOS

dot n punto m; "gwilson at transex, dot, co, dot, uk" g, wilson, arroba, transex, punto, co, punto, uk

◇ Internet *dot com* punto com f

◇ Internet *dot com company* empresa f punto com

◇ *dots per inch* puntos mpl por pulgada

dot-matrix printer n impresora f matricial or de agujas, Am impresora f de matriz de puntos

dotted quad n Internet dirección f IP

double-click 1 n doble clic m **2** vt hacer doble click en **3** vi hacer doble click (**on** en)

double-density disk n disco m de doble densidad

down adj (not working) **to be down** (computer) no funcionar; **the network is down** se ha caído la red; **the lines are down** no hay línea

◇ *down arrow* flecha f abajo

◇ *down arrow key* tecla f de flecha abajo

download Internet **1** n descarga f **2** vt descargar, bajar

3 *vi* descargarse; **graphic files take a long time to download** los archivos gráficos tardan mucho en descargarse

downloadable *adj* descargable

◇ *downloadable font* fuente *f* descargable

downtime *n* (*of machine*) paro *m* técnico

downward-compatible *adj* compatible con versiones anteriores

DP *n* (*abbr* **data processing**) proceso *m* de datos

dpi (*abbr* **dots per inch**) ppp

draft *n* borrador *m*

◇ *draft mode* modo *m* borrador

◇ *draft printout* impresión *f* en borrador

◇ *draft quality* (*of printout*) calidad *f* borrador

◇ *draft quality printing* impresión *f* en calidad borrador

◇ *draft version* borrador *m*

drag **1** *vt* (*icon*) arrastrar
2 *vi* **to drag and drop** arrastrar y soltar

drag-and-drop *n* arrastrar y soltar *m*

DRAM *n* (*abbr* **dynamic random access memory**) DRAM *f*

draw program *n* programa *m* de dibujo

drive *n* (*for disk*) unidad *f*; **a:/c: drive** unidad a:/c:

driver *n* (*software*) controlador *m*, driver *m*

drop *vt* (*icon*) soltar

drop cap *n* DTP letra *f* capitular

drop-down menu *n* menú *m* desplegable

drum scanner *n* DTP escáner *m* de tambor

DSL *n* (*abbr* **Digital Subscriber Line**) línea *f* digital por suscripción

DSP *n* (**a**) (*abbr* **digital signal processing**) procesado *m* digital de señales (**b**) (*abbr* **digital signal processor**) procesador *m* digital de señales

DTP *n* (*abbr* **desktop publishing**) autoedición *f*

◇ *DTP operator* autoeditor(ora) *m,f*

◇ *DTP software* software *m* de autoedición

dual-band *adj* Tel de banda dual

dual-mode *adj* Tel de modo doble

dump **1** *n* (**memory**) **dump** volcado *m* de memoria; (**screen**) **dump** pantallazo *m*, captura *f* de pantalla
2 *vt* (*memory*) volcar

duplex *n* dúplex *m*

DVD *n* (*abbr* **digital video disk**, **digital versatile disk**) DVD *m*

◇ *DVD drive* unidad *f* de DVD

◇ *DVD recordable* DVD *m* regrabable

◇ *DVD recorder* grabadora *f* de DVD

◇ *DVD rewritable* DVD *m* reescribible

◇ *DVD writer* grabadora *f* de DVD

DVD-R *n* (*abbr* **digital video disk-recordable**) DVD-R *m*

DVD-RAM *n* (*abbr* **digital video disk-random access memory**) DVD-RAM *f*

◇ *DVD-RAM drive* unidad *f* de DVD-RAM

DVD-ROM *n* (*abbr* **digital video disk-read only memory**) DVD-ROM *f*

◇ *DVD-ROM drive* unidad *f* de DVD-ROM

DVD-RW *n* (*abbr* **digital video disk-rewritable**) DVD-RW *m*

dynamic *adj* dinámico(a)

◇ *dynamic data exchange* intercambio *m* dinámico de datos

◇ *Internet* **dynamic HTML** HTML *m* dinámico

◇ *dynamic RAM* RAM *f* dinámica

Easter egg *n (program)* huevo *m* de Pascua

e-billing *n Internet* facturación *f* electrónica

e-book *n* libro *m* electrónico

EBPP *n Internet (abbr electronic bill presentment and payment)* facturación *f* electrónica

e-business *n Internet* comercio *m* electrónico

e-cash *n Internet* dinero *m* electrónico

echo *n* eco *m*

e-commerce *n Internet* comercio *m* electrónico
◇ *e-commerce site* sitio *m* de comercio electrónico

edge-to-edge printing *n DTP* impresión *f* a sangre

EDI *n Internet (abbr electronic data interchange)* EDI *m*, intercambio *m* electrónico de datos

edit **1** *n (menu heading)* edición *f*
2 *vt (text)* editar
◇ *edit keys* teclas *fpl* de edición
◇ *edit mode* modo *m* de edición

editing *n* edición *f*

editor *n (software)* editor *m*

EDO RAM *n (abbr extended data-out random access memory)* EDO RAM *f*

.edu *Internet* = en las direcciones de Internet, abreviatura que designa las páginas de universidades y entidades educativas

efficiency *n (of machine)* eficacia *f*

efficient *adj (machine)* eficaz

EFT *n Internet (abbr electronic funds transfer)* transferencia *f* electrónica de fondos

EFTPOS *n Internet (abbr electronic funds transfer at point of sale)* transferencia *f* electrónica de fondos en el punto de venta

EGA *(abbr enhanced graphics adaptor)* EGA

eject button *n* botón *m* de expulsión

electronic **1** *adj* electrónico(a)
2 *n* **electronics** electrónica *f*
◇ *electronic banking* banca *f* electrónica
◇ *Internet* *electronic billing* facturación *f* electrónica
◇ *electronic book* libro *m* electrónico

The Journey of an E-mail

1 Your computer

Your journey through the Internet begins in your computer. An **e-mail client** is used to write and send e-mail messages. The completed message travels between your computer and your **Internet Service Provider's** server via a telephone line through a **modem**, an **ADSL line** or an **ISDN** connection.

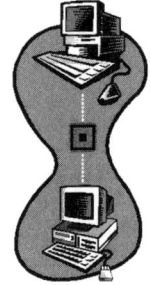

2 Your Internet Service Provider (ISP)

Your ISP acts as an intermediary between you and the Internet. When a message arrives at your ISP, a **router** redirects it to one of the Internet **backbones** - the real information highway.

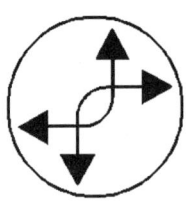

3 On the Internet

Data travels on the Net from router to router. Each time your message arrives at a router, it will be redirected to another router, getting closer each time to its destination. The longer the distance, the higher the number of routers through which your message may have to go.

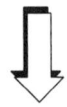

4 The end of the trip

At the end of the process, your message arrives at your recipient's ISP router where it can be collected. Depending on the traffic conditions on the Net, and the distance travelled, the whole trip can take anything from a few seconds to several hours.

◇ Internet **electronic business** comercio *m* electrónico

◇ Internet **electronic cash** dinero *m* electrónico

◇ Internet **electronic catalogue** catálogo *m* electrónico

◇ Internet **electronic commerce** comercio *m* electrónico

◇ **electronic crime** delito *m* electrónico

◇ Internet **electronic data interchange** intercambio *m* electrónico de datos

◇ **electronic data processing** tratamiento *m* or procesamiento *m* electrónico de datos

◇ Internet **electronic funds transfer** transferencia *f* electrónica de fondos

◇ Internet **electronic funds transfer at point of sale** transferencia *f* electrónica de fondos en el punto de venta

◇ Internet **electronic journal** periódico *m* electrónico

◇ Internet **electronic mail** correo *m* electrónico

◇ Internet **electronic mailbox** buzón *m* electrónico, *Am* casilla *f* de correo electrónico

◇ Internet **electronic mall** centro *m* comercial electrónico

◇ Internet **electronic marketing** márketing *m* electrónico

◇ **electronic media** medios *mpl* de comunicación electrónicos

◇ Internet **electronic money** dinero *m* electrónico

◇ **electronic office** oficina *f* informatizada *or* electrónica

◇ Internet **electronic payment system** sistema *m* de pago electrónico

◇ Internet **electronic point of sale** punto *m* de venta electrónico

◇ Internet **electronic publishing** edición *f* electrónica

◇ Internet **electronic purse** monedero *m* electrónico

◇ Internet **electronic shopping** compras *fpl* en línea

◇ Internet **electronic signature** firma *f* electrónica

◇ **electronic viewfinder** visor *m* electrónico

e-mail **1** *n* (system, message) correo *m* electrónico, e-mail *m*; **to contact sb by e-mail** ponerse en contacto con alguien por correo electrónico; **to send sth by e-mail** enviar algo por correo electrónico

2 *vt* (person) enviar un correo electrónico a; (document)

---

faq

¿**e-mail** o **email**? Cada vez más se empieza a ver la grafía "email" en inglés, sin guión, para referirse al correo electrónico. En este diccionario hemos utilizado la grafía con guión, pero conviene advertir que ambas formas son posibles.

enviar por correo electrónico; **e-mail us at...** contacte con nosotros por correo electrónico en la siguiente dirección…

◇ *e-mail account* cuenta *f* de correo electrónico

◇ *e-mail address* dirección *f* de correo electrónico

◇ *e-mail alias* alias *m inv* de correo electrónico

◇ *e-mail bomb* bomba *f* de correo electrónico

◇ *e-mail client* cliente *m* de correo electrónico

◇ *e-mail phone* teléfono *m* con correo electrónico

◇ *e-mail program* programa *m* de correo electrónico

◇ *e-mail software* software *m* de correo electrónico

e-mall *n Internet* centro *m* comercial electrónico

e-marketing *n Internet* márketing *m* electrónico

embed *vt* incrustar

embedded *adj* incrustado(a)

e-money *n Internet* dinero *m* electrónico

emoticon *n Internet* emoticono *m*, emoticón *m*

empty 1 *adj (wastebasket, recycle bin)* vacío(a)
2 *vt (wastebasket, recycle bin)* vaciar

EMS *n Tel (abbr* **enhanced messaging service)** EMS *m*

emulate *vt* emular

emulation *n* emulación *f*

enable *vt (option)* activar, habilitar

enabled *adj (option)* activado(a), habilitado(a)

encode *vt* codificar

encoder *n* codificador *m*

encoding *n* codificación *f*

encrypt *vt* encriptar, cifrar

encryption *n* encriptación *f*, cifrado *m*

◇ *Internet* **encryption key** llave *f* de encriptación *or* cifrado

end *n*

◇ *end key* tecla *f* fin

◇ *end user* usuario(a) *m,f* final

endnote *n* nota *f* de fin de documento

engaged *adj Br* **the line** *or* **number is engaged** está ocupado, *Esp* comunica; **I got the engaged tone** *or* **signal** estaba ocupado, *Esp* comunicaba

enhance *vt (image)* mejorar, aumentar la calidad de; **to enhance the quality of sth** mejorar la calidad de algo

enhanced *adj (image, quality)* mejorado(a)

◇ *enhanced keyboard* teclado *m* expandido

enhancement *n (of image)* mejora *f*, aumento *m* de calidad

enter 1 *n (key)* (tecla *f*) intro *m*
2 *vt (data)* introducir

◇ *enter key* tecla *f* intro

entry *n (of data)* introducción *f*

entry-level *adj (computer, program)* para principiantes, de gama baja

environment *n* entorno *m*

EPROM n (abbr **erasable programmable read only memory**) eprom f

EPS n (abbr **encapsulated PostScript®**) EPS m

e-publishing n Internet edición f electrónica

equal sign, equals sign n (signo m de) igual m

erasable adj regrabable

erase vt borrar

ergonomic adj ergonómico(a)

ergonomics n ergonomía f

error n error m
◇ **error checking** verificación f de errores
◇ **error code** código m de error
◇ **error message** mensaje m de error

escape 1 n (key) escape m
2 vi salir
◇ **escape key** tecla f de escape

esc key n tecla f esc

e-services npl Internet servicios mpl electrónicos

e-tailer n Internet tienda f digital or en Internet

e-tailing n Internet venta f en Internet

Ethernet® n Ethernet® f

EVF n (abbr **electronic viewfinder**) visor m electrónico

e-wear n hardware m vestible

exclamation mark, US **exclamation point** n signo m de admiración or exclamación

ex-directory adj (telephone number) que no figura en la guía telefónica

executable file n (archivo m) ejecutable m

execute vt (command, program) ejecutar

execution n (of command, program) ejecución f

exit 1 n salida f
2 vt (program, session) salir de
3 vi salir

expand vt (memory) ampliar, expandir

expandable adj (memory) ampliable, expandible; **98MB expandable to 392MB** 98MB ampliables or expandibles a 392MB

expanded adj expandido(a)
◇ **expanded keyboard** teclado m expandido
◇ **expanded memory** memoria f expandida

expansion n (of memory) ampliación f, expansión f
◇ **expansion card** tarjeta f de ampliación
◇ **expansion slot** ranura f de expansión

expert system n sistema m experto

export vt (file, data) exportar (**to** a)

exposure n DTP exposición f
◇ **exposure compensation** compensación f de la exposición

extended adj extendido(a)
◇ **extended keyboard** teclado m extendido

⋄ **extended memory** memoria *f* extendida

extensible markup language *n* lenguaje *m* extensible de marcado

extension *n* (**a**) *(for telephone)* extensión *f*, *RP* interno *m*; **can I have extension 946?** ¿me puede comunicar *or Esp* poner con la extensión 946?, *RP* ¿me puede dar con el interno 946? (**b**) *(of file)* extensión *f*

⋄ **extension manager** gestor *m* de extensiones

⋄ **extension number** número *m* de extensión

external *adj* externo(a)

⋄ **external command** comando *m* externo

⋄ **external device** periférico *m* externo

⋄ **external drive** unidad *f* externa

⋄ **external hard disk** disco *m* duro externo

⋄ **external modem** módem *m* externo

extract *vt (zipped file)* extraer

extranet *n Internet* extranet *f*

ezine *n* revista *f* electrónica

facing pages *n DTP* páginas *fpl* enfrentadas

fan *n (cooling device)* ventilador *m*

FAQ *n Internet (abbr* **frequently asked questions**) preguntas *fpl* más frecuentes

◇ *FAQ file* documento *m* con las preguntas más frecuentes

fascia *n (for mobile phone)* carcasa *f*

fasgrolia *n Internet* nueva jerga *f* electrónica

fatal error *n* error *m* fatal

favorites *npl Internet* favoritos *mpl*

fax **1** *n (machine, message)* fax *m*; **to send sb a fax** enviar un fax a alguien; **to send sth by fax** enviar algo por fax

2 *vt (message, document)* mandar por fax; **to fax sb** mandar un fax a alguien; **I'll fax the figures to you** le enviaré *or* mandaré un fax con las cifras

◇ *fax card* tarjeta *f* de fax

◇ *fax modem* módem *m* fax

◇ *fax number* número *m* de fax

feathering *n DTP* suavizado *m*

feed *vt (paper)* alimentar; **to**

feed data into a computer meter datos en un *Esp* ordenador *or Am* una computadora

feeder *n (for printer, scanner, photocopier)* alimentador *m*

fibre optic, *US* **fiber optic** *adj (cable)* de fibra óptica

fibre optics, *US* **fiber optics** *n* fibra *f* óptica

field *n (in database)* campo *m*

file *n* archivo *m*, fichero *m*; **file not found** *(message)* no se encuentra el archivo

◇ *file compression* compresión *f* de archivos *or* ficheros

◇ *file conversion* conversión *f* de archivos *or* ficheros

◇ *file format* formato *m* de archivo *or* fichero

◇ *file management* gestión *f* de archivos *or* ficheros

◇ *file management system* sistema *m* de gestión de archivos *or* ficheros

◇ *file manager* administrador *m* de archivos *or* ficheros

◇ *file name* nombre *m* de archivo *or* fichero

◇ *file name extension* extensión *f* del nombre del archivo *or* fichero

◇ *file protection* protección *f*

de archivos *or* ficheros

◇ **file server** servidor *m* de archivos *or* ficheros

◇ **file structure** estructura *f* del archivo *or* fichero

◇ **file transfer** transferencia *f* de archivos *or* ficheros

◇ Internet **file transfer protocol** protocolo *m* de transferencia de archivos *or* ficheros

◇ **file viewer** visualizador *m* de archivos *or* ficheros

fill *vt DTP* rellenar

film scanner *n* escáner *m* de película

filter *n* filtro *m*

◇ *DTP* **filter effect** efecto *m* de filtro

filtering software *n* Internet software *m* de filtrado

find *vt* buscar; **to find and replace** buscar y reemplazar

◇ **find command** comando *m* de búsqueda

finger *n* Internet finger *m*

firewall *n* Internet cortafuegos *m inv*, *Am* firewall *m*

FireWire® *n* FireWire® *m*

◇ **FireWire® port** puerto *m* FireWire®

firmware *n* firmware *m*

fixed disk *n* disco *m* fijo

flag **1** *n* comentario *m*, flag *m*
2 *vt (highlight)* destacar

flame Internet **1** *n* mensaje *m* ofensivo, llamada *f*
2 *vt* lanzar mensajes ofensivos *or* llamadas contra
3 *vi* lanzar mensajes ofensivos *or* llamadas

◇ **flame war** guerra *f* de mensajes ofensivos *or* llamadas

flamer *n* Internet = persona que manda un mensaje ofensivo

flaming *n* Internet envío *m* de mensajes ofensivos *or* llamadas

flash memory, flash RAM *n* memoria *f* flash

flat *adj*

◇ **flat file** archivo *m* sin formato

◇ **flat monitor** monitor *m* de pantalla plana

◇ **flat panel display** monitor *m* de pantalla plana

◇ Internet **flat rate** tarifa *f* plana

◇ **flat screen** pantalla *f* plana

flatbed scanner *n* escáner *m* plano *or* de sobremesa

flat-rate *adj*

◇ **flat-rate connection** *(to Internet)* conexión *f* con tarifa plana

◇ **flat-rate monthly charge** *(to ISP)* tarifa *f* plana mensual

flicker **1** *n (of screen)* parpadeo *m*
2 *vi* parpadear

floating *adj* flotante

◇ **floating palette** paleta *f* flotante

◇ **floating point** coma *f* flotante

◇ **floating point processor** procesador *m* de coma flotante

◇ **floating point unit** unidad *f* de coma flotante

◇ **floating window** ventana *f* flotante

floppy n disquete m; **on floppy** en disquete

◇ *floppy disk* disquete m

◇ *floppy (disk) drive* disquetera f

flowchart n organigrama m, diagrama m de flujo

flow control n Tel control m de flujo

flush adj **flush left/right** alineado(a) a la izquierda/derecha

folder n (directory) carpeta f

follow-up message n Internet (in newsgroups) mensaje m respuesta

font n fuente f

footer n pie m de página

footnote n nota f a pie de página

footprint n (of device) base f

foreground n primer plano m

form n Internet formulario m

◇ *form feed* avance m de página

format 1 n (of page) formato m 2 vt (disk, page, text) formatear

formatting n (a) (action) (of disk, text) formateado m (b) (format) (of text) formato m

FORTRAN n FORTRAN m

forum n Internet foro m

forward 1 vt (e-mail message) remitir 2 adj

◇ Internet **forward button** botón m adelante

◇ *forward search* búsqueda f hacia adelante

◇ *forward slash* barra f inclinada (hacia adelante); **"www, dot, bbc, dot, com, forward slash, news"** "www punto bbc punto com barra news"

four-colour, US **four-color** n DTP

◇ *four-colour process* cuatricromía f

◇ *four-colour separation* separación f de colores

FPU n (abbr **floating-point unit**) FPU f, unidad f de coma flotante

FQDN n Internet (abbr **Fully Qualified Domain Name**) nombre m de dominio totalmente cualificado

fragmentation n (of hard disk) fragmentación f

frame n (of web page) marco m, cuadro m

◇ *frame grabber* (in digital imaging) tarjeta f digitalizadora

free adj (expansion slot) disponible

freebie n regalito m

Freefone® n Br Tel **a Freefone number** un (número de) teléfono gratuito, Esp ≃ un teléfono 900; **call Freefone 400** llame al número gratuito 400

freenet n Internet red f ciudadana, Am freenet f

freeware n freeware m, programa m de dominio público (y gratuito)

freeze vi (screen, computer) bloquearse

friction feed n avance m de papel por fricción

front adj

◇ **front end** (of computer) frontal m

◇ **front-end computer** Esp ordenador m or Am computadora f frontal

◇ **front panel** panel m frontal

frozen adj (screen) bloqueado(a)

FTP Internet **1** n (abbr **File Transfer Protocol**) FTP m
2 vt enviar por FTP

◇ **FTP server** servidor m FTP

◇ **FTP site** sitio m FTP

full adj

◇ Tel **full duplex** dúplex m pleno

◇ **full Internet access** acceso m completo a Internet

◇ **full page display** monitor m de página completa

◇ **full screen** pantalla f completa

◇ **full stop** punto m

◇ **full version** (of software) versión f completa

full-screen adj a pantalla completa

function key n tecla f de función

future-proof 1 adj (computer) preparado(a) para futuras tecnologías
2 vt preparar para futuras tecnologías

fuzzy logic n lógica f difusa or borrosa

gamepad *n* gamepad *m*, mando *m* de juego

game port *n* puerto *m* de juegos

gamer *n* jugador(ora) *m,f*

gaming *n* juegos *mpl*

gamma correction *n DTP* corrección *f* de gamma

gateway *n Internet* pasarela *f*

GB *n* (*abbr* **gigabyte**) GB *m*

geek *n Fam* **a computer geek** un fanático de la informática

generate *vt* generar

generation *n* generación *f*; **a third/fourth generation computer** un *Esp* ordenador *or Am* computadora de tercera/cuarta generación

ghost site *n Internet* sitio *m* fantasma

GHz (*abbr* **gigahertz**) GHz

GIF *n* (*abbr* **Graphics Interchange Format**) GIF *m*

◇ *GIF file* archivo *m* GIF

gigabyte *n* gigabyte *m*

gigahertz *n* gigahercio *m*

GIGO (*abbr* **garbage in garbage out**) = información errónea genera resultados erróneos

glare *n*

◇ *glare filter* filtro *m* de pantalla

◇ *glare screen* filtro *m* de pantalla

global search *n* búsqueda *f* global

▸**go down** *vi* (*computer network*) caerse

▸**go into** *vt insep* (*file, program*) entrar en; **to go into a file** entrar en un archivo

gopher *n Internet* gopher *m*

Gothic *n DTP* letra *f* gótica

.gov = en las direcciones de Internet, abreviatura que designa las páginas de organismos gubernamentales

GPRS *n Tel* (*abbr* **General Packet Radio Service**) GPRS *m*

GPS *n Tel* (*abbr* **Global Positioning System**) GPS *m*

GPU *n* (*abbr* **graphics processing unit**) unidad *f* de procesamiento de gráficos

gradient fill *n DTP* degradado *m* lineal

graduated fill *n DTP* degradado *m* lineal

Graffiti® *n* (*on PDA*) (escritura *f* de) Graffiti® *m*

◇ *Graffiti area* área *f* (de escritura) de Graffiti

grammar checker *n* corrector *m* de gramática

graphical user interface *n* interfaz *f* gráfica de usuario

graphic interface *n* interfaz *f* gráfica

graphics *npl (images)* gráficos *mpl*

◇ *graphics accelerator* acelerador *m* gráfico

◇ *graphics accelerator card* tarjeta *f* aceleradora gráfica

◇ *graphics card* tarjeta *f* gráfica

◇ *graphics display* representación *f* gráfica

◇ *graphics mode* modo *m* gráfico

◇ *graphics package* software *m* de gráficos

◇ *graphics software* software *m* de gráficos

◇ *graphics spreadsheet* hoja *f* de cálculo con gráficos

◇ *graphics tablet* tableta *f* gráfica

grave accent *n* acento *m* grave

Greek text *n DTP* texto *m* simulado

grey, *US* **gray** *n* shades of grey niveles *mpl* de gris

◇ *grey levels* niveles *mpl* de gris

greyscale *US* **grayscale** *n* escala *f* de grises

◇ *greyscale monitor* monitor

m de escala de grises

grid *n* cuadrícula *f*

gridline *n* cuadrícula *f*

group dialling, *US* **group dialing** *n* marcado *m or Andes, RP* discado *m* múltiple

groupware *n* groupware *m*

GSM *n Tel (abbr* **global system for mobile communication)** GSM *m*

guarantee **1** *n (document, promise)* garantía *f*; **this printer has a five-year guarantee** esta impresora tiene cinco años de garantía; **under guarantee** en garantía; **extended guarantee** garantía ampliada; **on-site guarantee** garantía in situ; **return-to-base guarantee** garantía con devolución al distribuidor
2 *vt (product, appliance)* garantizar; **this printer is guaranteed for five years** esta impresora tiene cinco años de garantía

◇ *guarantee certificate* certificado *m* de garantía

guest *n* invitado(a) *m,f*

guestbook *n (of web page)* libro *m* de visitas

GUI *n (abbr* **graphical user interface)** interfaz *f* gráfica de usuario

guide *n (ruler)* guía *f*

gutter *n DTP* margen *m* interior

hack vi they hacked their way into the system accedieron al sistema burlando los códigos de seguridad

hacker n (**a**) *(illegal user)* pirata mf informático(a) (**b**) *(expert user)* hacker mf

hacking n *(illegal use)* piratería f informática

half-tone n DTP medio tono m

handheld n asistente m personal, organizador m personal

◊ *handheld computer* asistente m personal, organizador m personal

◊ *handheld scanner* escáner m de mano

handle n DTP manejador m

handset n (**a**) *(of telephone)* auricular m (**b**) *(mobile phone)* aparato m

hands-free adj *(phone, dialling)* de manos libres; phone with hands-free facility or kit teléfono con (opción de) manos libres

handshake n Tel diálogo m de establecimiento de comunicación

handshaking n Tel establecimiento m de comunicación

hanging indent n DTP sangría f francesa

▸ **hang up** vi *(on telephone)* colgar

hard adj

◊ *hard copy* copia f impresa

◊ *hard disk* disco m duro

◊ *hard drive* unidad f de disco duro

◊ *hard hyphen* guión m indivisible

◊ *hard return* retorno m manual

◊ *hard space* espacio m indivisible

hardware n hardware m

◊ *hardware problem* problema m de hardware

hash n Br *(signo m)* número m; *(on telephone, IRC channel)* almohadilla f, Am numeral m

HD (**a**) *(abbr hard disk)* disco m duro (**b**) *(abbr high density)* alta densidad f

head n *(on printer)* cabezal m

header n encabezamiento m, encabezado m

heading n encabezamiento m, encabezado m

headphones *npl* auriculares *mpl*

◇ *headphones socket* entrada *m* para auriculares

heat sink *n* sumidero *m* térmico

help *n* ayuda *f*

◇ *help button* botón *m* de ayuda

◇ *help desk* (for computing queries) servicio *m* de asistencia

◇ *help key* tecla *f* de ayuda

◇ *help line* servicio *m* de asistencia

◇ *help menu* menú *m* de ayuda

◇ *help screen* pantalla *f* or ventana *f* de ayuda

helper application *n* aplicación *f* auxiliar

helpline *n* (for computing queries) servicio *m* de asistencia

Hex *adj* (abbr **hexadecimal**) hexadecimal

hexadecimal *adj* hexadecimal

hidden *adj* oculto(a)

◇ *hidden file* archivo *m* or fichero *m* oculto

◇ *hidden text* texto *m* oculto

hide *vt* (files, records) ocultar

hierarchical *adj* jerárquico(a)

◇ *hierarchical file system* sistema *m* de archivos jerárquicos

◇ *hierarchical menu* menú *m* jerárquico

high-density *adj* (disk, graphics, printing) de alta densidad

high-end *adj* de gama alta

high-level language *n* lenguaje *m* de alto nivel

highlight *vt* (text) seleccionar, realzar

high memory *n* memoria *f* alta

high resolution *n* alta resolución *f*

high-resolution *adj* de alta resolución

high-speed *adj* de alta velocidad

hi-res *adj* Fam (abbr **high-resolution**) de alta resolución

history list *n* Internet historial *m*

hit **1** *n* Internet (visit to web site) acceso *m*, visita *f*; (in search) resultado *m*; **this web site counted 20,000 hits last week** esta página web registró 20.000 accesos or visitas durante la semana pasada

2 *vt* (key) pulsar

hoax *n* (e-mail) mensaje *m* con una falsa alarma

hold **1** *n* **to put sb on hold** (on telephone) poner a alguien en espera; **to be on hold** estar en espera

2 *vt* (**a**) (store) almacenar; **how much data will this disk hold?** ¿cuánta información puede almacenar este disco?; **the commands are held in the memory** los comandos se almacenan en la memoria

(**b**) (on telephone) **hold the line please** espere un momento or no cuelgue, por favor; **hold all my calls** no me pase ninguna llamada

3 *vi (on telephone)* esperar; **the line's** *Br* **engaged** *or US* **busy, will you hold?** está ocupado *or Esp* comunicando, ¿le importaría esperar?

▸ **hold down** *vt sep (key, mouse button)* mantener apretado(a)

home *n*

◊ *home banking* banca *f* electrónica, telebanco *m*

◊ *home cinema* cine *m* en casa

◊ *home computer Esp* ordenador *m* doméstico, *Am* computadora *f* doméstica

◊ *home computing* informática *f* personal

◊ *home key* tecla *f* de inicio

◊ *Internet home page (initial page)* portada *f*, página *f* inicial *or* de inicio; *(start page in browser)* página *f* inicial *or* de inicio; *(personal page)* página *f* personal

◊ *home server* servidor *m* doméstico

◊ *home shopping* telecompra *f*

hook *n (of telephone)* **to leave the phone off the hook** dejar el teléfono descolgado; **to put the phone back on the hook** colgar el teléfono

▸ **hook up 1** *vt sep* conectar

2 *vi* conectarse

hop *n Internet* salto *m*

horizontal *adj* horizontal

◊ *horizontal justification* justificación *f* horizontal

◊ *horizontal orientation* orientación *f* horizontal

host 1 *n* **host (computer)** host *m*, sistema *m* central

2 *vt Internet (web site)* alojar, hospedar

◊ *host address* dirección *f* de host

hosting *n Internet (of web site)* alojamiento *m*, hospedaje *m*

hot *adj*

◊ *hot key* tecla *f* personalizada

◊ *Tel hot line* línea *f* directa

◊ *hot line support* asistencia *f* por línea directa

◊ *hot link* vínculo *m* activo

◊ *Internet hot list* lista *f* de los mejores enlaces

◊ *hot spot* punto *m* interactivo

◊ *hot swap (of devices)* reemplazo *m* en caliente

HSCSD *n Tel (abbr High Speed Circuit Switched Data)* HSCSD *m*

HTML *n Internet (abbr Hyper Text Markup Language)* HTML *m*

◊ *HTML editor* editor *m* de HTML

HTTP *n Internet (abbr Hyper Text Transfer Protocol)* HTTP *m*

◊ *HTTP server* servidor *m* de HTTP

hub *n* hub *m*

hybrid *adj (CD-ROM)* híbrido(a)

hyperlink *n Internet* hiperenlance *m*

hypermedia *n* hipermedia *f*

hypertext *n* hipertexto *m*

◇ *hypertext link* enlace *m* hipertextual

hyphen *n* guión *m*

hyphenation *n* partición *f* de palabras, partición *f* silábica

IAP n Internet (abbr **Internet Access Provider**) proveedor m de acceso a Internet

I-beam pointer n puntero m en forma de I

IBM-compatible adj compatible (con) IBM

icon n icono m
◇ **icon bar** barra f de iconos
◇ **icon editor** editor m de iconos

ID n (abbr **identification**) identificación f

IDE n (abbr **integrated drive electronics**) IDE m

identifier n identificador m

identity n (in e-mail program) identidad f

idle adj (machine) inactivo(a)

illegal adj (character, file name, instruction) ilegal

illustration n ilustración f
◇ **illustration software** software m de diseño gráfico

image n imagen f
◇ **image bank** banco m de imágenes
◇ **image editing** edición f de imágenes
◇ **image editing program** programa m de edición de imágenes
◇ **image editor** editor m de imágenes
◇ **image format** formato m de imagen
◇ DTP **image layer** capa f
◇ **image manipulation** manipulación f de imágenes
◇ Internet **image map** mapa m interactivo
◇ **image processing** tratamiento m de imagen

imagesetter n DTP filmadora f

IMAP n Internet (abbr **Internet Message Access Protocol**) IMAP m

IMEI n Tel (abbr **International Mobile Equipment Identity**) IMEI m

impact printer n impresora f de impacto

import vt (file, data) importar (**from** de)

impression n Internet (hit) impresión f
◇ **impression banner** banner m de impresiones

in box, inbox n (for e-mail) buzón m de entrada, Am casilla f de correo de entrada

incoming *adj* incoming calls llamadas *fpl or Am* llamados *mpl* de fuera; **incoming mail** correo *m* recibido

incompatibility *n* incompatibilidad *f* (**with** con)

incompatible *adj* incompatible (**with** con)

incremental *adj* incremental

◇ *incremental backup* copia *f* de seguridad incremental

◇ *incremental plotter* plotter *m* incremental

indent *vt* sangrar, *Am* indentar

indentation *n* sangrado *m*, *Am* indentado *m*

index **1** *n* (*in book, database*) índice *m* (alfabético)
2 *vt* (*database*) indexar, indizar

infect *vt* (*file, disk*) infectar

infoaddict *n Fam* Internet infoadicto(a) *m,f*

infobahn *n* infopista *f*, autopista *f* de la información

infohighway *n* infopista *f*, autopista *f* de la información

information *n* (**a**) (*data*) información *f*
(**b**) *Tel* información *f*, *Am* informaciones *fpl*

◇ *Internet information highway* autopista *f* de la información

◇ *information processing* proceso *m* de datos

◇ *information retrieval* recuperación *f* de información

◇ *information society* sociedad *f* de la información

◇ *information storage* almacenamiento *m* de información

◇ *Internet information superhighway* superautopista *f* de la información

◇ *information technology* tecnologías *fpl* de la información

infrared *n* infrarrojo *m*

◇ *infrared mouse Esp* ratón *m or Am* mouse *m* de infrarrojos

◇ *infrared keyboard* teclado *m* de infrarrojos

initialization *n* (*of computer, modem, printer*) inicialización *f*

initialize *vt* (*computer, modem, printer*) inicializar

ink cartridge *n* cartucho *m* de tinta

inkjet printer *n* impresora *f* de chorro de tinta

inline image *n* Internet imagen *f* integrada

input **1** *n* (*action*) input *m*, entrada *f*; (*data*) datos *mpl* introducidos
2 *vt* (*data*) introducir

◇ *input device* dispositivo *m* de entrada

input/output *n* entrada *f* y salida

◇ *input/output device* dispositivo *m* de entrada y salida

insert **1** *n* inserción *f*
2 *vt* insertar

◇ *insert key* tecla *f* de inserción

◇ *insert mode* modo *m* de inserción

insertion point *n* punto *m* de inserción

install *vt (equipment, software)* instalar

◇ *install program* programa *f* de instalación

installation disk *n* disco *m* de instalación

installer *n (program)* instalador *m*

instant *adj (immediate)* instantáneo(a)

◇ *instant message* mensaje *m* instantáneo

◇ *instant messaging* mensajería *f* instantánea

instruction *n* instrucción *f*; **instructions** *(in program)* instrucciones

◇ *instruction manual* manual *m* de instrucciones

integrated *adj (fax, modem)* integrado(a)

◇ *integrated package* paquete *m* integrado

◇ *integrated services digital network* red *f* digital de servicios integrados

◇ *integrated software* software *m* integrado

intelligent terminal *n* terminal *m* inteligente

interact *vi* interactuar (**with** con)

interactive *adj* interactivo(a)

◇ *interactive CD* CD *m* interactivo

◇ *interactive CD-ROM* CD-ROM *m* interactivo

◇ *interactive video* *Esp* vídeo *m* or *Am* video *m* interactivo

interface *n* interfaz *m* or *f*, interface *m* or *f*

interlaced *adj (monitor)* entrelazado(a)

internal *adj* interno(a)

◇ *internal clock* reloj *m* interno

◇ *internal drive* unidad *f* de disco interna

◇ *internal modem* módem *m* interno

international *adj*

◇ *international call* llamada *f* or *Am* llamado *m* internacional

◇ *Br* *international dialling code* indicativo *m* internacional

internaut *n* internauta *mf*

Internet *n* **the Internet** Internet *f*; **on the Internet** en Internet; **to surf the Internet** navegar por Internet

◇ *Internet 2* Internet *f* 2

◇ *Internet access provider* proveedor *m* de acceso a Internet

◇ *Internet account* cuenta *f* de Internet

◇ *Internet address* dirección *f* de Internet

◇ *Internet banking* banca *f* por Internet

◇ *Internet café* cibercafé *m*

◇ *Internet connection* conexión *f* a Internet

◇ *Internet number* número *m* de Internet

◇ *Internet phone* teléfono *m* por Internet

◇ *Internet presence provider* proveedor *m* de presencia en Internet

◇ *Internet protocol* protocolo *m* de Internet

The Internet

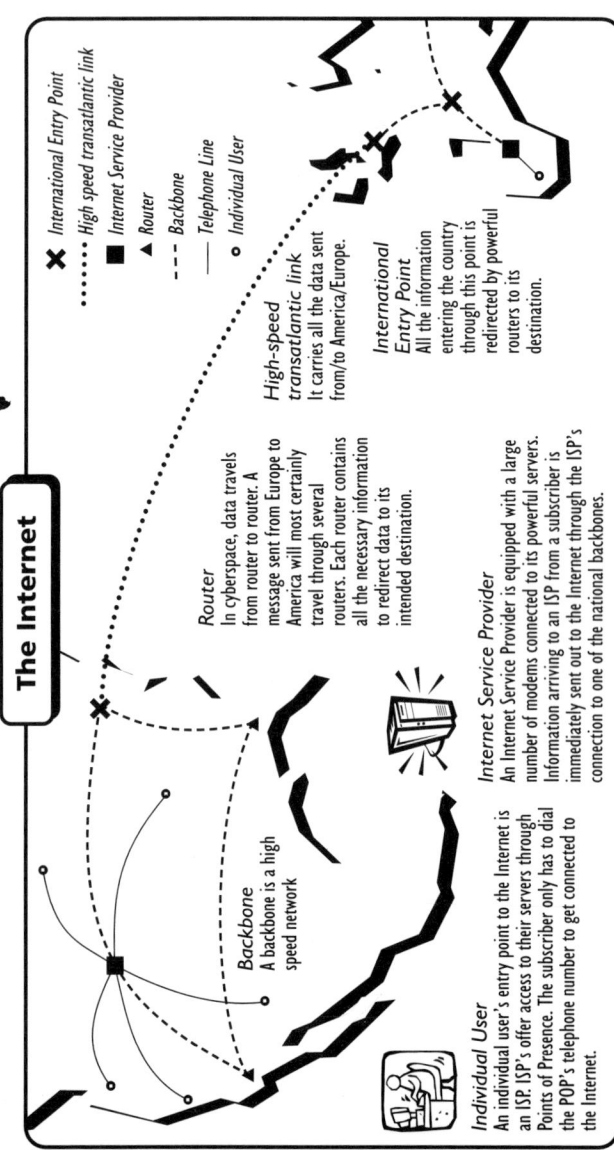

Key:
- ✕ International Entry Point
- ••••• High speed transatlantic link
- ■ Internet Service Provider
- ▲ Router
- --- Backbone
- — Telephone Line
- ○ Individual User

Router
In cyberspace, data travels from router to router. A message sent from Europe to America will most certainly travel through several routers. Each router contains all the necessary information to redirect data to its intended destination.

High-speed transatlantic link
It carries all the data sent from/to America/Europe.

International Entry Point
All the information entering the country through this point is redirected by powerful routers to its destination.

Backbone
A backbone is a high speed network

Internet Service Provider
An Internet Service Provider is equipped with a large number of modems connected to its powerful servers. Information arriving to an ISP from a subscriber is immediately sent out to the Internet through the ISP's connection to one of the national backbones.

Individual User
An individual user's entry point to the Internet is an ISP. ISP's offer access to their servers through Points of Presence. The subscriber only has to dial the POP's telephone number to get connected to the Internet.

◇ **Internet Relay Chat** charla *f* interactiva por Internet

◇ **Internet service provider** proveedor *m* de acceso a Internet

◇ **Internet Society** Sociedad *f* Internet

◇ **Internet surfer** internauta *mf*

◇ **Internet telephone** teléfono *m* por Internet

◇ **Internet telephony** telefonía *f* por Internet

◇ **Internet user** internauta *mf*, usuario(a) *m,f* de Internet

◇ **Internet TV** TV *f* por Internet

Internet-ready *adj* listo(a) para Internet, preparado(a) para Internet

interoperability *n* interoperabilidad *f*

interpolation *n* interpolación *f*

interpreter *n (software)* intérprete *m*

interstitial *n* Internet *(advertisement)* banner *m* flotante

intranet *n* intranet *f*

invalid *adj (file name)* inválido(a)

inverted commas *n* comillas *fpl*

invisible file *n* archivo *m* invisible

I/O *n (abbr* **input/output)** E/S, entrada/salida

IP *n (abbr* **Internet Protocol)**

◇ **IP address** dirección *f* IP

◇ **IP number** número *m* IP

IRC *n* Internet *(abbr* **Internet Relay Chat)** IRC *m*

◇ **IRC channel** canal *m* IRC

IrDA *n (abbr* **Infrared Data Association)**

◇ **IrDA port** puerto *m* de infrarrojos

ISDN 1 *n (abbr* **integrated services digital network)** RDSI *f* **2** *vt Fam* **to ISDN sth** enviar algo por RDSI

◇ **ISDN card** tarjeta *f* RDSI

◇ **ISDN line** línea *f* RDSI

◇ **ISDN modem** módem *m* RDSI

ISOC *n* Internet *(abbr* **Internet Society)** Sociedad *f* Internet

ISP *n* Internet *(abbr* **Internet Service Provider)** PSI *m*, proveedor *m* de acceso a Internet

IT *n (abbr* **information technology)** TI *fpl*, tecnologías *fpl* de la información

italic 1 *n* italic(s) cursiva *f*; **in italics** en cursiva **2** *adj* cursiva; **italic(s) face** or **type** letra cursiva

item *n (on menu)* ítem *m*

jaggies *npl DTP* serretado *m*

Java® *n Internet* Java® *m*

JavaScript® *n Internet* Java-Script® *m*

Jaz® *n*

◇ **Jaz**® **disk** disco *m* Jaz®

◇ **Jaz**® **drive** unidad *f* Jaz®

job *n (task)* tarea *f*

joining fee *n Internet* tarifa *f* de alta

joystick *n* joystick *m*

JPEG *n (abbr* **Joint Photographic Experts Group**) JPEG *m*

◇ **JPEG file** archivo *m* JPEG

Jughead *n Internet* Jughead

jump *vi* saltar; **to jump from** one web page to another saltar de una página web a otra

jumper *n (pin)* jumper *m*, puente *m*

junk e-mail *n Internet* correo *m* basura

justification *n (of text)* justificación *f*; **left/right justification** justificación a la izquierda/derecha; **vertical justification** justificación vertical

justified *adj (text)* justificado(a); **left/right justified** justificado a la izquierda/derecha; **vertically justified** justificado verticalmente

justify *vt (text)* justificar

K *n* (*abbr* **kilobyte**) K *m*; **how many K are left?** ¿cuántos K quedan?

KB *n* (*abbr* **kilobyte**) KB *m*

Kb *n* (*abbr* **kilobit**) Kb *m*

Kbps (*abbr* **kilobits per second**) kbps

kerning *n DTP* interletraje *m*

key *vt* (*data, text*) teclear, *Am* tipear

◇ *key combination* combinación *f* de teclas

▸ **key in, key up** *vt sep* (*data, text*) teclear, *Am* tipear

keyboard **1** *n* (*of typewriter, computer*) teclado *m*
2 *vt* (*data, text*) teclear, *Am* tipear
3 *vi* teclear, *Am* tipear

◇ *keyboard layout* disposición *f* del teclado

◇ *keyboard map* mapa *m* de caracteres

◇ *keyboard shortcut* atajo *m* de teclado

keyboarder *n* teclista *mf*, operador(ora) *m,f*

keypad *n* teclado *m* numérico

keystroke *n* pulsación *f*; **keystrokes per minute/hour** caracteres por minuto/hora

keyword *n* palabra *f* clave

killer app *n* aplicación *f* rompedora

kilobit *n* kilobit *m*

kilobyte *n* kilobyte *m*

kiosk *n* terminal *m* interactivo

kit *n* kit *m*

knowbot *n Internet* robot *m* de conocimiento

knowledge *n*

◇ *knowledge base* base *f* de conocimientos

◇ *knowledge economy* economía *f* de conocimientos

◇ *knowledge management* gestión *f* de conocimientos

knowledge-based system *n* sistema *m* experto

The Spanish keyboard
(Traditional Sort)

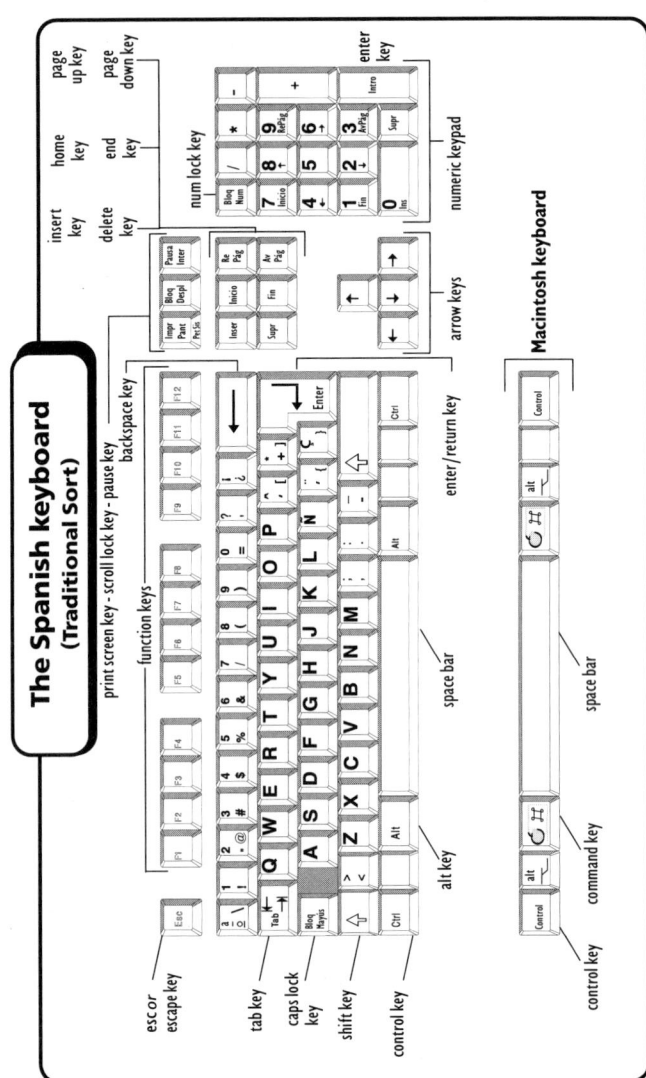

esc or escape key

tab key

caps lock key

shift key

control key

alt key

print screen key - scroll lock key - pause key

function keys

backspace key

enter/return key

space bar

insert key

delete key

page up key

page down key

home key

end key

num lock key

numeric keypad

enter key

arrow keys

Macintosh keyboard

control key

command key

space bar

LAN n (abbr **local area network**) red f de área local

land line n Tel línea f terrestre

landscape n (paper format) formato m apaisado; **to print sth in landscape** imprimir algo en apaisado

◇ **landscape mode** modo m apaisado

language n lenguaje m

laptop (computer) n Esp ordenador m or Am computadora f portátil

laser n láser m

◇ **laser printer** impresora f láser

lasso tool n DTP herramienta f lazo

latency n latencia f

launch vt arrancar, abrir

layer n DTP capa f

layout n diseño m, formato m; **to do the layout for sth** maquetar algo

◇ **layout application** programa m de maquetación

LCD n (abbr **liquid crystal display**) LCD, pantalla f de cristal líquido

◇ **LCD finder** visor m de cristal líquido

◇ **LCD monitor** monitor m de cristal líquido

◇ **LCD screen** pantalla f de cristal líquido

leading n DTP interlineado m

leased line n línea f arrendada or alquilada

LED n (abbr **light-emitting diode**) LED m, diodo m emisor de luz

left arrow n flecha f izquierda

◇ **left arrow key** tecla f de flecha izquierda

left-click 1 vt hacer clic or pinchar con el botón izquierdo en **2** vi hacer clic or pinchar con el botón izquierdo (**on** en)

legacy software n software m anticuado

legal n (paper size) = tamaño de papel de 216 x 356mm, utilizado sobre todo en los Estados Unidos

letter n (paper size) tamaño m carta; = tamaño de papel de 216 x 279mm, utilizado sobre todo en los Estados Unidos

◇ **letter quality** calidad f de carta

levels of grey, US **levels of gray** n DTP niveles mpl de gris

library n (of programs) biblioteca f, librería f

licence, US **license** n licencia f

◇ **licence agreement** acuerdo m de licencia

light pen n lápiz m óptico

Li-Ion battery n batería f de litio-ión

line n (a) (telephone connection) línea f; **the line is** Br **engaged** or US **busy** está ocupado, Esp comunica; **hold the line please** espere un momento, por favor; **it's a good/bad line** te oigo bien/mal; **she's on the other line** está hablando por otra línea
(b) (of text) línea f

◇ **line break** salto m de línea

◇ **line end** fin m de línea

◇ **line feed** avance m de línea

◇ **lines per inch** líneas fpl por pulgada

◇ Tel **line noise** ruido m en la línea

◇ Tel **line rental** alquiler m or Méx renta f de la línea

◇ **line spacing** interlineado m

linear programming n programación f lineal

link 1 n (hyperlink) enlace m, vínculo m (**to** a)
2 vt conectar (**to** a)
3 vi **to link to** conectar a

linkrot n Fam Internet desactualización f de enlaces

Linux n Linux m

liquid crystal display n pantalla f de cristal líquido

list 1 vt listar
2 n lista f

◇ Internet **list server** servidor m de listas

lite version n (of software) versión f limitada

lithium-ion battery n batería f de litio-ión

live cam n Internet webcam f

load 1 vt (disk, program) cargar; **to load a program into the memory** cargar un programa en la memoria
2 vi (software, program) cargarse

▸ **load up** vt sep (disk, program) cargar

loader n cargador m

local adj local

◇ **local area network** red f de área local

◇ Tel **local call** llamada f local or urbana, Am llamado m local or urbano

◇ **local rate number** número m con tarifa local

localization n localización f

localize vt localizar

location n Internet dirección f

lock vt (a) (file, diskette) bloquear (b) (mobile phone) bloquear

▸ **log in** vi (user) entrar, abrir una sesión

▸ **log off 1** vt sep salir de
2 vi salir

▸ **log on 1** vt sep entrar en, abrir una sesión en
2 vi (user) entrar, abrir una

sesión; **to log onto a system** entrar en un sistema

▸ **log out** *vi (user)* salir

log file *n* registro *m* de actividad

logic 1 *n* lógica *f*
2 *adj* lógico(a)
◇ *logic board* placa *f* lógica
◇ *logic bomb* bomba *f* lógica
◇ *logic card* tarjeta *f* lógica
◇ *logic circuit* circuito *m* lógico
◇ *logic operator* operador *m* lógico

logical *adj* lógico(a)

login *n* conexión *f*
◇ *login name* nombre *m* del usuario

logoff *n* desconexión *f*

long-distance 1 *adj* **a long-distance (telephone) call** *Esp* una conferencia, *Am* un llamado de larga distancia
2 *adv* **to telephone long-distance** *Esp* poner una conferencia, *Am* hacer un llamado de larga distancia

look-up table *n* tabla *f* de referencia

loop *n* bucle *m*, referencia *f* circular

lossless *adj (compression)* sin pérdidas

lossy *adj (compression)* con pérdidas

lost cluster *n* cluster *m* perdido

low-density *adj* de baja densidad

low-end *adj* de gama baja

lower-case 1 *n* minúsculas *fpl*
2 *adj* en minúsculas

low-level language *n* lenguaje *m* de bajo nivel

low-res *adj Fam (abbr* **low-resolution***)* de baja resolución

low resolution *n* baja resolución *f*

low-resolution *adj* de baja resolución

lurk *vi Internet* mirar, fisgar

lurker *n Internet* mirón(ona) *m,f*, fisgón(ona) *m,f*

Mac *n* Mac *m*; **available for the Mac** disponible para (el) Mac

◇ *Mac disk* disco *m* de Mac

◇ *Mac OS* sistema *m* operativo Mac

Mac-compatible *adj* compatible con (el) Mac

machine *n* (computer) *Esp* ordenador *m*, *Am* computadora *f*

◇ *machine code* código *m* máquina

◇ *machine language* lenguaje *m* máquina

◇ *machine translation* traducción *f* automática

machine-readable *adj* legible para *Esp* el ordenador *or* *Am* la computadora

macro *n* macro *f*

◇ *macro language* lenguaje *m* macro

◇ *macro virus* virus *m* de macro

magnetic *adj* magnético(a)

◇ *magnetic card* tarjeta *f* magnética

◇ *magnetic card reader* lector *m* de tarjetas magnéticas

◇ *magnetic disk* disco *m* magnético

◇ *magnetic strip* (on card) banda *f* magnética

◇ *magnetic tape* cinta *f* magnética

magneto-optical *adj* magneto-óptico(a)

magnify *vt* aumentar

mail *n* (e-mail) correo *m* (electrónico)

◇ *mail account* cuenta *f* de correo

◇ *mail address* dirección *f* de correo electrónico

◇ *mail bomb* bomba *f* de correo electrónico

◇ *mail forwarding* remisión *f* de correo

◇ *mail gateway* pasarela *f* de correo

◇ *mail merge* combinación *f* de correspondencia

◇ *mail path* = camino que ha seguido un correo electrónico

◇ *mail reader* lector *m* de correo

◇ *mail server* servidor *m* de correo

mailbot *n* Internet generador *m* automático de respuestas

mailbox *n* (for e-mail) buzón *m*, *Am* casilla *f* de correo

mailing list *n* Internet lista *f* de correo *or* de distribución

mainframe (computer) n *Esp* ordenador m central, *Am* computadora f central

main memory n memoria f principal

maintenance n mantenimiento m

management information system n sistema m de gestión de la información

margin n margen m; **to set the margins** fijar los márgenes

marquee n *DTP* marco m rectangular

mask n *DTP* máscara f

mass storage n almacenamiento m masivo

mast n *(for mobile phone)* antena f

master adj
◇ **master disk** disco m maestro
◇ **master file** archivo m maestro

math co-processor n *US* coprocesador m matemático

maths co-processor n *Br* coprocesador m matemático

matrix n matriz f

maximize vt *(window)* agrandar, maximizar

MB n *(abbr* **megabyte)** MB m

Mb n *(abbr* **megabit)** Mb m

Mbps *(abbr* **megabits per second)** Mbps

m-commerce n comercio m móvil

media n **storage media** sistemas mpl de almacenamiento

meg n *Fam* mega m; **128 meg memory** 128 megas de memoria

megabit n megabit m

megabyte n megabyte m; **128 megabyte memory** 128 megabytes de memoria

megaflop n megaflop m

megahertz n megahercio m; **500 megahertz** 500 megahercios

megapixel n megapíxel m

memory n memoria f
◇ **memory address** dirección f de memoria
◇ **memory bank** banco m de memoria
◇ **memory card** tarjeta f de memoria
◇ **memory chip** chip m de memoria
◇ **memory management** gestión f de memoria
◇ **memory manager** gestor m de memoria
◇ **memory mapping** mapeado m de memoria
◇ **memory upgrade** ampliación f de memoria

memory-intensive adj *(application)* que requiere mucha memoria

memory-resident adj residente en memoria

menu n menú m
◇ **menu bar** barra f de menús
◇ **menu item** ítem m del menú
◇ **menu option** opción f del menú

menu-driven adj a base de menús

merge 1 *vt (files)* fusionar, unir **2** *n* fusión *f*

◇ *merge codes* códigos *mpl* de fusión

message *n (e-mail)* mensaje *m*

◇ *message board* tablón *m* de anuncios

◇ *message body* cuerpo *m* del mensaje

◇ *message box* ventana *f* de diálogo

◇ *message header* encabezado *m* del mensaje

meta ad *n Internet* anuncio *m* vinculado a búsqueda

MHz *(abbr* **megahertz)** Mhz

micro *n (microcomputer) Esp* microordenador *m*, *Am* microcomputadora *f*

microbrowser *n Tel* micronavegador *m*

microchip *n* microchip *m*

microcomputer *n Esp* microordenador *m*, *Am* microcomputadora *f*

micropayment *n Internet* micropago *m*

microprocessor *n* microprocesador *m*

MIDI *(abbr* **musical instrument digital interface)** MIDI

mid-range *adj* de gama media

millennium bug *n* efecto *m* 2000

millisecond *n* milisegundo *m*

MIME *n Internet (abbr* **Multipurpose Internet Mail Extensions)** MIME *m*

minicomputer *n Esp* miniordenador *m*, *Am* minicomputadora *f*

MiniDisc® *n* MiniDisc® *m*

minimize *vt (window)* minimizar

mini tower *n* minitorre *f*

minus sign *n* signo *m* menos

mips *(abbr* **million instructions per second)** mips

mirror site *n Internet* sitio *m* espejo *or* réplica

MIS *n (abbr* **management information system)** sistema *f* de gestión de la información

.misc *Internet (abbr* **miscellaneous)** *(in newsgroups)* = abreviatura que designa a los foros de discusión abiertos a todo tipo de temas

misconvergence *n* falta *f* de convergencia

MMS *n Tel (abbr* **multimedia messaging service)** MMS *m*

MMX *n (abbr* **multimedia extensions)** MMX *m*

mobile 1 *n Br* móvil *m*, *Am* celular *m* **2** *adj* móvil

◇ *mobile chip* chip *m* móvil

◇ *mobile Internet* Internet *f* desde el móvil

◇ *Br mobile phone* teléfono *m* móvil, *Am* teléfono *m* celular

◇ *mobile telephony* telefonía *f* móvil, *Am* telefonía *f* celular

mode *n* modo *m*

model *vt* modelar

The multimedia computer

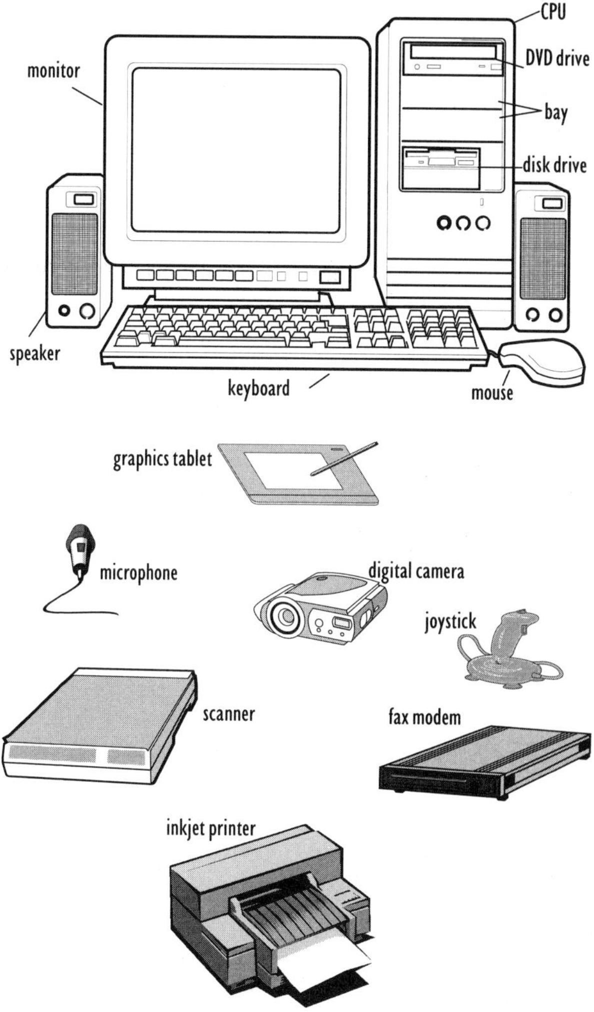

monitor

CPU

DVD drive

bay

disk drive

speaker

keyboard

mouse

graphics tablet

microphone

digital camera

joystick

scanner

fax modem

inkjet printer

modelling, US **modeling** n
modelado m

modem 1 n módem m; **to send
sth to sb by modem** enviar algo
a alguien por módem
2 vt **to modem sth to sb** enviar
algo a alguien por módem

◇ **modem card** tarjeta f de módem

◇ **modem port** puerto m del módem

moderated list n Internet lista f moderada

moderator n Internet moderador(ora) m,f

modifier key n tecla f modificadora

moire n DTP moiré m

monitor n (screen) monitor m

mono adj (printing mode) en blanco y negro

monochrome adj monocromo(a)

monospaced adj DTP monoespaciado(a)

monospacing n DTP monoespaciado m

morph vt (image) transformar metamorfoseando or con morfing

morphing n (of image) metamorfosis f inv, morphing m

motherboard n placa f madre, Am motherboard f

motorized tray n bandeja f motorizada

mouse n Esp ratón m, Am mouse m

◇ **mouse ball** bola f del Esp ratón or Am mouse

◇ **mouse button** botón m del Esp ratón or Am mouse

◇ **mouse click** clic m (del Esp ratón or Am mouse)

◇ **mouse driver** controlador m del Esp ratón or Am mouse

◇ Br **mouse mat** alfombrilla f, Am mouse pad m

◇ **mouse pad** alfombrilla f, Am mouse pad m

◇ **mouse port** puerto m del Esp ratón or Am mouse

movie mode n (on digital camera) modo m película

MP3 n (abbr **MPEG1 Audio Layer 3**) MP3 m

◇ **MP3 file** archivo m de MP3

◇ **MP3 player** reproductor m de MP3

MPEG n (abbr **Moving Pictures Expert Group**) MPEG m

MS-DOS® n (abbr **Microsoft Disk Operating System**) MS-DOS® m

MUD n Internet (abbr **multi-user dungeon**) entorno m MUD

multi-access adj multiusuario, de acceso múltiple

multicast n Internet multidifusión f

multifunctional key n tecla f multifuncional

multi-image processing n DTP multiprocesado m de imágenes

multimedia 1 n multimedia f
2 adj multimedia

◇ **multimedia computer** Esp

ordenador *m or Am* computadora *f* multimedia

multiple mailboxes *npl* buzón *m* múltiple, *Am* casillas *fpl* de correo múltiples

multiprocessor *n* multiprocesador *m*

multiprogramming *n* multiprogramación *f*

multiscan, multiscanning *n* multifrecuencia *f*

multi-session *adj*

◇ *multi-session disk* disco *m* multisesión

◇ *multi-session mode* modo *m* multisesión

multi-station, multistation *adj* multipuesto

multitasking *n* multitarea *f*

multithreading *n* multiproceso *m*

multi-user, multiuser *adj* multiusuario *inv*

◇ *multi-user software* software *m* multiusuario

◇ *multi-user system* sistema *m* multiusuario

name server *n Internet* servidor *m* de nombres

nanosecond *n* nanosegundo *m*

nanotechnology *n* nanotecnología *f*

national call *n Tel* llamada *f* *or Am* llamado *m* nacional

navigate *Internet* **1** *vt* navegar por; **to navigate the Net** navegar por Internet
2 *vi (around web site)* navegar

navigation *n Internet (around web site)* navegación *f*

◇ **navigation bar** barra *f* de navegación

negative scanner *n* escáner *m* de negativos

nerd *n Fam* **a computer nerd** un(a) pirado(a) por la informática

Net *n Fam* **the Net** la Red

◇ **Net surfer** internauta *mf*
◇ **Net user** internauta *mf*

.net *Internet* = en las direcciones de Internet, abreviatura que designa las páginas de entidades oficiales relacionadas con la administración de Internet

nethead *n Fam Internet* pirado(a) *m,f* por Internet

netiquette *n Internet* netiqueta *f*

netizen *n Internet* ciudadano(a) *m,f* de la Red, ciuredano(a) *m,f*

netlag *n Internet* paralización *f* del tráfico

netspeak *n Internet* jerga *f* de Internet

network **1** *n* red *f*
2 *vt* conectar en red

◇ **network administrator** administrador(ora) *m,f* de red
◇ **network card** tarjeta *f* de red
◇ **network controller** controlador *m* de red
◇ **network driver** controlador *m* de red
◇ **network interface card** tarjeta *f* de red
◇ **network server** servidor *m* de red
◇ **network software** software *m* de red
◇ **network traffic** tráfico *m* de la red

networked systems *npl* sistemas *mpl* en red

networking *n (of computer system)* conexión *f* en red; **to have networking capabilities**

Network topologies

Centralized

A central computer controls access to the network

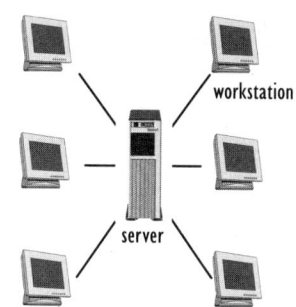

Star network
Its physical layout resembles a star. At its centre is a central network processor.

workstation

server

Decentralized

Each workstation can access the network independently and establish its own connections with other workstations

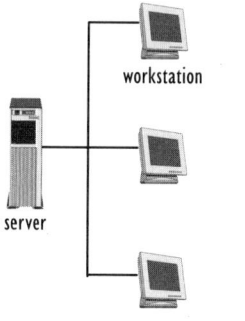

workstation

server

Bus network
A single connecting line, the bus, is shared by a number of nodes, including workstations and shared printers.

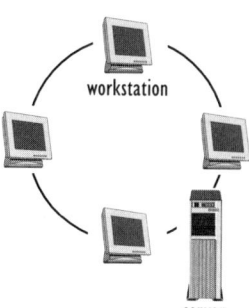

workstation

server

Ring network
A number of nodes are arranged around a closed loop cable.

(terminal) poderse conectar a una red

neural network *n* red *f* neuronal

newbie *n* *Fam* *Internet* novato(a) *m,f*

news *n* *Internet* grupos *mpl* de noticias, noticias *fpl*

◊ *news reader* lector *m* de noticias

◊ *news server* servidor *m* de grupos de noticias

newsgroup *n* *Internet* grupo *m* de noticias

NIC *n* (*abbr* **network interface card**) tarjeta *f* de red

nick *n* *Fam* *Internet* apodo *m*, pseudónimo *m*

nickname *n* *Internet* apodo *m*, pseudónimo *m*

NNTP *n* *Internet* (*abbr* **Network News Transfer Protocol**) protocolo *m* de transferencia de grupos de noticias

node *n* nodo *m*

noise *n* *Tel* ruido *m*

non-interlaced *adj* no

entralazado(a)

notebook (computer) *n* *Esp* ordenador *m* portátil, *Am* computadora *f* portátil

notepad *n* (*software*) bloc *m* de notas

number *n* número *m*

◊ *number crunching* cálculos *mpl* numéricos largos y complicados

◊ *number key* tecla *f* numérica

◊ *numbers lock* bloqueo *m* numérico

◊ *numbers lock key* tecla *f* de bloqueo numérico

numeric *adj* numérico(a)

◊ *numeric field* campo *m* numérico

◊ *numeric keypad* teclado *m* numérico

numerical *adj* numérico(a)

◊ *numerical keypad* teclado *m* numérico

num lock *n* (*abbr* **numbers lock**) bloqueo *m* numérico

◊ *num lock key* tecla *f* de bloqueo numérico

object *n (in document)* objeto *m*

object-orientated *adj* orientado(a) a objeto

oblique *n* barra *f* oblicua

OCR *n* (a) (*abbr* **optical character reader**) OCR *m*, lector *m* óptico de caracteres (b) (*abbr* **optical character recognition**) OCR *m*, reconocimiento *m* óptico de caracteres

◊ **OCR software** software *m* de OCR

off-hook, offhook *adj* descolgado(a)

◊ **off-hook signal** señal *f* de descolgado

office *n*

◊ **office automation** ofimática *f*

◊ **office IT** ofimática *f*

off-line, offline 1 *adj (processing)* fuera de línea, off-line; *(printer)* desconectado(a); **to be off-line** *(person)* estar desconectado(a); **to go off-line** desconectarse

2 *adv* **to work off-line** trabajar desconectado *or* sin conexión

◊ **off-line mode** modo *m* desconectado *or* off-line

◊ **off-line reader** lector *m* off-line *or* fuera de línea

off-topic *adj Internet* que no tiene que ver con la discusión

one-step *adj* **one-step set-up/web access** configuración/acceso a Internet en un solo paso

on-hook, onhook *adj* colgado(a)

◊ **on-hook signal** señal *f* de colgado

on-line, online 1 *adj (processing)* en línea, on-line; *(printer)* conectado(a); **to be on-line** *(of person)* estar conectado(a); **to go on-line** conectarse; **the disk contains all you need to get on-line** el disco contiene todo lo necesario para conectarse; **the company went on-line in November** *(have Internet presence)* la empresa comenzó a ofrecer sus servicios por Internet en noviembre; *(have Internet connection)* la empresa tiene acceso a Internet desde noviembre; **to put the printer on-line** conectar la impresora **2** *adv* en línea, on line; **to buy/order on-line** comprar/hacer pedidos en línea *or* on-line; **to shop on-line** comprar en línea *or* on-line; **to work on-line** trabajar en línea *or* on-line

◇ *on-line banking* banca *f* electrónica

◇ *on-line help* ayuda *f* en línea *or* on-line

◇ *on-line mode* modo *m* en línea *or* on-line

◇ *on-line registration* inscripción *f* en línea *or* on-line

◇ *on-line service* servicio *m* en línea *or* on-line

◇ *on-line shopping* compras *fpl* en línea *or* on-line

◇ *on-line time* tiempo *m* de conexión

on/off switch *n* interruptor *m* de encendido/apagado

on-screen, onscreen 1 *adj* en pantalla
2 *adv Esp* en el ordenador, *Am* en la computadora; **to work on-screen** trabajar *Esp* en el ordenador *or Am* en la computadora

◇ *on-screen help* ayuda *f* en pantalla

on-site *adj* in situ

◇ *on-site guarantee* garantía *f* in situ

◇ *on-site service* servicio *m* in situ

opening tag *n* etiqueta *f* de apertura

open line *n Tel* línea *f* abierta

operating system *n* sistema *m* operativo

operation *n* operación *f*

operator *n* *Tel* (*person*) **(switchboard) operator** telefonista *mf*, operador(ora) *m,f*

optical *adj* óptico(a)

◇ *optical character reader* lector *m* óptico de caracteres

◇ *optical character recognition* reconocimiento *m* óptico de caracteres

◇ *optical disk* disco *m* óptico

◇ *optical fibre or US fiber* fibra *f* óptica

◇ *optical mouse Esp* ratón *m or Am* mouse *m* óptico

◇ *optical scanner* escáner *m* óptico

◇ *optical zoom* zoom *m* óptico

optimization *n* optimización *f*

optimize *vt* optimizar

optimizer *n* optimizador *m*

opt-in e-mail *n Internet* correo *m* promocional solicitado

option key *n* tecla *f* de opción

.org *Internet* = en las direcciones de Internet, abreviatura que designa las páginas de organizaciones sin ánimo de lucro

organizer *n* (*software*) organizador *m*

orphan *n DTP* (línea *f*) huérfana *f*

OS *n* (*abbr* **operating system**) sistema *m* operativo

out box, outbox *n* (*for e-mail*) buzón *m* de salida, *Am* casilla *f* de correo de salida

outgoing *adj* (*telephone call, e-mail*) saliente

output 1 *n* (*of data, information*) salida *f*
2 *vt* (*data, information*) sacar (**to** a)

◇ *output device* dispositivo *m* de salida

outside line *n Tel* línea *f* exterior

overburning *n* sobrequemado *m*, grabación *f* por encima de la capacidad máxima

overclock *vt* hacer funcionar por encima de la velocidad teórica

overflow *n (of data)* desbordamiento *m*

oversampling *n* sobremuestreo *m*

overwrite *vt (file)* sobreescribir

◇ **overwrite mode** modo *m* de sobreescritura

package *n (software)* paquete *m*

packet *n (of data)* paquete *m*
◇ *Internet* **packet loss** pérdida *f* de paquetes
◇ *Internet* **packet switching** conmutación *f* de paquetes
◇ **packet writing** *(to CD-RW)* escritura *f* de paquetes

page *n (of document, computer file)* página *f*
◇ **page break** salto *m* de página
◇ **page design** diseño *m* de página
◇ **page down** avance *m* de página
◇ **page down key** tecla *f* de avance de página
◇ **page format** formato *m* de página
◇ **page layout** diseño *m* de página
◇ **page preview** previsualización *f*, vista *f* preliminar
◇ **page scanner** escáner *m* de páginas
◇ **page setup** ajuste *m or* configuración *f* de página
◇ **page up** retroceso *m* de página
◇ **page up key** tecla *f* de retroceso de página
▸ **page down** *vi* desplazarse hasta la página siguiente, avanzar una página

▸ **page up** *vi* desplazarse hasta la página anterior, retroceder una página

pager *n* buscapersonas *m inv*, *Esp* busca *m*, *Méx* localizador *m*, *RP* radiomensaje *m*

paginate *vt* paginar

pagination *n* paginación *f*

paint program *n* programa *m* de dibujo

palette *n* paleta *f*

palmtop *n* palm(top) *m or f*, asistente *m* personal

pane *n* ventana *f*

paper *n* papel *m*
◇ **paper advance** *(on printer)* avance *m* del papel
◇ **paper feed** alimentación *f* de papel
◇ **paper jam** atasco *m* de papel
◇ **paper tray** bandeja *f* de papel

paperless office *n* oficina *f* electrónica *or* informatizada

paragraph *n* párrafo *m*
◇ **paragraph break** salto *m* de párrafo
◇ **paragraph format** formato *m* de párrafo

◇ *paragraph mark* marca *f* de párrafo

parallel *adj* paralelo(a)

◇ *parallel interface* interfaz *f* paralela

◇ *parallel port* puerto *m* paralelo

◇ *parallel printer* impresora *f* en paralelo

◇ *parallel processing* procesado *m* en paralelo

parameter *n* parámetro *m*

parity *n* paridad *f*

◇ *parity bit* bit *m* de paridad

◇ *parity check* prueba *f* de paridad

partition 1 *n (of disk)* partición *f*
2 *vt (hard disk)* crear particiones en

PASCAL *n* PASCAL *m*

password *n* contraseña *f*, clave *f*

◇ *password protection* protección *f* por contraseña *or* clave

password-protected *adj* protegido(a) por contraseña *or* clave

paste *vt (text)* pegar (**into/onto** en)

patch *n (correction)* parche *m*, *Am* patch *m*

path *n* camino *m*, localización *f*

pathname *n* camino *m*, localización *f*

pause *n* pausa *f*

◇ *pause key* tecla *f* de pausa

pay-as-you-go *n Internet, Tel* pago *m* por uso

payment gateway *n Internet* pasarela *f* de pago

PC *n (abbr* **personal computer)** PC *m*; **available for the PC** disponible para (el) PC

◇ *PC disk* disco *m* de PC

PC-compatible *adj* compatible con (el) PC

PCI *n (abbr* **peripheral component interface)** PCI *m*

PCMCIA *n (abbr* **PC memory card international association)** PCMCIA

PDA *n (abbr* **personal digital assistant)** PDA *m*, asistente *m* personal

PDF *n (abbr* **portable document format)** PDF *m*

Pentium® *n* Pentium® *m*

perforated paper *n* papel *m* perforado

period *n (punctuation)* punto *m*

peripheral *n* periférico *m*

◇ *peripheral device* (dispositivo *m*) periférico *m*

◇ *peripheral unit* (dispositivo *m*) periférico *m*

Perl *n (abbr* **practical extraction and report language)** Perl *m*

personal *adj* personal

◇ *personal computer Esp* ordenador *m* personal, *Am* computadora *f* personal

◇ *personal computing* informática *f* personal

◇ *personal digital assistant* asistente *m* personal

◇ *Internet personal home page* página *f* personal

◇ **personal organizer** (electronic) organizador *m* personal

PGP *n* Internet (abbr **Pretty Good Privacy**) sistema *m* de cifrado PGP

phone book *n* guía *f* telefónica, listín *m* de teléfonos, *Am* directorio *m* de teléfonos

phonecard *n* tarjeta *f* telefónica

photo *n*

◇ **photo CD** photo CD *m*, foto CD *m*

◇ **photo editing** edición *f* fotográfica

◇ *Tel* **photo messaging** mensajería *f* con fotos

◇ **photo realism** fotorrealismo *m*

photocomposition *n* DTP fotocomposición *f*

photocopier *n* fotocopiadora *f*

photocopy **1** *n* fotocopia *f* **2** *vt* fotocopiar

photocopying machine *n* fotocopiadora *f*

photographic paper *n* papel *m* fotográfico

photo-quality paper *n* papel *m* fotográfico

photorealism *n* fotorrealismo *m*

photorealistic *adj* fotorrealista

phreaker *n* Fam = persona que manipula las líneas telefónicas para obtener llamadas gratis

pie chart *n* gráfico *m* circular or de sectores

PIM *n* (abbr **personal information manager**) agenda *f* personal

pin *n* pin *m*

ping *n* Internet ping *m*

pipe *n* (symbol) pleca *f*, barra *f* vertical

pirate **1** *adj* (copy, version) pirata **2** *vt* piratear

pitch *n* grado *m* de inclinación, pitch *m*

pixel *n* píxel *m*

pixellated *adj* (image) pixelado(a)

pixellation *n* (of image) pixelación *f*

plain-paper fax *n* fax *m* con papel normal

platform *n* (hardware standard) plataforma *f*

platform-independent *adj* que funciona en cualquier plataforma

player *n* reproductor *m*

playlist *n* lista *f* de canciones

plotter *n* (device) plóter *m*, plotter *m*

plug *n* (electrical) enchufe *m*

plug and play *n* conectar y funcionar, enchufar y usar

plug-in *n* conector *m*, plug-in *m*

plus sign *n* signo *m* más

PNG *n* (abbr **portable network graphics**) PNG *m*

point *n DTP* punto *m*

◇ *point size* tamaño *m* en puntos

pointer *n* puntero *m*

point-to-point protocol *n Internet* protoloco *m* punto a punto

POP *n Internet* (**a**) (*abbr* **post office protocol**) POP *m*
(**b**) (*abbr* **point of presence**) punto *m* de acceso *or* conexión

pop-up menu *n* menú *m* desplegable

port 1 *n* (*socket*) puerto *m*
2 *vt* (*transfer*) transferir

portability *n* (*of program, software*) portabilidad *f*

portable 1 *n* (*computer*) portátil *m*
2 *adj* (**a**) (*computer*) portátil
(**b**) (*program*) portable

portal *n Internet* portal *m*

portrait *n* (*paper format*) formato *m* vertical *or* de retrato; **to print sth in portrait** imprimir algo en vertical

◇ *portrait mode* modo *m* vertical

position *vt* (*cursor, image*) colocar

post *Internet* **1** *vt* (*to newsgroup*) enviar
2 *n* envío *m*

posterization *n DTP* posterización *f*

posterize *vt DTP* posterizar

posting *n Internet* (*to newsgroup*) envío *m*, mensaje *m*

postmaster *n Internet* (*for e-mail*) administrador(ora) *m,f or* jefe(a) *m,f* de correo

post office protocol *n Internet* protocolo *m* POP

PostScript® *n* PostScript® *m*

◇ *Postscript font* fuente *f* PostScript®

pound sign *n* (**a**) (*symbol "£"*) símbolo *m or* signo *m* de la libra
(**b**) *US* (*symbol "#"*) almohadilla *f, Am* numeral *m*

power *n* (*electricity*) electricidad *f*

◇ *power pack* batería *f*

◇ *power save mode* modo *m* de apagado automático

◇ *power supply* fuente *f* de alimentación

◇ *power switch* interruptor *m* de encendido

◇ *power unit* alimentador *m* de corriente

◇ *power user* usuario(a) *m,f* experto(a)

▸ **power down 1** *vt sep* apagar
2 *vi* apagarse

▸ **power up 1** *vt sep* encender, *Am* prender
2 *vi* encenderse, *Am* prenderse

power-on key *n* tecla *f* de encendido

powersave mode *n* (*of printer, computer*) modo *m* de apagado automático

ppi (*abbr* **pixels per inch**) ppp

ppm (*abbr* **pages per minute**) ppm

PPP *n Internet* (*abbr* **point-to-point protocol**) PPP *m*

predictive text input *n Tel*

predicción *f* de introducción de texto

pre-emptive multitasking *n* multitarea *f* preferencial

preferences *npl* preferencias *fpl*

prefix *n* prefijo *m*

preformatted *adj (disk)* preformateado(a)

preinstall *vt (software)* preinstalar

preinstalled *adj (software)* preinstalado(a)

pre-pay package *n (for mobile phones)* paquete *m* de prepago

prepress *n DTP* preimpresión *f*

preprogram *vt* preprogramar

preprogrammed *adj* preprogramado(a)

presentation *n*
◊ *presentation graphics* gráficos *mpl* para presentaciones
◊ *presentation graphics program* programa *m* de presentaciones

press *vt (key)* apretar, pulsar

preview *n* previsualización *f*

print 1 *vt* imprimir
  2 *vi (document)* imprimirse; *(printer)* imprimir
◊ *print buffer* buffer *m* de impresión
◊ *print format* formato *m* de impresión
◊ *print head* cabezal *m* de impresión

◊ *print job* trabajo *m* de impresión
◊ *print media* soporte *m* de impresión
◊ *print menu* menú *m* de impresión
◊ *print preview* previsualización *f*, vista *f* preliminar
◊ *print quality* calidad *f* de impresión
◊ *print queue* cola *f* de impresión
◊ *print screen* impresión *f* de pantalla
◊ *print screen key* tecla *f* de impresión de pantalla
◊ *print speed* velocidad *f* de impresión
▸ **print out** *vt sep* imprimir

printer *n* impresora *f*
◊ *printer cable* cable *m* de impresora
◊ *printer carriage* carro *m* de la impresora
◊ *printer driver* controlador *m* de impresora
◊ *printer paper* papel *m* de impresora
◊ *printer port* puerto *m* de la impresora
◊ *printer speed* velocidad *f* de la impresora

printout *n* copia *f* impresa

privacy *n* privacidad *f*

private line *n Tel* línea *f* privada

privilege *n (for access to network, database)* privilegio *m*

proceed *vi (in dialogue box)* continuar

process *vt (data)* procesar

Types of printer

Dot-Matrix

▷ Uses an inked ribbon to make an impression on the paper
▷ able to print on multi-part forms and continuous paper
▷ low cost per printed page
▷ higher noise level
▷ lower print quality

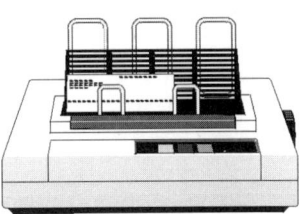

Inkjet

▷ Uses a fine jet of ink to form characters on the paper
▷ affordable colour printing
▷ high cost per printed page
▷ quiet printing

Laser

▷ Uses laser to print text on the paper
▷ low cost per printed page
▷ quiet printing
▷ fast
▷ colour laser printers are expensive

◇ *DTP* **process colours** cuatri-cromía *f*

processing *n (of data)* proce-so *m*, procesado *m*

◇ *processing speed* velocidad *f* de proceso

◇ *processing time* tiempo *m* de procesamiento

processor *n* procesador *m*

◇ *processor speed* velocidad *f* del procesador

product activation *n* acti-vación *f* de producto

program 1 *n* programa *m*
2 *vt* programar; **to program a computer to do sth** programar *Esp* un ordenador *or Am* una computadora para que haga algo
3 *vi* programar; **to program in assembly language** programar en lenguaje ensamblador

◇ *program disk* disco *m* de programa

◇ *program language* lenguaje *m* de programación

◇ *program library* biblioteca *f* or librería *f* de programas

programmer *n* programa-dor(ora) *m,f*

programming *n* programa-ción *f*

◇ *programming error* error *m* de programación

◇ *programming language* len-guaje *m* de programación

prompt *n* mensaje *m*; **return to the C:\ prompt** volver a C:\

properties *npl (of file, drive)* propiedades *fpl*

proportional spacing *n DTP* espaciado *m* proporcio-nal, monoespaciado *m*

protection *n* protección *f*

protocol *n* protocolo *m*

provider *n Internet* proveedor *m*

proxy *n Internet* proxy *m*

◇ *proxy server* servidor *m* proxy

public domain *n* dominio *m* público

◇ *public domain software* software *m* de dominio pú-blico

publish *vt (web page)* publicar

▸ **pull down** *vt sep (menu)* desplegar

pull-down menu *n* menú *m* desplegable

pull technology *n Internet* tecnología *f* informática por solicitud, tecnología *f* de atrac-ción

pulse *n Tel* pulso *m*

push technology *n Internet* tecnología *f* informática por suscripción

quality *n* calidad *f*

quarantine *vt (infected file)* poner en cuarentena

query 1 *n* consulta *f*
2 *vt (database)* consultar

question mark *n* signo *m* de interrogación

queue 1 *n* cola *f*

2 *vt (print jobs)* poner en cola

quit 1 *vt (database, program)* salir de
2 *vi* salir

quote *vt (in e-mail)* citar

quoting *n (in e-mail)* cita *f*

QWERTY keyboard *n* teclado *m* QWERTY

rackmounted *adj* monta-do(a) en estante

radio button *n* botón *m* de tipo radio

RAID *n* (*abbr* **redundant array of independent disks**) RAID *m*

◇ *RAID drive* unidad *f* RAID

RAM *n* (*abbr* **random access memory**) (memoria *f*) RAM *f*

random *adj* aleatorio(a)

◇ *random access* acceso *m* aleatorio

◇ *random access memory* memoria *f* de acceso aleatorio

raster graphics *npl* gráficos *mpl* rasterizados

rasterize *vt* rasterizar

raw *adj* (*data, statistics*) en bruto

RDBMS *n* (*abbr* **relational database management system**) sistema *m* de gestión de bases de datos relacionales

RDRAM *n* (*abbr* **Rambus dynamic random access memory**) RDRAM *f*

read *vt* leer

▸ **read out** *vt sep* (*data*) visualizar

readdress *vt* (*e-mail message*) redireccionar

reader *n* lector *m*

read-me file *n* documento *m* léeme

read-only *adj* that file is read-only ese archivo es de sólo lectura; **to make a file read-only** hacer que un archivo sea de sólo lectura

◇ *read-only memory* memoria *f* de sólo lectura

read-write head *n* cabeza *f* lectora/grabadora

ready mode *n* (*of printer*) modo *m* preparada

real time *n* tiempo *m* real

real-time *adj* en tiempo real

reboot 1 *vt* reinicializar **2** *vi* reinicializarse

.rec *Internet* (*abbr* **recreation**) (*in newsgroups*) = abreviatura que designa a los foros de discusión abiertos a temas de tipo lúdico

recall button *n* (*on telephone*) botón *m* de rellamada *or Andes, RP* de rediscado

reception *n* the reception is poor here aquí hay poca cobertura

recipient *n* (*of e-mail message*) destinatario(a) *m,f*

reconfigure *vt* reconfigurar

reconnect 1 *vt* reconectar
2 *vi* reconectarse

record *n (in database)* registro *m*

recover *vt (file, data)* recuperar

recovery *n (of file, data)* recuperación *f*

recycle bin *n* papelera *f* de reciclaje

red-eye effect *n DTP* efecto *m* de ojos rojos

redial *Tel* **1** *n* redial **(feature)** (botón *m* de) rellamada *f*, *Andes, RP* rediscado *m*
2 *vt (number)* volver a marcar *or Andes, RP* discar
3 *vi* volver a marcar *or Andes, RP* discar

redirect *vt (e-mail message)* redireccionar (**to** hacia)

redo *vt* repetir

redraw *vt* redibujar

reference *n* referencia *f*

refill card *n US (for mobile phone)* tarjeta *f* de recarga

reformat *vt* reformatear

refresh 1 *n* refresco *m*
2 *vt (screen)* actualizar, refrescar
◇ *refresh rate* velocidad *f* de refresco

register 1 *n (of memory)* registro *m*
2 *vt (software)* registrar

registered user *n* usuario(a) *m,f* registrado(a)

registration *n* registro *m*
◇ *registration card* tarjeta *f* de registro
◇ *registration number* número *m* de registro

registry *n (Windows file)* registro *m*

reinitialize *vt* reinicializar

reinsert *vt (block)* volver a insertar

reinstall *vt* reinstalar

relational database *n* base *f* de datos relacional

release *n (of software)* versión *f*

reload *vt* volver a cargar

remailer *n Internet* redireccionador *m* de correo

remote *adj (user)* remoto(a)
◇ *remote access* acceso *m* remoto
◇ *remote login* conexión *f* remota
◇ *remote server* servidor *m* remoto
◇ *remote terminal* terminal *m* remoto

removable *adj (disk, media)* extraíble, removible

rename *vt (file)* renombrar, cambiar de nombre

render *vt DTP* renderizar

rendering *n DTP* renderizado *m*

rental *n (for telephone)* alquiler *m*, *Méx* renta *f*

repaginate *vt* repaginar

repetitive strain injury *n* lesión *f* por esfuerzo *or* movimiento repetitivo

replace *vt* reemplazar; **replace all** *(command)* reemplazar todos

replenishment card *n US (for mobile phone)* tarjeta *f* de recarga

report *n (of database)* informe *m*

reprogram *vt* reprogramar

reprogrammable *adj (key)* reprogramable

rerun *vt (program)* volver a ejecutar

resample *vt DTP (image)* remuestrear

reset *vt* reinicializar

◇ *reset button* botón *m* de reinicio

◇ *reset switch* botón *m* de reinicio

resident *adj* residente

resizable *adj* redimensionable

resize *vt* redimensionar

resolution *n (of image)* resolución *f*

response time *n* tiempo *m* de respuesta

restart **1** *n (of system)* reinicio *m*

2 *vt (system)* reiniciar

3 *vi (system)* reiniciarse

restore *vt* restaurar

resume *vt* continuar

retouch *vt (photograph)* retocar

retrieval *n* recuperación *f*

retrieve *vt* recuperar

retry *vi* volver a intentar

return *n (key)* retorno *m*

◇ *return address* *(of e-mail)* dirección *f* del remitente

◇ *return key* tecla *f* de retorno

reverse *vt Br Tel* **to reverse the charges** llamar a cobro revertido

◇ *reverse slash* barra *f* oblicua invertida

◇ *reverse sort* ordenación *f* a la inversa

reverse-charge call *n Br Tel* llamada *f or Am* llamado *m* a cobro revertido

revert *vi (undo)* volver

rewritable *adj (media)* regrabable

RGB *(abbr* **red, green and blue)** RGB

ribbon *n (under menu bar)* cinta *f*

right arrow *n* flecha *f* derecha

◇ *right arrow key* tecla *f* de flecha derecha

right-click **1** *vt* hacer clic *or* pinchar con el botón derecho en

2 *vi* hacer clic *or* pinchar con el botón derecho (**on** en)

ring network *n* red *f* en anillo

ringtone *n (on phone)* señal *f* de llamada; *(on mobile phone)* melodía *f*

RISC *n (abbr* **reduced instruction set chip** *or* **computer)**

◇ *RISC processor* procesador *m* RISC

roam *vi Tel (mobile phone user)* viajar

roaming n Tel (of mobile phone) itinerancia f

robot n Internet robot m

rocker switch n conmutador m basculante

rollover button n botón m dinámico or cambiante

ROM n (abbr **read only memory**) (memoria f) ROM f

roman n DTP (letra f) redonda f or redondilla f

root directory n directorio m raíz

router n Internet encaminador m, router m

routine n rutina f

row n (in table, spreadsheet) fila f

RSI n (abbr **repetitive strain injury**) lesión f por esfuerzo or movimiento repetitivo

RTF (abbr **rich text format**) RTF

◇ **RTF file** archivo m RTF

ruler n (**a**) (in word processor) regla f
(**b**) DTP regla f

◇ **ruler line** raya f

run 1 vt (program) ejecutar; **this computer runs most software** con Esp este ordenador or Am esta computadora se puede ejecutar la mayoría del software
2 vi **this software runs on DOS** este software funciona en DOS; **do not interrupt the program while it is running** no interrumpa el programa mientras se está ejecutando

runtime (version) n versión f run-time, = versión limitada de un programa de apoyo que acompaña a una aplicación

satellite (speaker) *n* altavoz *m* satélite

saturation *n DTP (of image)* saturación *f*

save 1 *vt (document)* guardar; **to save sth to disk** guardar algo en el disco; **do you want to save changes?** ¿desea guardar cambios?; **save as...** guardar como…

2 *vi* guardar cambios; **this file is taking a lot of time to save** este archivo está tardando mucho en guardarse

scalability *n* escalabilidad *f*

scalable font *n DTP* fuente *f* escalable

scan 1 *n* escaneo *m*
2 *vt* escanear

▸ **scan in** *vt sep (graphics)* escanear

scanner *n* escáner *m*

scheduler *n (package)* software *m* de planificación (de proyectos)

.sci *Internet (abbr* **science**) *(in newsgroups)* = abreviatura que designa a los foros de discusión sobre temas científicos

scrapbook *n (on Macintosh)* apuntador *m*

scratchpad *n US* bloc *m* de notas

screen *n* pantalla *f*; **to work on screen** trabajar en pantalla; **to bring up the next screen** visualizar la siguiente pantalla

◇ **screen capture** captura *f* de pantalla

◇ **screen dump** pantallazo *m*, captura *f* de pantalla

◇ *US Internet* **screen name** apodo *m*, pseudónimo *m*

◇ **screen refresh** refresco *m* de pantalla

◇ **screen shot** captura *f* de pantalla

screensaver *n* salvapantallas *m inv*

script *n* guión *m*, script *m*

scroll *vi* desplazarse por la pantalla

◇ **scroll arrow** flecha *f* de desplazamiento

◇ **scroll bar** barra *f* de desplazamiento

◇ **scroll lock key** tecla *f* de bloqueo de desplazamiento

◇ **scroll wheel** *(on mouse)* rueda *f* de desplazamiento

▸ **scroll down 1** *vt insep* **to scroll down a document** desplazarse hacia abajo por un documento

2 *vi (person)* desplazarse hacia abajo

▸ **scroll through** *vt insep (text)* recorrer

▸ **scroll up** **1** *vt insep* **to scroll up a document** desplazarse hacia arriba por un documento

2 *vi (person)* desplazarse hacia arriba

SCSI *n (abbr* **small computer systems interface)** SCSI *m*

◊ ***SCSI address*** dirección *f* SCSI

◊ ***SCSI card*** tarjeta *f* SCSI

◊ ***SCSI chain*** cadena *f* SCSI

SDRAM *n (abbr* **synchronous dynamic random access memory)** (memoria *f*) SDRAM *f*

search **1** *n* búsqueda *f*; **to do a search** hacer una búsqueda; **to do a search for sth** buscar algo

2 *vt (file, directory)* buscar; **to search and replace sth** buscar y reemplazar algo

3 *vi* buscar

◊ *Internet* ***search engine*** motor *m or* página *f* de búsqueda

◊ ***search time*** tiempo *m* de búsqueda

searchable *adj* **a product searchable by name/price** un producto que se puede buscar por nombre/precio

second-generation *adj* de segunda generación

sector *n (of disk)* sector *m*

secure *adj Internet* seguro(a)

◊ ***secure electronic transaction***

transacción *f* electrónica segura

◊ ***secure HTTP*** HTTP *m* seguro

◊ ***secure server*** servidor *m* seguro

◊ ***secure sockets layer*** protocolo *m* SSL

security *n* seguridad *f*

◊ *Internet* ***security certificate*** certificado *m* de seguridad

◊ ***security level*** nivel *m* de seguridad

seek time *n* tiempo *m* de búsqueda

select *vt* seleccionar; **to select an option** seleccionar una opción

selection *n* selección *f*

self-extracting file *n* archivo *m* autodescomprimible

self-replicating *adj* que se autorreproduce

self-test **1** *n* autotest *m*

2 *vi* efectuar un autotest

semicolon *n* punto *m* y coma

separator *n* separador *m*

sequence *n* secuencia *f*

sequential *adj* secuencial

◊ ***sequential access*** acceso *m* secuencial

◊ ***sequential processing*** procesado *m* secuencial

serial *adj*

◊ ***serial cable*** cable *m* de serie

◊ ***serial device*** periférico *m* en serie

◊ ***serial interface*** interfaz *m or f* de serie

◊ ***serial port*** puerto *m* (de) serie

◇ **serial printer** impresora *f* en serie

server *n* servidor *m*

service *n*

◇ **service bureau** servicio *m* de filmación

◇ *Internet* **service provider** proveedor *m* de servicios

session *n* (**a**) *Internet* sesión *f* (**b**) *(when writing to CD-R)* sesión *f*

SET® *n* *Internet* (*abbr* **secure electronic transaction**) protocolo *m* SET®

set 1 *n* *(of characters)* juego *m*; *(of instructions)* conjunto *m*
2 *vt* *(tabs, format)* configurar

▸ **set up** *vt sep* *(computer, system)* configurar

setting *n* configuración *f*; **settings** configuración *f*

setup *n*

◇ **setup CD-ROM** CD-ROM *m* de instalación

◇ *Internet* **setup charge** cuota *f* de conexión

◇ *Internet* **setup fee** cuota *f* de conexión

◇ **setup program** programa *m* de configuración

SGML *n* (*abbr* **Standard Generalized Markup Language**) SGML *m*

shade *n* sombreado *m*

◇ **shades of grey** *or US* **gray** tonos *mpl* de gris

shadow printing *n* impresión *f* subordinada

shareware *n* shareware *m*

sheet feeder *n* alimentador *m* de hojas sueltas

shell *n* (**a**) *(of program)* shell *m* (**b**) *(of mouse)* carcasa *f*

shift *n* mayúsculas *fpl*; **an asterisk is shift 8** para el asterisco hay que presionar mayúsculas y 8

◇ **shift key** tecla *f* de mayúsculas

shopbot *n* *Internet* robot *m* de compras

shopping basket *n* *Internet* cesta *f or* carrito *m* de la compra

shopping cart *n* *US Internet* cesta *f or* carrito *m* de la compra

shortcode *n* *Tel* código *m* de marcado *or Andes, RP* discado abreviado

◇ **shortcode dialling** marcado *m or Andes, RP* discado *m* abreviado

shortcut *n* atajo *m*, acceso *m* directo

◇ **shortcut key** tecla *f* de atajo

show *vt* *(files, records)* mostrar

▸ **shut down 1** *vt sep* *(computer)* apagar
2 *vi* *(system)* apagarse

shutdown *n* apagado *m*

shutter *n* *DTP* obturador *m*

◇ **shutter priority** prioridad *f* a la obturación

signal *n* *Tel* señal *f*; **I can't get a signal** *(on mobile phone)* no tengo cobertura

signature *n* *(on e-mail)* firma *f*

◇ **signature file** archivo *m* de firma

◊ *signature line* línea *f* con la firma

SIM *n* (*abbr* **subscriber identity module**)

◊ *SIM card* (*in mobile phone*) tarjeta *f* SIM

SIM-free phone *n* Tel teléfono *m* sin SIM

SIMM *n* (*abbr* **single in-line memory module**) SIMM *m*

simulate *vt* simular

simulation *n* simulación *f*

simulator *n* simulador *m*

single-mode *adj* Tel de banda única

single-user licence, US **single-user license** *n* licencia *f* para un único usuario

site *n* Internet sitio *m*

◊ *site map* mapa *m* del sitio

size **1** *n* (*of file, font*) tamaño *m* **2** *vt* cambiar de tamaño

skin *n* (*of program*) máscara *f*

skip *vt* (*command*) saltarse

slash *n* barra *f*

slashdot effect *n* Internet = efecto que hace que un sitio se colapse por recibir demasiadas visitas

sleep *vi* dormir, reposar; **to put a notebook to sleep** poner un portátil a dormir *or* reposar

slide show *n* proyección *f* de diapositivas

SLIP *n* (*abbr* **serial line Internet protocol**) protocolo *m* SLIP

slot *n* ranura *f*, Am slot *m*

small caps *npl* versalita *f*

smart *adj*

◊ *smart card* tarjeta *f* inteligente

◊ *smart quotes* comillas *fpl* tipográficas

SmartMedia® card *n* tarjeta *f* SmartMedia®

smiley *n* Internet emoticono *m*, emoticón *m*

SMS Tel (*abbr* **short message service**) **1** *n* (*service*) SMS *m*; (*message*) mensaje *m* de texto **2** *vt* enviar un mensaje de texto a

◊ *SMS message* mensaje *m* SMS

SMTP *n* Internet (*abbr* **Simple Mail Transfer Protocol**) protocolo *m* SMTP

snail mail *n* Fam correo *m* caracol *or* tortuga, correo *m* tradicional

snap-on cover *n* (*for mobile phone*) carcasa *f*

.soc Internet (*abbr* **social**) (*in newsgroups*) = abreviatura que designa a los foros de discusión abiertos temas que versan sobre la sociedad

socket *n* (**a**) (*slot*) zócalo *m* (**b**) Internet socket *m*, puerto *m*

soft *adj*

◊ *soft copy* copia *f* en formato electrónico

◊ *soft key* botón *m* inteligente

◊ *soft hyphen* guión *m* corto, guión *m* de final de renglón

◊ *soft return* retorno *m* automático

software *n* software *m*

◇ *software company* empresa *f* de software

◇ *software developer* desarrollador(ora) *m,f* de software

◇ *software engineer* ingeniero(a) *m,f* de software

◇ *software error* error *m* de software

◇ *software house* casa *f* de software

◇ *software package* paquete *m* de software

◇ *software piracy* piratería *f* informática

◇ *software platform* plataforma *f* de software

◇ *software problem* problema *m* de software

◇ *software tool* herramienta *f* de software

SOHO *adj* (*abbr* **small office home office**) para teletrabajadores

solids modelling, *US* **solids modeling** *n* modelado *m* de sólidos

sort 1 *n* (*arranging in list*) ordenación *f*; **the program will do an alphabetical sort** el problema va a realizar una ordenación alfabética

2 *vt* (*arrange in list*) ordenar; **to sort sth alphabetically** ordenar algo alfabéticamente; **to sort sth in ascending/descending order** clasificar algo por orden ascendente/descendente

sound card *n* tarjeta *f* de sonido

source *n*

◇ *source code* código *m* fuente

◇ *source disk* disco *m* original

◇ *source document* documento *m* original

space *n* (*in text*) espacio *m*

◇ *space bar* barra *f* espaciadora

spacing *n* espacio *m*

spam *Internet* **1** *n* correo *m* basura

2 *vt* enviar correo basura a

3 *vi* enviar correo basura

spammer *n* *Internet* = persona que envía correo basura

spamming *n* *Internet* envío *m* de correo basura

S/P-DIF *n* (*abbr* **Sony/Philips Digital Interface**) S/P-DIF *m*

speaker *n* (*loudspeaker*) altavoz *m*

specification *n* especificaciones *fpl or* características *fpl* técnicas

specs *n* especificaciones *fpl or* características *fpl* técnicas

speech recognition *n* reconocimiento *m* del habla

speed *n* velocidad *f*; **a 32 speed CD-ROM** un CD-ROM de velocidad 32x

◇ *Tel* *speed dial* marcado *m* rápido, marcación *f* rápida, *Andes, RP* discado *m* rápido

spellcheck 1 *n* **to do** *or* **run a spellcheck on a document** pasar el corrector ortográfico a un documento

2 *vt* **to spellcheck a document** pasar el corrector ortográfico a un documento

spellchecker *n* corrector *m* ortográfico

spelling checker n corrector m ortográfico

spider n Internet araña f

spidering n Internet arañeo m

splash page n Internet página f introductoria

split vt (file, image) dividir

◇ **split screen** ventana f dividida

spot colour, US **spot color** n DTP color m plano or directo

spreadsheet n (document, software) hoja f de cálculo

spyware n Internet software m espía

SQL n (abbr **structured query language**) SQL m

SSL n Internet (abbr **secure sockets layer**) protocolo m SSL

stand-alone adj independiente, autónomo(a)

standard memory n memoria f estándar

standby n (of mobile phone) tiempo m en espera, autonomía f en espera

◇ **standby mode** (of printer, computer) modo m de reposo, modo m de suspensión del sistema

◇ **standby time** (of mobile phone) tiempo m en espera, autonomía f en espera

star network n red f en estrella

start vi

◇ **start button** (in Windows) botón m de inicio

◇ **start menu** (in Windows) menú m (de) inicio

▸ **start up 1** vt sep (computer) arrancar
2 vi (computer) arrancar

starter pack n Internet kit m de conexión

start-up n (a) (of computer) arranque m
(b) Internet (company) nueva empresa f

◇ **start-up disk** disco m de arranque

◇ **start-up screen** pantalla f de arranque

status n

◇ **status bar** barra f de estado

◇ **status line** línea f de estado

sticky adj Internet (web site) adherente, atractivo(a)

stop button n Internet botón m (de) detener

storage n (of data) almacenamiento m

◇ **storage capacity** capacidad f de almacenamiento

◇ **storage device** dispositivo m de almacenamiento

◇ **storage media** sistemas mpl de almacenamiento

store vt (data) almacenar

stream vt (data, audio) reproducir en tiempo real

streaming n (of data, audio) reproducción f en tiempo real; **audio/data streaming** audio/datos en tiempo real

strike-through mode n efecto m de tachado

string n (of characters) cadena f

stroke n (oblique) barra f inclinada

stub antenna n (on mobile phone) antena f (externa)

style n estilo m
◇ *style bar* barra f de estilos
◇ *style sheet* hoja f de estilos

stylechecker n corrector m de estilo

stylus n (for PDA) lápiz m óptico

subdirectory n subdirectorio m

subfolder n subdirectorio m

subject n (of e-mail message) asunto m

submenu n submenú m

subnet n subred f

subroutine n subrutina f

subscribe vi (to ISP) abonarse

subscriber n (to ISP, telephone network) usuario(a) m,f, cliente mf

subscript n subíndice m; **subscript "a"** "a" (escrita como) subíndice

subscription n (to ISP) cuota f de conexión

subwoofer n subwoofer m

suite n (of software) paquete m integrado

supercomputer n Esp superordenador m, Am supercomputador m

superhighway n Internet autopista f de la información

superscript n superíndice m; **superscript "a"** "a" (escrita como) superíndice, "a" volada

support vt this package is supported by all workstations este paquete funciona en todas las estaciones de trabajo; **56K supported** funciona con 56K
◇ *support line* línea f de asistencia técnica

surf vt to surf the Net navegar por Internet

surface modelling, US **surface modeling** n modelado m de superficies

surfer n internauta mf

surge protector n protector m de sobrecarga

surround sound n sonido m envolvente

SVGA (abbr Super Video Graphics Array) SVGA

switch vi press this key to switch between screens pulse esta tecla para pasar de una pantalla a otra

switchboard n Tel centralita f, Am conmutador m
◇ *switchboard operator* telefonista mf

swung dash n tilde f, virguilla f

symbol n símbolo m

synchronous adj síncrono(a)

syntax n sintaxis f
◇ *syntax error* error m de sintaxis

SYSADMIN n (abbr **Systems Administrator**) administrador(ora) m, f del sistema

SYSOP n (abbr **Systems Opera-**

tor) operador(ora) *m,f* del sistema

system *n* sistema *m*

◇ **systems analysis** análisis *m inv* de sistemas

◇ **systems analyst** analista *mf* de sistemas

◇ **system disk** disco *m* de sistema

◇ **systems engineer** ingeniero(a) *m,f* de sistemas

◇ **system error** error *m* del sistema

◇ **system failure** *Esp* fallo *m or Am* falla *f* del sistema

◇ **system file** archivo *m* del sistema

◇ **system folder** carpeta *f* del sistema

◇ **systems management** gestión *f* de sistemas

◇ **system software** software *m* de sistema

◇ **system unit** unidad *f* central, CPU *f*

tab 1 *n* tabulador *m*
2 *vt (text)* tabular
◇ *tab key* tecla *f* de tabular, tabulador *m*

tab-delimited *adj* separado(a) por tabuladores

table *n (diagram)* tabla *f*

tablet *n* tableta *f*

tabulate *vt* tabular

tabulator *n* tabulador *m*
◇ *tabulator key* tecla *f* de tabular, tabulador *m*

tag 1 *n (code)* etiqueta *f*
2 *vt* etiquetar

talktime *n Tel* tiempo *m* de conversación, autonomía *f* en llamada

tape *n* cinta *f*
◇ *tape backup* copia *f* de seguridad en cinta
◇ *tape backup system* sistema *m* de copias de seguridad en cinta
◇ *tape backup unit* unidad *f* de copias de seguridad en cinta
◇ *tape unit* unidad *f* de cinta

target disk *n* disco *m* de destino

task *n* tarea *f*

taskbar *n* barra *f* de tareas

TCP/IP *n Internet (abbr* **transmission control protocol/Internet protocol)** TCP/IP *m*

TDMA *n Tel (abbr* **time division multiple access)** TDMA *m*

tear-off menu *n* menú *m* flotante

techie *n Fam* experto(a) *m,f* en informática

technical *adj* técnico(a)
◇ *technical assistance* asistencia *f* técnica
◇ *technical support* servicio *m* de asistencia técnica, soporte *m* técnico

teleconference *n* teleconferencia *f*

teleconferencing *n* teleconferencias *fpl*

telematics *n* telemática *f*

telephone 1 *n* teléfono *m*
2 *vt* telefonear; **to telephone New York** telefonear a Nueva York
3 *vi* telefonear
◇ *telephone banking* telebanca *f*, banca *f* telefónica
◇ *telephone bill* factura *f* del teléfono
◇ *telephone book* guía *f* telefónica, listín *m* de teléfonos,

Am directorio *m* de teléfonos

◇ *telephone call* llamada *f* telefónica, *Am* llamado *m* telefónico

◇ *telephone directory* guía *f* telefónica, listín *m* de teléfonos, *Am* directorio *m* de teléfonos

◇ *telephone exchange* central *f or* centralita *f* telefónica

◇ *telephone line* línea *f* de teléfono

◇ *telephone message* mensaje *m* telefónico

◇ *telephone number* número *m* de teléfono

◇ *telephone operator* telefonista *mf*, operador(ora) *m,f*

◇ *telephone order* pedido *m* por teléfono

◇ *telephone receiver* auricular *m*, *RP, Ven* tubo *m*

◇ *telephone subscriber* abonado(a) *m,f* al teléfono

teleprocessing *n* teleproceso *m*

teletex *n* teletexto *m*

Telnet *n* *Internet* Telnet *m*

template *n* plantilla *f*

temporary file *n* archivo *m* temporal

terabyte *n* terabyte *m*

terminal *n* terminal *m*

◇ *terminal emulation* emulación *f* de terminal

◇ *terminal emulator* emulador *m* de terminal

◇ *terminal server* servidor *m* de terminales

terminator *n* (of chain) terminador *m*

text 1 *n* texto *m*

2 *vt* *Tel* (send text message to) enviar un mensaje de texto a

3 *vi* *Tel* (send text messages) enviar mensajes de texto

◇ *text block* bloque *m* de texto

◇ *text editing* edición *f* de textos

◇ *text editor* editor *m* de textos

◇ *text field* campo *m* de texto

◇ *text file* archivo *m* de texto

◇ *text layout* formato *m* del texto

◇ *Tel* *text message* mensaje *m* de texto

◇ *Tel* *text messaging* envío *m* de mensajes de texto

◇ *text mode* modo *m* (de) texto

◇ *text processing* procesado *m or* tratamiento *m* de textos

◇ *text processor* procesador *m* de textos

◇ *text wrap* contorneo *m* de texto

texter *n* *Tel* persona *f* que manda mensajes de texto

texting *n* *Tel* envío *m* de mensajes de texto

texture *n* *DTP* textura *f*

TFT *n* (abbr **thin film transistor**) TFT *m*

◇ *TFT display* pantalla *f* TFT

◇ *TFT screen* pantalla *f* TFT

thermal *adj* térmico(a)

◇ *thermal paper* papel *m* térmico

◇ *thermal printer* impresora *f* térmica

thesaurus *n* diccionario *m* de sinónimos

third-generation *adj* *Tel* de

tercera generación

third-party *adj* de terceras partes

◇ *third-party developer* desarrollador(ora) *m,f* de terceras partes

◇ *third-party software* software *m* de terceras partes

thread *n (in newsgroup)* hilo *m* de discusión

three-button mouse *n Esp* ratón *m or Am* mouse *m* de tres botones

3G *Tel (abbr* **third generation**) 3G

throughput *n* rendimiento *m*, capacidad *f* de procesamiento

thumbnail *n* miniatura *f*

TIFF *n (abbr* **Tagged Image File Format**) TIFF *m*

◇ *TIFF file* archivo *m* TIFF

tile *vt (windows)* poner en mosaico

timeout *n Internet* tiempo *m* expirado

time sharing *n* tiempo *m* compartido

title bar *n* barra *f* de título

toggle *vi* **to toggle between two applications** moverse de un programa a otro apretando una tecla

◇ *toggle key* = tecla o botón que permite activar o desactivar una función

◇ *toggle switch* = tecla o botón que permite activar o desactivar una función

token ring *n* red *m* en anillo, token ring *m*

toll call *n US Tel* llamada *f or Am* llamado *m* de larga distancia, *Esp* conferencia *f*

toll-free *US Tel* **1** *adj* **toll-free number** (número *m* de) teléfono *m* gratuito

2 *adv* **to call toll-free** llamar gratuitamente

tone *n* (**a**) *Tel* tono *m* (**b**) *DTP (of colour)* tono *m*

toner *n* tóner *m*

◇ *toner cartridge* cartucho *m* de tóner

tool bar, toolbar *n* barra *f* de herramientas

toolbox *n* caja *f* de herramientas

topic *n Internet* tema *m*, asunto *m*

◇ *topic drift* desviación *f* del tema

top-level domain *n Internet* dominio *m* de alto nivel

top-up card *n Br (for mobile phone)* tarjeta *f* de recarga

touch *n*

◇ *touch pad Esp* ratón *m or Am* mouse *m* táctil, touchpad *m*

◇ *touch screen* pantalla *f* táctil

touch-sensitive *adj* táctil

touch-tone telephone *n* teléfono *m* de tonos, teléfono *m* de marcado *or Andes, RP* discado por tonos

tower *n (CPU)* torre *f*

◇ *tower system* torre *f*

track *n (of disk)* pista *f*

trackball *n Esp* ratón *m or Am* mouse *m* de bola, trackball *m*

trackpad *n Esp* ratón *m or Am* mouse *m* táctil, trackpad *m*

traffic *n Internet (on web site)* tráfico *m*

transceiver *n* transceptor *m*

transfer **1** *n (of data)* transferencia *f*
2 *vt* (**a**) *Tel (call)* pasar, transferir; **I'm transferring you now** le paso ahora mismo
(**b**) *(data)* transferir
◇ *transfer rate* velocidad *f* de transferencia
◇ *transfer speed* velocidad *f* de transferencia

translate *vt (software)* traducir

translator *n (of software)* traductor(ora) *m,f*

transmission *n (of data)* transmisión *f*

transparency (scanning) adaptor *n (for scanner)* adaptador *m* para transparencias

trash *n US* papelera *f* (de reciclaje)
◇ *trash can* papelera *f*

tray *n* bandeja *f*

tree *n (of data)* árbol *m*
◇ *tree diagram* diagrama *m* en árbol
◇ *tree structure* diagrama *m* en árbol

trial version *n (of software)* versión *f* de prueba

tri-band, triple-band *adj Tel* de triple banda

Trojan Horse *n* troyano *m*

troubleshooter *n* técnico(a)

m,f (en resolución de problemas)

troubleshooting *n* resolución *f* de problemas

true-colour, *US* **true-color** *adj (image)* de color verdadero

TrueType® font *n DTP* fuente *f* TrueType®

trunk call *n* llamada *f or Am* llamado *m* de larga distancia, *Esp* conferencia *f*

trusted third party *n (for Internet transactions)* tercero *m* de confianza

TTP *n (abbr* **trusted third party***) (for Internet transactions)* tercero *m* de confianza

tunneling *n* tunelado *m*

tutorial *n* tutorial *m*, curso *m*
◇ *tutorial program* tutorial *m*, curso *m*

TV *n* televisión *f*, TV *f*
◇ *TV out* salida *f* de TV
◇ *TV tuner card* tarjeta *f* sintonizadora de TV

twisted pair *n* par *m* trenzado

type **1** *n (text)* tipo *m*, letra; **in large/small type** en letra grande/pequeña; **in bold type** en negrita
2 *vt* escribir a máquina, mecanografiar; **to type sth into a computer** pasar algo *Esp* a ordenador *or Am* a la computadora
3 *vi* escribir a máquina, mecanografiar
◇ *type size* tamaño *m* de letra

typeface *n* tipo *m* de letra

typesetter *n DTP* filmadora *f*

UDP *n Internet (abbr* **User Datagram Protocol***)* UDP *m*

UML *n (abbr* **unified modelling language***)* UML *m*

UMTS *n Tel (abbr* **Universal Mobile Telecommunications Services***)* UMTS *m*

unauthorized *adj* no autorizado(a)

◊ **unauthorized access** acceso *m* no autorizado

undo *vt (command)* deshacer; **undo changes** deshacer cambios; **undo last** deshacer el último cambio

unedited *adj (text)* sin editar

unformatted *adj (disk)* sin formatear

uninitialized *adj* sin inicializar

uninstall *vt* desinstalar

uninterruptible power supply *n* sistema *m* de alimentación ininterrumpida, *Méx* regulador *m*, *RP* estabilizador *m*

unique visitor *n Internet* visitante *m* único

Unix *n* Unix *m*

Unix-based *adj* basado(a) en Unix

unlimited e-mail addresses *npl* direcciones *fpl* de correo ilimitadas

unlisted *adj (telephone number)* que no figura en la guía (telefónica)

unlock *vt* (**a**) *(file, diskette)* desbloquear
(**b**) *(mobile phone) (from service provider)* liberalizar; *(keypad)* desbloquear

unreadable *adj (file, data)* ilegible

unsubscribe *vi (to ISP, mailing list)* cancelar la suscripción

unzip *vt (file)* descomprimir

up arrow *n* flecha *f* arriba

◊ **up arrow key** tecla *f* de flecha arriba

update 1 *n (of software package)* actualización *f*
2 *vt* actualizar

upgradability *n* capacidad *f* de actualización

upgradable *adj (hardware, system)* actualizable; *(memory)* ampliable

upgrade 1 *n (of hardware, software, system)* actualización *f*; *(of memory)* ampliación *f*
2 *vt (hardware, software,*

system) actualizar; *(memory)* ampliar

◇ **upgrade kit** kit *m* de actualización

upload *Internet* **1** *n* carga *f*
2 *vt* cargar, subir

upper-case 1 *n* mayúsculas *fpl*
2 *adj* en mayúsculas

UPS *n* (*abbr* **uninterruptible power supply**) SAI *m*, *Méx* regulador *m*, *RP* estabilizador *m*

upward-compatible *adj* compatible con versiones anteriores

urban legend *n* Internet leyenda *f* urbana

URL *n* Internet (*abbr* **uniform resource locator**) URL *m*, dirección *f*

USB *n* (*abbr* **universal serial bus**) USB *m*

◇ **USB cable** cable *m* USB
◇ **USB port** puerto *m* USB

Usenet *n* Internet Usenet *f*

user *n* *(of computer)* usuario(a) *m,f*

◇ **user account** *(in Windows)* cuenta *f* de usuario

◇ **user group** grupo *m* de usuarios

◇ **user ID, user identification** nombre *m* de usuario

◇ **user interface** interfaz *m or f* de usuario

◇ **user language** lenguaje *m* de usuario

◇ **user manual** manual *m* del usuario

◇ **user name** nombre *m* de usuario

◇ **user software** software *m* de usuario

◇ **user support** asistencia *f* técnica al usuario

user-definable *adj (characters, keys)* definible por el usuario

user-friendliness *n* facilidad *f* de manejo

user-friendly *adj* fácil de manejar

utility *n* *(program)* utilidad *f*

◇ **utility program** utilidad *f*

validate *vt* validar

validation *n* validación *f*

variable *n* variable *f*

VDU *n* (*abbr* **visual display unit**) monitor *m*

◇ **VDU operator** persona *f* que trabaja en pantalla

vector *n DTP*

◇ **vector graphics** gráficos *mpl* vectoriales

◇ **vector tool** herramienta *f* de vectores

vendor *n* vendedor(ora) *m,f*

Veronica *n Internet* Verónica

version *n* versión *f*

vertical *adj* vertical

◇ **vertical justification** justificación *f* vertical

◇ **vertical orientation** orientación *f* vertical

VGA (*abbr* **Video Graphics Array**) VGA; **Super VGA** Super VGA

vibrating alert *n* (*on mobile phone*) vibración *f* de llamada

video *n Esp* vídeo *m*, *Am* video *m*

◇ **video accelerator card** acelerador *m* de *Esp* vídeo *or Am* video

◇ **video board** placa *f* de *Esp* vídeo *or Am* video

◇ **video card** tarjeta *f* de *Esp* vídeo *or Am* video

◇ **video clip** clip *m* de *Esp* vídeo *or Am* video

◇ **video memory** memoria *f* de *Esp* vídeo *or Am* video

videoconference *n* videoconferencia *f*

videoconferencing *n* videoconferencias *fpl*

video-on-demand *n Esp* vídeo *m or Am* video *m* a la carta

view *vt* (*codes, document*) visualizar

viewable area *n* (*of monitor*) área *f* visible

viewer *n* (*program*) visualizador *m*

viral marketing *n Internet* márketing *m* viral *or* boca a boca

virtual *adj* virtual

◇ **virtual memory** memoria *f* virtual

◇ **virtual reality** realidad *f* virtual

◇ **virtual reality simulator** simulador *m* de realidad virtual

virus n virus m inv; **to disable a virus** desactivar un virus

⋄ **virus check** detección f de virus; **to run a virus check on a disk** comprobar la presencia de virus en un disco

⋄ **virus detector** detector m de virus

⋄ **virus program** programa m virus

virus-free adj sin virus

visit vt (web page) visitar

visual display unit n monitor m

voice n voz f

⋄ **voice** Br **dialling** or US **dialing** marcado m por voz, marcación f por voz, Andes, RP discado m por voz

⋄ **voice mail** correo m de voz

⋄ **voice mailbox** buzón m de voz

⋄ **voice mail retrieval** acceso m a correo de voz

⋄ **voice recognition** reconocimiento m de voz

⋄ **voice synthesizer** sintetizador m de voz

⋄ **voice tag** (on mobile phone) comando m de voz

voice-activated adj activado(a) por la voz

VoIP n Internet (abbr **voice over Internet protocol**) VOIP m

volume n volumen m

VPN n (abbr **virtual private network**) VPN f

VRAM n (abbr **video random access memory**) VRAM f

VRML n (abbr **virtual reality modelling language**) VRML m

W3 *n* (*abbr* World Wide Web) WWW *f*

WAIS *n* Internet (*abbr* Wide Area Information Service) servidores *mpl* de información de área amplia

wallpaper *n* (*for screen*) papel *m* tapiz

WAN *n* (*abbr* wide area network) red *f* de área extensa

WAP *n* (*abbr* Wireless Application Protocol) WAP *m*

◇ *WAP phone* teléfono *m* WAP

warez *n Fam* software *m* pirata

warm *adj*

◇ *warm boot* arranque *m* en caliente

◇ *warm start* arranque *m* en caliente

warranty *n* garantía *f*; **this printer has a five-year warranty** esta impresora tiene cinco años de garantía; **under warranty** en garantía; **extended warranty** garantía ampliada; **on-site warranty** garantía in situ; **return-to-base warranty** garantía con devolución al distribuidor

◇ *warranty certificate* certificado *m* de garantía

wastebasket *n* papelera *f*

watchdog program *n Internet* programa *m* de vigilancia *or* control

---

faq

¿**Web site** o **Website**, **web site** o **website**? Esta es la cuestión. Dentro de las expresiones "the World Wide Web" y "the Web", el término "Web" se suele escribir en mayúsculas; la situación es menos clara en lo que respecta a los nombres compuestos en los que figura esta palabra, donde se puede encontrar como una sola palabra o como dos palabras, con "w" mayúscula o minúscula. En este diccionario hemos optado por utilizar la "w" minúscula y las dos palabras para la presentación de términos compuestos como "web site", aunque conviene advertir que se puede encontrar también "website" y que ambas se pueden utilizar indistintamente.

WAV n (abbr **waveform audio**) WAV m

◇ **WAV file** archivo m WAV

WCDMA n Tel (abbr **wideband code division multiple access**) WCDMA m

Web n the Web la Web

◇ **web address** dirección f web

◇ **web authoring** creación f de páginas web

◇ **web authoring program** programa m para la creación de páginas web

◇ **web authoring tool** herramienta f para la creación de páginas web

◇ **web browser** navegador m

◇ **web consultancy** consultoría f sobre páginas web

◇ **web design agency** agencia f de diseño de páginas web

◇ **web designer** diseñador(ora) m,f de páginas web

◇ **web forum** fórum m en la web

◇ **web hosting** hospedaje m or alojamiento m de páginas web

◇ **web page** página f web

◇ **web phone** teléfono m web

◇ **web publishing** publicación f en la web

◇ **web ring** anillo m de webs

◇ **web server** servidor m web

◇ **web site** sitio m web, web m or f

◇ **web space** espacio m web

◇ **web streaming** reproducción f en tiempo real por la web

webcam n cámara f web

webcast Internet **1** n emisión f por la web
2 vt emitir por la web

webcaster n Internet emisora f por la web

webcasting n Internet emisiones fpl por la web

webmail n webmail m, correo m en la web

Webmaster n Internet administrador(ora) m,f de (sitio) web, webmaster mf

website n sitio m web

welcome message n mensaje m de bienvenida

wheelmouse n Esp ratón m or Am mouse m con rueda de desplazamiento

white balance n DTP balance m de blancos

wide area network n red f de área extensa

widow n DTP viuda f

wildcard n comodín m

◇ **wildcard character** carácter m comodín

WIMP (interface) n (abbr **windows, icon, mouse, pointer**) interfaz m or f WIMP

window n (on screen) ventana f

Windows Explorer® n explorador m de Windows®

▸ **wire up** vt sep (devices) conectar con cables (**to** a)

wireframe modelling, US **wireframe modeling** n modelado m de alambres

wireless *adj* inalámbrico(a)

◇ *wireless keyboard* teclado *m* inalámbrico

◇ *wireless LAN* red *f* local inalámbrica

◇ *wireless mouse* *Esp* ratón *m* or *Am* mouse *m* inalámbrico

◇ *wireless network* red *f* inalámbrica

◇ *wireless network card* tarjeta *f* de red inalámbrica

wizard *n* asistente *m*

Word *n* Word *m*; **it's in Word** está en Word; **a Word document/file** un documento/archivo de Word

word *n* palabra *f*

◇ *word count* *(on menu)* contar palabras; **to do a word count** contar las palabras

◇ *word processing* tratamiento *m* or procesamiento *m* de textos

◇ *word processor* procesador *m* de textos

◇ *word wrap* salto *m* de línea automático

word-process *vt* pasar a tratamiento de textos

work area *n* área *f* de trabajo

workstation *n* estación *f* de trabajo

World Wide Web *n* World Wide Web *f*, Web *f*

WORM (*abbr* **write once read many times**) WORM

worm *n* gusano *m*

WP *n* (**a**) (*abbr* **word processing**) tratamiento *m* or procesamiento *m* de textos
(**b**) (*abbr* **word processor**) procesador *m* de textos

wrist rest *n* apoyamuñecas *m inv*, reposamuñecas *m inv*

write **1** *vt* *(CD-ROM)* escribir; **to write sth to disk** escribir algo en el disco
2 *vi* escribir

◇ *write protection* protección *f* contra escritura

◇ *write speed* velocidad *f* de escritura

write-protect *vt* proteger contra escritura

write-protected *adj* protegido(a) contra escritura

WWW *n* (*abbr* **World Wide Web**) WWW *f*

WYSIWYG *n* (*abbr* **what you see is what you get**) WYSIWYG, = se imprime lo que ves

XGA *n* (*abbr* **extended graphics array**) XGA *m*

XML *n* (*abbr* **Extensible Markup Language**) XML *m*

Y2K compliant *adj* (*abbr* **year 2000 compliant**) adaptado(a) al *or* a prueba del efecto 2000

year 2000 compliant *adj* adaptado(a) al *or* a prueba del efecto 2000

Yellow Pages *npl* **the Yellow Pages** las páginas amarillas

zap *vt (file)* borrar

Zip® *n*

◇ **Zip® cartridge** cartucho *m* Zip®

◇ **Zip® disk** disco *m* Zip®

◇ **Zip® drive** unidad *m* Zip®

zip *vt (file)* comprimir

◇ **zip file** archivo *m* zip

zombie *n* (*computer*) = *Esp* ordenador *or* *Am* computadora bajo el control de un hacker sin conocimiento de su propietario

zoom box *n* cuadro *m* de zoom

LOS CORREOS ELECTRÓNICOS EN INGLÉS

En un espacio de tiempo relativamente breve el correo electrónico se ha convertido en una de las formas de comunicación más extendidas y populares, tanto en el ámbito personal como en el comercial. Aunque se trata sin duda de un fenómeno internacional, cada país adopta unas convenciones y un estilo propio al escribir correos electrónicos. En este suplemento encontrarás todo lo que necesitas saber para escribir un correo electrónico en inglés que suene natural.

Estructura de un correo electrónico

Los correos electrónicos constan de dos partes principales. El **encabezamiento** ("header") muestra el nombre del destinatario y su dirección, el nombre y la dirección de todas las personas a las que se envía una copia, y el asunto del mensaje.

El **cuerpo** ("body") contiene el texto del mensaje propiamente dicho.

Las direcciones de correo electrónico se dividen en dos partes, separadas por el símbolo @ (pronunciado "at"):

jbloggs@lexiworld.com

La primera parte es el **nombre del usuario** ("user name"), que identifica el buzón de correo individual del destinatario ("jbloggs" en el ejemplo anterior). La parte que sigue a la arroba se conoce como dominio y suele ser el nombre de una empresa u organización ("lexiworld" en el ejemplo anterior), seguido de un punto y a continuación la extensión. Esta parte final del **nombre del dominio** ("domain name") indica el tipo de organización (p. ej. **.com** o **.org**) y a menudo también el país en que se encuentra el servidor (p. ej. **.co.uk**) El "." se lee "dot", por eso se dice "dot com" o "dot co dot uk"

Cómo escribir un correo electrónico

Hay algunas diferencias importantes entre el lenguaje usado en el correo tradicional y el de los correos electrónicos.

- En primer lugar, el estilo de los correos electrónicos es mucho menos rígido y formal, incluso en el contexto de la correspondencia comercial o al dirigirse a desconocidos. Las estrictas normas que rigen la correspondencia formal enviada por correo postal no suelen observarse en este caso.

- La rapidez en la comunicación constituye el aspecto principal del correo electrónico, y por consiguiente los mensajes suelen estar escritos con un estilo un tanto telegráfico. No hace falta escribir frases enteras ni seguir las normas gramaticales al pie de la letra para transmitir la información esencial.

- Al igual que sucede con los mensajes de texto, las abreviaturas se suelen utilizar en los correos electrónicos entre amigos a fin de ahorrar tiempo (ver pág. 10). Las personas que se conocen a veces firman su mensaje sólo con la inicial de su nombre, p. ej. "P" en lugar de "Peter".

- Los **emoticonos** ("emoticons" o "smileys") son símbolos creados mediante la combinación de distintos caracteres del teclado (ver pág. 15). Se usan en correos electrónicos personales para expresar diferentes estados de ánimo de forma aparentemente más explícita de lo que sería posible mediante la escritura convencional, o para aclarar el sentido de una frase ambigua. No se considera apropiado utilizarlos en correos electrónicos comerciales.

- Hay quienes añaden el equivalente del énfasis hablado a una o varias palabras de su mensaje mediante un asterisco antes y después de la palabra que quieren resaltar, p. ej. "You *really* mustn't miss this movie".

Cómo empezar un mensaje

Casi siempre conocemos el nombre del destinatario por su dirección electrónica, de modo que los correos electrónicos nunca empiezan con los impersonales "Dear Sir" o "Dear Madam" propios de las cartas formales enviadas por correo tradicional. Incluso si mandamos un mensaje a un servicio de asistencia técnica en línea y desconocemos el nombre del destinatario, conviene empezar nuestro mensaje con un saludo mucho menos formal, como "Hello" o "Hi".

Aunque es posible que un mensaje comercial formal dirigido a una persona a la que no conocemos muy bien empiece con "Dear Mr o Dear Mrs", seguido del apellido de dicha persona (p. ej. Dear Mr Green), si la conocemos es mucho más normal usar su nombre de pila (p. ej. Dear Margaret).

"Hi" es sin duda la forma más frecuente de empezar un correo electrónico dirigido a un amigo o a un compañero de trabajo. Este saludo puede ir seguido del nombre de pila de la persona en cuestión (p. ej. Hi Mark), pero a menudo se usa solo. Al contestar a un mensaje de un colega o de un compañero, o incluso de un servicio de asistencia técnica en línea, es habitual prescindir de estos saludos iniciales y empezar directamente con la respuesta.

Cómo acabar un mensaje

Al contestar a mensajes de amigos o de compañeros de trabajo algunas personas no suelen molestarse en firmar su respuesta, aunque hay quienes consideran bastante descortés no incluir la firma. De todos modos, las fórmulas de despedida más frecuentes en los correos electrónicos son mucho menos formales que las empleadas en el correo postal. Fórmulas fijas como "Yours sincerely", "Yours faithfully" y "Yours truly" no se usan casi nunca. "Best wishes" y "All the best" son despedidas habituales para mensajes a personas a las que no conozcas demasiado, aunque hay quien prefiere prescindir de estas frases y sólo escribe su nombre.

En los Estados Unidos los mensajes comerciales suelen ser un poco más formales que los británicos, y la despedida "Sincerely" se utiliza habitualmente cuando no se conoce bien al destinatario. También se usan "All the best" y "Best regards." Hay quienes usan sólo "Best" para despedirse de manera más informal.

Los amigos y los compañeros de trabajo emplean distintas despedidas informales, como "Bye for now" (a menudo abreviada a BFN). Como hemos explicado más arriba, estas despedidas pueden ir seguidas del nombre de pila de la persona en cuestión.

Netiqueta

Aunque no se observen las convenciones propias del correo tradicional, quienes escriben correos electrónicos deberían ceñirse al código de comportamiento conocido como **netiqueta** ("netiquette"), o etiqueta de la red. Si respetas unas cuantas normas básicas evitarás molestar u ofender a los destinatarios de tus mensajes y así podras comunicarte más eficazmente con ellos.

- **Resume claramente el contenido de tu mensaje en la línea del asunto.**

  Los mensajes con un título claro facilitan la clasificación del correo. Las personas ocupadas ni siquiera se molestarán en abrir los mensajes si el título no indica de qué tratan.

- **Escribe mensajes cortos y que vayan al grano.**

  Esta norma tiene especial relevancia en el ámbito laboral. Como hemos explicado antes, la rapidez en la comunicación constituye la gran ventaja de los correos electrónicos, y de todos modos no suele prestarse atención a los mensajes largos.

- **Evita escribir todo el mensaje con mayúsculas.**

  SI ESCRIBES TODO EL MENSAJE CON MAYÚSCULAS AL DESTINATARIO LE PARECERÁ QUE ESTÁS GRITANDO. ADEMÁS, CUESTA MÁS LEERLO.

- **No cites demasiados mensajes anteriores en tus respuestas.**

  Al contestar a un mensaje puedes incluir el texto de dicho mensaje en tu respuesta con la función "Responder". Sin embargo, cabe recordar que ser breve e ir al grano son las normas de estilo básicas para la redacción de un correo electrónico.

  Por tanto, no es conveniente citar el mensaje anterior completo, y menos aún si forma parte de una cadena de mensajes, ya que esto hace que sea mucho más difícil para el destinatario encontrar tu respuesta. Sólo deberías citar las partes del mensaje o de los mensajes anteriores que guarden relación con tu contestación. Pueden intercalarse en tus respuestas punto por punto (ver como ejemplo el mensaje: "Pregunta rápida a tu jefe en la oficina y su correspondiente respuesta").

- **Utiliza los emoticonos con cuidado.**

  Los emoticonos sólo deberían usarse en el correo electrónico personal y no para asuntos comerciales o, por regla general, en la oficina. Si hace falta aclarar una frase, suele ser mejor redactarla de otra forma para que su significado quede claro por sí solo. Es preferible usar los emoticonos únicamente para transmitir un cierto tono de voz, es decir, para dar énfasis a lo que has escrito. No conviene escribir una frase despectiva seguida de un emoticono feliz para insinuar que no lo has dicho en serio.

- **No abuses de las abreviaturas.**

  No todo el mundo está familiarizado con abreviaturas como BTW (by the way) o BFN (bye for now) y hay personas que pueden ser reacias a admitir que no las entienden. Es preferible usar abreviaturas sólo cuando estés seguro de que los destinatarios las conocen.

Éstos son los puntos más importantes que se deben tener en cuenta a la hora de escribir un correo electrónico. Hay otras convenciones que también se deberían observar, como no adjuntar ficheros grandes sin pedir permiso antes al destinatario, no enviar mensajes ofensivos o llamaradas (conocidos como flames), y mandar mensajes sólo a aquellas personas a quienes realmente les puedan interesar en lugar de usar la función Copia (CC) para enviarle una copia a todo el mundo.

Ejemplos de correos electrónicos

A un amigo

A continuación encontrarás un ejemplo de un correo electrónico escrito a un amigo. El mensaje muestra el estilo informal y telegráfico a que nos hemos referido antes.

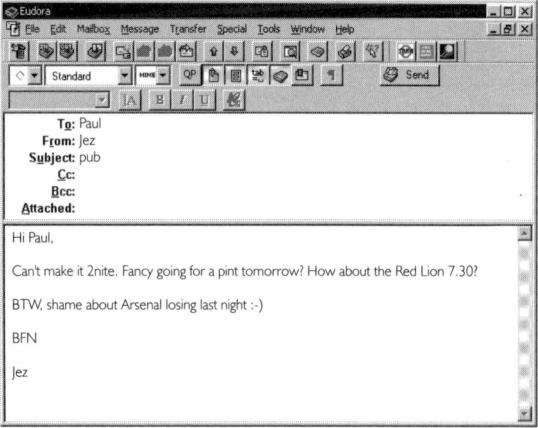

Solicitud de información a un servicio de asistencia técnica

Ya que en este caso desconocemos el nombre del destinatario, el mensaje comienza simplemente con "Hi". Además va al grano y proporciona la información necesaria para que se entienda bien el problema, que está resumido claramente en la línea del asunto. Se considera cortés acabar los mensajes en los que se pide ayuda con "Thanks".

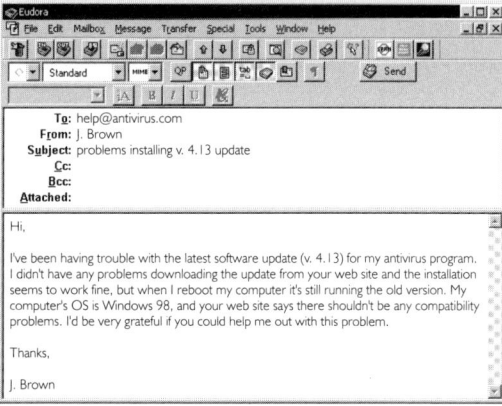

Respuesta a la pregunta de un usuario

Éste es uno de los contextos en los que un correo electrónico es casi tan formal como una carta con la misma función.

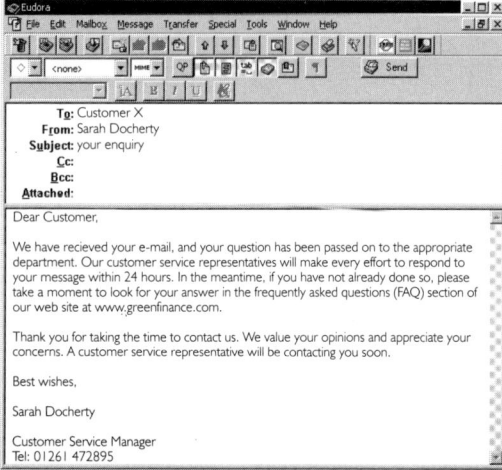

Pregunta y respuesta entre colaboradores

Al igual que sucede en los correos entre amigos, se usan encabezamientos y cierres informales, pero sin emoticonos ni abreviaturas, ya que éste es principalmente un correo electrónico de trabajo. La primera línea de cada correo es más personal, por lo que el estilo de esta parte es más telegráfico que el de la parte comercial del mensaje.

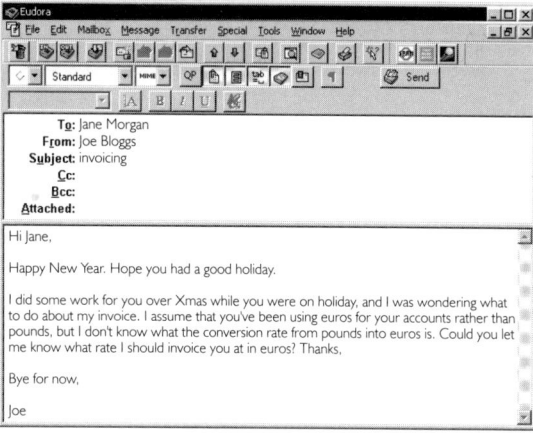

Hi Jane,

Happy New Year. Hope you had a good holiday.

I did some work for you over Xmas while you were on holiday, and I was wondering what to do about my invoice. I assume that you've been using euros for your accounts rather than pounds, but I don't know what the conversion rate from pounds into euros is. Could you let me know what rate I should invoice you at in euros? Thanks,

Bye for now,

Joe

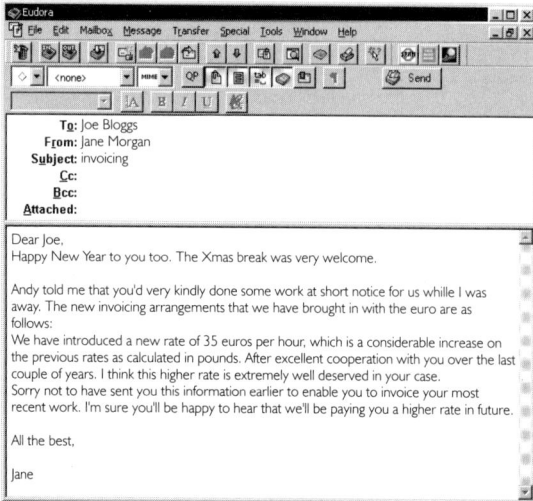

Dear Joe,
Happy New Year to you too. The Xmas break was very welcome.

Andy told me that you'd very kindly done some work at short notice for us while I was away. The new invoicing arrangements that we have brought in with the euro are as follows:
We have introduced a new rate of 35 euros per hour, which is a considerable increase on the previous rates as calculated in pounds. After excellent cooperation with you over the last couple of years, I think this higher rate is extremely well deserved in your case.
Sorry not to have sent you this information earlier to enable you to invoice your most recent work. I'm sure you'll be happy to hear that we'll be paying you a higher rate in future.

All the best,

Jane

Mensaje más formal a un colega al que no conoces bien

El estilo de este tipo de mensaje es similar al de una carta equivalente enviada por correo tradicional. Sin embargo, fíjate en el cierre "With best wishes" en lugar de "Yours sincerely" y también en el uso de "Thanks" en lugar del más formal "Thank you" al principio del penúltimo párrafo, lo cual muestra que, incluso en los contextos más formales, los correos electrónicos suelen escribirse con un estilo más propio de la lengua hablada.

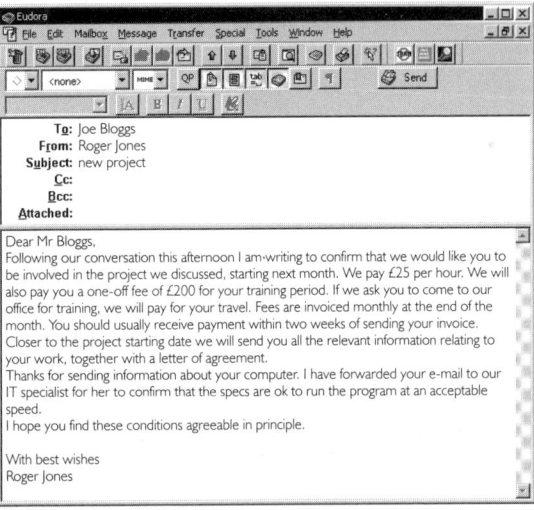

To: Joe Bloggs
From: Roger Jones
Subject: new project
Cc:
Bcc:
Attached:

Dear Mr Bloggs,
Following our conversation this afternoon I am writing to confirm that we would like you to be involved in the project we discussed, starting next month. We pay £25 per hour. We will also pay you a one-off fee of £200 for your training period. If we ask you to come to our office for training, we will pay for your travel. Fees are invoiced monthly at the end of the month. You should usually receive payment within two weeks of sending your invoice. Closer to the project starting date we will send you all the relevant information relating to your work, together with a letter of agreement.
Thanks for sending information about your computer. I have forwarded your e-mail to our IT specialist for her to confirm that the specs are ok to run the program at an acceptable speed.
I hope you find these conditions agreeable in principle.

With best wishes
Roger Jones

Pregunta rápida a tu jefe y su correspondiente respuesta

Este intercambio muestra cómo citar correctamente algunas partes de mensajes anteriores mediante la función "Responder". Las preguntas y las respuestas deben ser breves e ir al grano. Observa que en la contestación se ha eliminado la línea introductoria del mensaje original, dado que no guarda relación con la respuesta.

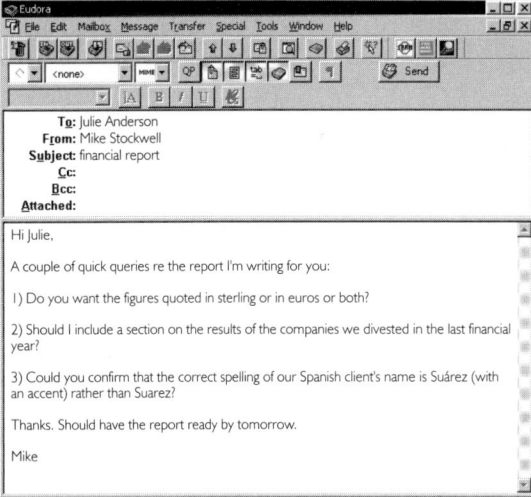

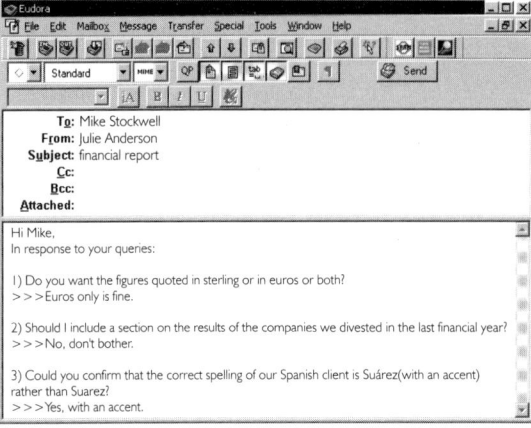

Lista de abreviaturas usadas en mensajes de texto, correos electrónicos y chats en línea

Incluimos a continuación una lista con algunas de las abreviaturas más frecuentes usadas en mensajes de texto (mensajes SMS), correos electrónicos y chats en línea. Cabe mencionar que la mayoría se emplean de forma mucho más habitual en mensajes de texto que en correos electrónicos, mientras que la frecuencia con que aparecen en los chats en línea se encuentra a medio camino entre estos dos.

El uso de abreviaturas en correos electrónicos depende mucho de quién sea el destinatario y del tipo de mensaje enviado. Sin embargo, sería perfectamente posible emplear cualquiera de las abreviaturas que aparecen más abajo entre amigos, especialmente si ambos son aficionados a enviar mensajes de texto. Se están inventando constantemente nuevas abreviaturas, de modo que la lista que incluimos a continuación es tan sólo una muestra de las muchas que puedes encontrarte.

1CE	Once	**AIIC**	As If I Care (*me trae sin cuidado*)
2DAY	Today		
2MORO	Tomorrow	**AISI**	As I See It (*desde mi punto de vista*)
2NITE	Tonight		
2U2	To You Too (*y para ti también*)	**AIUI**	As I Understand It (*si lo he entendido bien*)
4EVER	Forever (*para siempre*)	**ASAP**	As Soon As Possible (*lo antes posible*)
AAMOF	As A Matter of Fact (*de hecho*)	**ATB**	All The Best (*saludos*)
		B	Be
Adv	Advice (*consejo*)	**B4**	Before (*antes*)
AFAICT	As Far As I Can Tell (*por lo que yo sé*)	**BAK**	Back At Keyboard (*vuelvo a estar al teclado*)
AFAIK	As Far As I Know (*que yo sepa*)	**BBFN**	Bye Bye For Now (*hasta luego*)
AFK	Away From Keyboard (*no estoy al teclado*)	**BBL**	Be Back Later (*vuelvo luego*)

B/C	Because (*porque*)	**DK**	Don't Know (*no sé*)
BCNU	Be Seeing You (*nos vemos*)	**Doc**	Document (*documeto*)
BFN	Bye For Now (*hasta luego*)	**DUCWIM**	Do You See What I Mean? (*¿entiendes lo que quiero decir?*)
BOC	But Of Course (*claro que sí*)	**DYJIW**	Don't You Just Hate It When (*¿no te saca de quicio que...?*)
BRB	Be Right Back (*vuelvo en seguida*)		
BST	But Seriously Though (*bromas aparte*)	**EOD**	End Of Discussion (*fin de la discusión*)
		EOF	End Of File (*fin del fichero*)
BTDT	Been There Done That (*indica que algo está muy visto*)	**ETLA**	Extended Three Letter Acronym (*sigla de más de tres letras*)
BTW	By The Way (*por cierto*)		
C	See	**EZ**	Easy (*fácil*)
CD	Could	**F2F**	Face To Face (*cara a cara*)
CID	Consider It Done (*dalo por hecho*)	**F2T**	Free To Talk (*ahora puedo hablar*)
cld	Could	**FAQ**	Frequently Asked Questions (*preguntas más frecuentes*)
COZ	Because (*porque*)		
CU	See You (*hasta la vista*)	**FOAF**	Friend Of A Friend (*el amigo de un amigo*)
CUL	See You Later (*hasta luego*)	**FOC**	Free Of Charge (*gratis*)
CUL8R	See You Later (*hasta luego*)	**Foll**	Following, to follow (*siguiente, seguir*)
CUM	Come	**FOTFLOL**	Falling On The Floor Laughing Out Loud (*me parto de risa*)
CYA	See Ya (*hasta la vista*)		
DA	The		

FWD	Forward (*reenviar*)	**IIRC**	If I Recall Correctly (*si mal no recuerdo*)
FWIW	For What It's Worth (*por si sirve de algo*)	**IJWTK**	I Just Want To Know (*sólo quería saber...*)
FYA	For Your Amusement (*para que te diviertas*)	**IJWTS**	I Just Want To Say (*sólo quiero decir que*)
FYI	For Your Information (*para tu información*)	**IM**	I'm
G2G	Got To Go (*tengo que irme*)	**IMHO**	In My Humble Opinion (*en mi humilde opinión*)
GA	Go Ahead (*adelante*)	**IMNSHO**	In My Not So Humble Opinion (*en mi no tan humilde opinión*)
GAL	Get A Life (*¿no tienes nada mejor que hacer?*)		
GGN	Gotta Go Now (*me tengo que ir*)	**IMO**	In My Opinion (*en mi opinión*)
GR8	Great (*estupendo*)	**IOW**	In Other Words (*en otras palabras*)
H8	Hate	**IRL**	In Real Life (*en la vida real*)
HAND	Have A Nice Day (*que pases un buen día*)	**ISTM**	It Seems To Me (*me parece*)
HHOJ	Ha Ha, Only Joking (*ja, ja, era broma*)	**ISTR**	I Seem To Recall (*creo recordar*)
HHOS	Ha Ha, Only Serious (*ja, ja, va en serio*)	**ITRO**	In The Region Of (*alrededor de*)
HTH	Hope This Helps (*espero que esto te sirva*)	**IWBNI**	It Would Be Nice If (*estaría bien si*)
IAC	In Any Case (*en cualquier caso*)	**ISWYM**	I See What You Mean (*te entiendo*)
IAE	In Any Event (*en cualquier caso*)	**JK**	Just Kidding (*¡es broma!*)
IDTS	I Don't Think So (*creo que no*)	**KIT**	Keep In Touch (*mantente en contacto*)

L8	Late (*tarde*)	**NW!**	No Way! (*¡de ninguna manera!*)
L8R	Later (*hasta luego*)		
LO	Hello (*hola*)	**OBTW**	Oh, By The Way (*ah, a propósito*)
LOL	Laughing Out Loud (*me desternillo*)	**OIC**	Oh, I See (*ah, ya veo*)
LTNS	Long Time No See (*¡cuánto tiempo sin verte!*)	**OMG**	Oh, My God (*¡Dios mío!*)
LUV	Love	**OT**	Off Topic (*indica que algo se aparta del tema*)
LV	Love		
M8	Mate (*colega, amigo*)	**OTOH**	On The Other Hand (*por otra parte*)
MSG	Message (*mensaje*)		
MYOB	Mind Your Own Business (*no te metas en lo que no te importa*)	**OTT**	Over The Top (*exagerado*)
		OTW	On The Whole (*en conjunto*)
NBD	No Big Deal (*no pasa nada*)	**PAW**	Parents Are Watching (*mis padres vigilan*) (*Observa que el equivalente en EE UU es P911, en alusión al número de teléfono para emergencias*)
NE	Any		
NE1	Anyone		
NETHNG	Anything		
NM	Nothing Much (*poca cosa; una posible respuesta a WU*)	**PCM**	Please Call Me (*llámame, por favor*)
NO1	No-one	**PD**	Public Domain (*dominio público*)
NP	No Problem (*no hay problema*)	**PITA**	Pain In The Arse (*rollo*)
NRN	No Reply Necessary (*no hace falta que respondas*)	**PLS**	Please (*por favor*)
		POD	Piece Of Data (*dato*)
NTL	Nevertheless (*sin embargo*)	**POV**	Point Of View (*punto de vista*)

PPL	People	**TVM**	Thanks Very Much (*muchas gracias*)
prhps	Perhaps		
R	Are	**TYVM**	Thank You Very Much (*muchas gracias*)
RITE	Right		
ROTFL	Rolling on the Floor Laughing (*me parto de risa*)	**TXT**	Text (*texto*)
		U	You
RSN	Real Soon Now (*dentro de muy poco*)	**U2**	You Too (*tú también*)
		URAQT	You Are A Cutie (*eres un encanto*)
RTFM	Read The Fucking Manual (*¡lee el puto manual!*)	**W8**	Wait
		WAN2	Want To
RUOK?	Are You Ok? (*¿estás bien?*)	**WBS**	Write Back Soon (*contéstame pronto*)
SOZ	Sorry (*lo siento*)	**WD**	Would
SPK	Speak	**WDYT?**	What Do You Think? (*¿qué te parece?*)
SUM1	Someone		
THRU	Through	**WIBNI**	Wouldn't It Be Nice If (*estaría muy bien si*)
THX	Thanks (*gracias*)		
TIA	Thanks In Advance (*gracias por adelantado*)	**WKND**	Weekend (*fin de semana*)
		W/O	Without
TLA	Three Letter Acronym (*sigla de tres letras*)	**WOT**	What
		WRT	With Regard To (*en lo que respecta a*)
TNX	Thanks (*gracias*)	**WU?**	What's Up? (*¿qué pasa?*)
TTYL	Talk To You Later (*hasta luego*)		
		X	Ex
TTYRS	Talk To You Real Soon (*hasta muy pronto*)	**XLNT**	Excellent (*excelente*)
		XOXOXO	Hugs and kisses (*besos y abrazos*)

XTRA	Extra	**YR**	Your
Y	Why	**YRE**	You're
YHM	You Have Mail (*tienes correo*)	**YYSSW**	Yeah Yeah Sure Sure Whatever (*indica una indiferencia absoluta*)

Emoticonos

:-)	Contento	:-)X	Llevar pajarita
:-))	Muy contento	<|-)	Chino
:-D	Reírse a carcajadas	3:-)	Vaca
:-(	Triste	8-)	Llevar gafas
:-((	Muy triste	|-)	Dormir
:´-(	Llorar	:-¡	Fumador
:-||	Muy enfadado	:-?	Fumador en pipa
:-C	Muy disgustado	:-/	Indeciso
:-O	Escandalizado	C|:-)	Llevar bombín
:-@	Gritar	d:-)	Llevar gorra
;-)	Guiñar el ojo	[:-)	Llevar cascos
:-|	Fruncir las cejas	|-O	Bostezar
(:-)	Calvo	:-*	Beso
:-)>	Barbudo	:-*)	Borracho

WRITING E-MAILS IN SPANISH

In a relatively short space of time, e-mail has become one of the most widespread and popular forms of both personal and business communication. Although it is very much an international phenomenon, each country nevertheless has its own conventions and style for writing e-mail messages. This section provides you with everything you need to know in order to write a natural-sounding e-mail in Spanish.

Structure of an e-mail

E-mail messages have two main parts.

The **header** ("encabezamiento") shows the recipient's name and address, the name and address of anyone to whom the message is being copied, and the subject of the message.

The **body** ("cuerpo") contains the actual text of the message.

E-mail addresses are divided into two parts, separated by the @ symbol (pronounced "arroba"):

jalonso@novalingua.com

The first part is the **user name** ("nombre de usuario") which identifies the recipient's individual mailbox ("jalonso" in the example above). The part after the @ symbol is known as the **domain name** ("nombre de dominio") and is usually the name of a company or organization ("novalingua" in the example above), followed by a dot and then three or more letters. This final part of the domain name shows the type of organization (e.g. **.com** or **.org**) and often also the country where the host server is located (e.g. **.es**). The "." is pronounced "punto", hence "punto com" or "punto es".

How to write an e-mail

There are several significant differences between the type of language used in conventional snail-mail letters and that used in e-mails.

- First and foremost, the style of e-mails is much less formal and rigid. This applies even to contexts such as business communications or when writing to people who you don't know. The strict rules that govern formal snail-mail letter writing in these contexts are not generally observed in the case of e-mails.

- While messages between work colleagues prefer the "tú" form prevalent in all informal communication, certain business messages, for example ones from a customer services department, can still be written in formal snail-mail style, and this type of message uses the "usted" form.

- E-mails in Spanish are often written in a slightly less telegraphic style than tends to be the case in English, this being mainly due to the fact that Spanish contains fewer of the abbreviated forms that characterize so much of this type of communication in English.

- As with text messaging, abbreviations are sometimes used in e-mail messages between friends as a means of saving time (see p. 25).

- **Smileys** or **emoticons** ("emoticonos") are symbols created by combinations of keyboard characters (see p. 26). They are used in personal e-mails to express different emotions in a supposedly more graphic manner than is possible using ordinary text, or to clarify the sense in which an ambiguous phrase is intended. It is not considered appropriate to use them in business e-mails.

- Some people add the equivalent of spoken emphasis to a word or words in their e-mail by enclosing the words to be emphasized in asterisks, e.g. "es *muy* difícil".

How to start a message

You almost always know the name of the person you are writing to from their e-mail address, which means that e-mail messages virtually never begin with the impersonal "Señor" or "Señora" used in formal snail-mail letters. Even if you are sending a message to an online technical support service and do not know the name of the person you are writing to, you should begin your message with something much less formal, such as "Hola".

While a formal business message to a person who you do not know may very well still begin with "Estimado señor/Estimada señora" followed by the person's surname (e.g. Estimado Sr. Morán), if you do know them then it would be much more usual to use their Christian name (e.g. Querida Amelia).

"Hola" is by far the most common way of starting an e-mail written to a friend or a work colleague. This can be followed by the person's Christian name (e.g. Hola, Juan), but it is often just used on its own. When answering a message from a work colleague or friend, or indeed from an online technical support service, it is common not to bother with such introductory greetings at all but simply to go straight into the main text of your reply.

How to end a message

When answering messages from friends or colleagues, people will also often not bother to sign off the message with their name, although there are those who consider this to be rather impolite. In any case, the most common ways of signing off an e-mail message are much less formal than those used in snail-mail letters. Set formulae such as "Reciba un atento saludo"and "Le saluda atentamente" are virtually never used. "Atentamente" and "Saludos" are common endings for messages to people who you do not know particularly well, although some people prefer to dispense with such phrases altogether and just write their name.

Friends and work colleagues use a variety of informal endings, such as "Hasta pronto" and "Un saludo". As explained above, these endings may or may not be followed by the person's Christian name.

Netiquette

Although the conventions of snail-mail letter writing are not observed, people writing e-mails are expected to stick to the code of behaviour known as **netiquette** ("netiqueta"), which is the same in Spanish as in English. If you follow a few basic rules you will avoid annoying or offending the people you write to and thus communicate more effectively with them.

- **Clearly summarize the contents of your message in the subject line.**

   Clearly titled messages make it easier for people to sort and prioritize their e-mail. Busy people often won't even open messages if they can't tell what they are about from the title.

● **Keep your messages short and to the point.**

This is particularly true in a business environment. As explained above, the great advantage of e-mails is speed of communication, and long messages tend to be ignored anyway.

● **Avoid writing your whole message in capital letters.**

IF YOU USE ALL CAPITAL LETTERS THE RECIPIENT WILL PER-CEIVE IT AS SHOUTING. IT IS ALSO HARDER TO READ.

● **Don't overquote previous messages in your replies.**

When responding to a message, you can include the text of the message you are replying to in your answer by using the "Reply" function. However, it should be remembered that being brief and to the point is the key to good e-mail style. Consequently, it is not a good idea to quote the whole of the previous message, even less so if it is part of a chain of messages, since this makes it much harder for the recipient to find your answer. You should only quote the parts of the previous message or messages that are relevant to your response. These can be interspersed with your replies, point by point (see example e-mail *Quick query and response to your boss at work*).

● **Use emoticons with care.**

Smileys should only be used in personal e-mail and not for business or, as a rule, in the office. If a statement needs an emoticon for clarification it is usually better to try and rephrase it so its meaning is clear in its own right. It is best to stick to using smileys to convey a particular tone of voice, i.e. to give a particular emphasis to what you have written. It is considered rude to write something derogatory followed by a happy smiley to imply that you don't mean it seriously.

● **Don't overuse abbreviations.**

Not everyone is familiar with abbreviations like "xq" (porque) or "mñn" (mañana) and people may be reluctant to admit that they don't understand them. It is best only to use abbreviations when writing to people who you know to be conversant with them.

These are the most important things to bear in mind as far as the actual writing of your e-mail message is concerned. There are a number of other conventions that should also be observed, such as not attaching large files without the recipient's prior permission, not sending insulting messages, and only sending messages to people for whom they are really relevant rather than using the Carbon Copy (CC) function to copy them to everyone.

Example e-mail messages

To a friend

This example of an e-mail written to a friend demonstrates the informal, rather telegraphic style referred to above. Full sentences are dispensed with in the interests of brevity. The message is introduced with the informal "Hola" and ended with the abbreviation "a2" (adiós). Abbreviations and emoticons are used liberally.

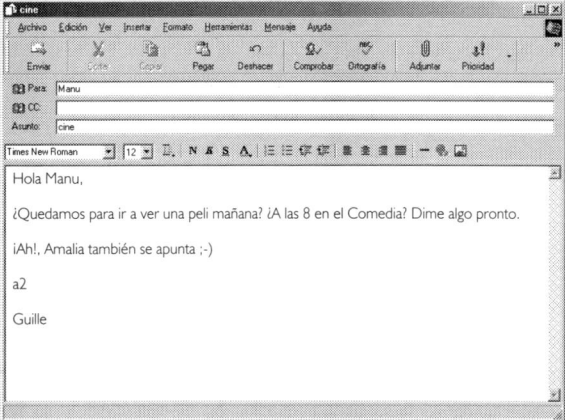

Writing to an online technical support service

Since in this case the name of the recipient is unknown, the message simply begins with "Hola". Note the use of the "usted" form indicating a greater degree of formality than a similar message would have in English. The message is to the point and the problem is summarized clearly in the subject line. It is polite to end messages requesting help with "Gracias".

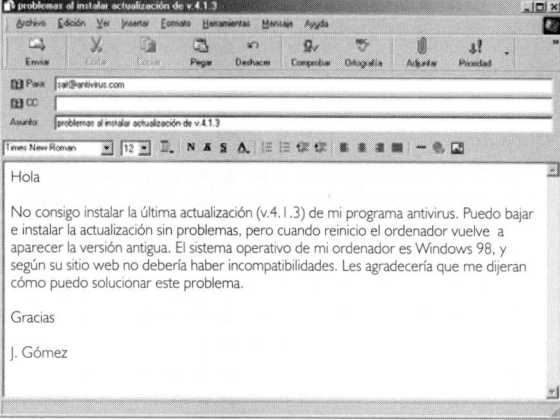

Response to a customer enquiry

This is one context in which an e-mail is almost as formal as an equivalent snail-mail letter with the same function.

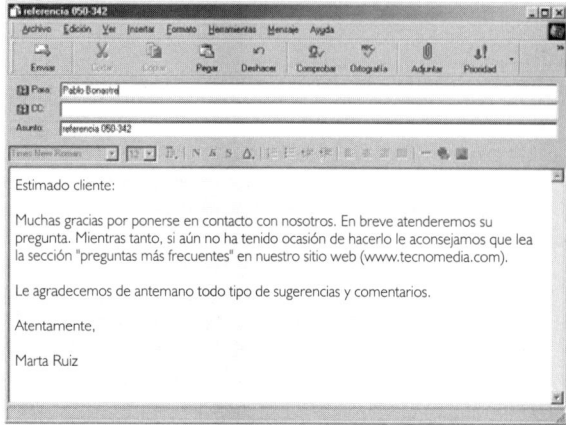

Query and response between business colleagues who know each other quite well

As in the e-mail between friends, informal openings and endings are used, but note the absence of smileys and abbreviations, since this is mainly a work message rather than a personal one. The first line of each message is more personal, and consequently the style for this part is more telegraphic than the business part of the message.

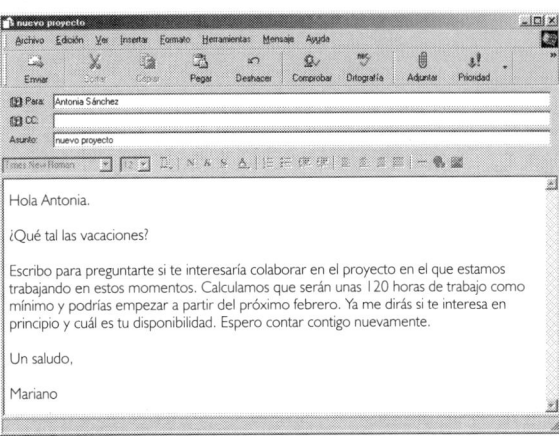

Hola Antonia.

¿Qué tal las vacaciones?

Escribo para preguntarte si te interesaría colaborar en el proyecto en el que estamos trabajando en estos momentos. Calculamos que serán unas 120 horas de trabajo como mínimo y podrías empezar a partir del próximo febrero. Ya me dirás si te interesa en principio y cuál es tu disponibilidad. Espero contar contigo nuevamente.

Un saludo,

Mariano

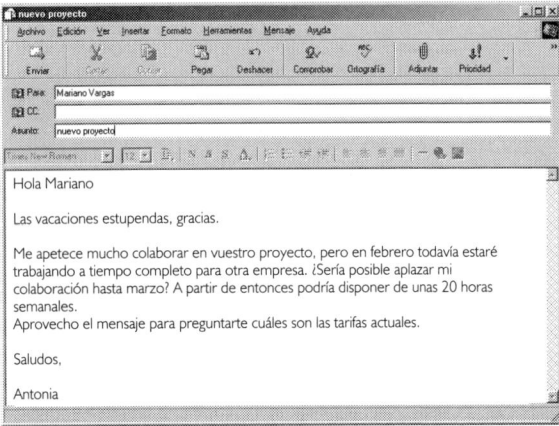

Hola Mariano

Las vacaciones estupendas, gracias.

Me apetece mucho colaborar en vuestro proyecto, pero en febrero todavía estaré trabajando a tiempo completo para otra empresa. ¿Sería posible aplazar mi colaboración hasta marzo? A partir de entonces podría disponer de unas 20 horas semanales.
Aprovecho el mensaje para preguntarte cuáles son las tarifas actuales.

Saludos,

Antonia

More formal message to a business contact who you don't know well

E-mail is becoming more and more widely used in the Spanish working environment, although it is probably not yet as well established a method of business correspondence as it is in the English-speaking world.

The style of this formal message is similar to that of an equivalent snail-mail letter.

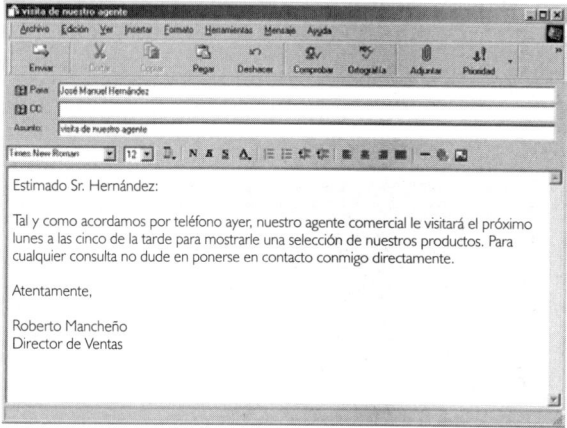

Quick query to your boss and response

This exchange shows the correct way to quote parts of previous messages using the "Reply" function. Both queries and answers are kept as short and to the point as possible. Note that in the reply, the introductory line of the original message has been deleted, since it is not relevant to the response.

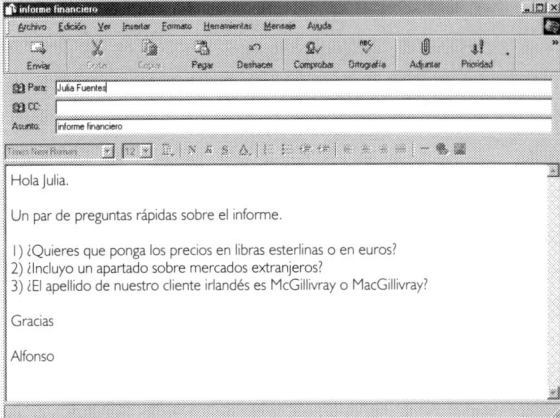

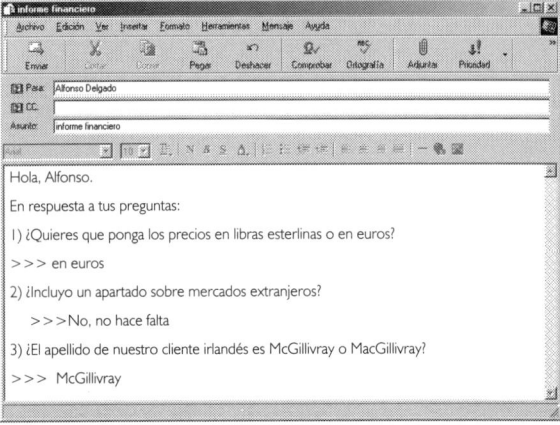

List of abbreviations and acronyms used in texting, e-mails and online chat

The following is a list of some of the more common abbreviations and acronyms used in texting, e-mails and online chat. It should be noted that the majority are much more commonly used in text messages than in e-mails, with their frequency in online chat falling somewhere between these two. The use of acronyms and abbreviations in e-mails is partly a matter of individual taste and also very much dependent on who the recipient is and the type of message being sent. However, it would be perfectly possible for any of the abbreviations and acronyms listed below to be used in e-mails between friends, especially if they are both keen texters. New "texting slang" terms are being invented all the time, so the terms listed only seek to give a flavour of what you might expect to come across.

Note that because English is the main language of the Internet, English acronyms and abbreviations (see section in Spanish supplement) are much more established than Spanish ones.

When writing text messages in Spanish, you should bear in mind the following basic rules:

- Accents are not used.

- Vowels are omitted from the most common words (e.g. "donde" becomes "dnd").

- The letter "h", which is not pronounced in Spanish, is always omitted (e.g. "hola" becomes "ola").

- The letter "ll" is replaced by "y" and "ch" is replaced by "x". Thus, "botella" becomes "boteya" and "chica" becomes "xica".

- Question marks and exclamation marks are used in the same way as in English, i.e. they are only written at the end of a sentence, and not also at the beginning as in conventional written Spanish.

A2	adiós *(bye for now)*
bboo	besos *(love and kisses)*
cnd	cuando, cuándo *(when)*
dnd	donde, dónde *(where)*
find	fin de semana *(weekend)*
kdms	quedamos, quedemos *(let's meet...)*
ke	que, qué *(which, that, who, what)*

ktl ?	¿qué tal? *(how's things?)*
LAP	lo antes posible *(as soon as possible)*
M1Ml	mándame un mensaje luego *(get back to me later)*
mjr	mejor *(better)*
mññ	mañana *(tomorrow)*
muxo	mucho *(a lot, a lot of)*
q	que, qué *(which, that, who, what)*
salu2	saludos *(all the best)*
tb	también *(also)*
tq	te quiero *(love you)*
wapa	guapa *(gorgeous)*
x	por *(because of, by, etc)*
xa	para *(for)*
xdon	perdón *(sorry)*
xq	porque, por qué *(because, why)*

Smileys

Smileys, or emoticons, are probably used more in English than in Spanish, but it is worth illustrating some of the most common ones.

:-)	Happy	**:-)X**	Bow tie
:-))	Really happy	**<|-)**	Chinese
:-D	Laughing out loud	**3:-)**	Cow
:-(	Sad	**8-)**	Glasses
:-((	Really sad	**|-)**	Sleep
:´-(	Crying	**:-¡**	Smoker
:-||	Really angry	**:-?**	Pipe smoker
:-C	Really upset	**:-/**	Undecided
:-O	Surprised	**C|:-)**	Bowler hat
:-@	Screaming	**d:-)**	Baseball cap
;-)	Wink	**[:-)**	Headphones
:-|	Frown	**|-O**	Yawn
(:-)	Bald	**:-***	Kiss
:-)>	Beard	**:-*)**	Drunk

abierto, -a *adj (archivo)* open

abonarse *vpr (a proveedor de acceso)* to subscribe

abrir *vt (archivo)* to open

acceder *vi* **acceder a algo** to access sth

acceso *nm* access; *(a página web)* hit; **acceso a Internet** Internet access; **tener acceso a Internet** to have access to the Internet; **esta página web registró 20.000 accesos durante la semana pasada** this web site counted 20,000 hits last week

◇ *acceso aleatorio* random access

◇ *acceso no autorizado* unauthorized access

◇ *Internet acceso completo a Internet* full Internet access

◇ *acceso directo (a red)* direct access; *(en Windows)* shortcut

◇ *Internet acceso por línea conmutada* dial-up access

◇ *acceso remoto* remote access

◇ *acceso secuencial* sequential access

◇ *Internet acceso telefónico* dial-up access

accesorio de escritorio *nm* desk accessory

aceleración *nf* acceleration

acelerador *nm* accelerator

◇ *acelerador gráfico* graphics accelerator

◇ *acelerador de Esp vídeo o Am video* video accelerator

acelerar *vt* to accelerate

acento *nm* accent

◇ *acento agudo* acute accent

◇ *acento circunflejo* circumflex accent

◇ *acento grave* grave accent

acrónimo *nm* acronym

activación de producto *nf* product activation

activado, -a *adj* activated, enabled; **activado por la voz** voice-activated

activar *vt* to activate, to enable

actualización *nf (de software, hardware)* upgrade

actualizar *vt (software, hardware)* to upgrade

acuerdo de licencia *nm Br* licence o *US* license agreement

acumulador *nm* accumulator

acuse de recibo *nm Internet* acknowledgement, *US* acknowledgment

adaptador *nm* adapter, adaptor

◇ *adaptador para transparencias* transparency (scanning) adapter *o* adaptor

◇ *adaptador de Esp vídeo o Am vídeo* video adapter *o* adaptor

adjuntar *vt* to attach; **adjuntar un archivo a un correo electrónico** to attach a file to an e-mail; **se adjunta...** please find attached...

adjunto, -a *adj (archivo)* attached

administrador, -ora **1** *nm,f (persona)* administrator **2** *nm (software)* manager

◇ *administrador de archivos* file manager

◇ *administrador de bases de datos* database administrator

◇ *Internet administrador de correo* postmaster

◇ *administrador de dispositivos* device manager

◇ *administrador de extensiones* extension manager

◇ *administrador de red* network administrator

◇ *administrador del sistema* system administrator

◇ *Internet administrador de (sitio) web* Webmaster

ADSL *nm (abrev de asymmetrical digital subscriber line)* ADSL

AENOR *nf (abrev de Asociación Española para la Normalización y Certificación)* = Spanish body which certifies quality and safety standards for manufactured goods, *Br* ≃ BSI, *US* ≃ ANSI

agencia *nf*

◇ *agencia de creación de páginas web* web design agency

◇ *Agencia de Protección de Datos* Data Protection Agency

agenda *nf (en programa de correo)* address book

agente *nm (software)* agent

◇ *agente de usuario* user agent

agrandar *vt (ventana)* to maximize

ajuste de página *nm* page setup

alfa *nf* alpha

alfanumérico, -a *adj* alphanumeric

alfanúmero *nm* alphanumeric string

alfombrilla *nf* mouse pad, *Br* mouse mat

ALGOL *nm (abrev de Algorithmic Oriented Language)* ALGOL

algorítmico, -a *adj* algorithmic

algoritmo *nm* algorithm

alias *nm inv* (**a**) *(en correo electrónico)* alias (**b**) *(en escritorio)* alias

◇ *alias de correo electrónico* e-mail alias

alimentación *nf* feed

◇ *alimentación hoja a hoja* cut sheet feed

◇ *alimentación de papel* paper feed

alimentador *nm (para escáner, impresora)* feeder

◇ *alimentador automático de documentos* *(en escáner)* automatic document feeder

◇ *alimentador de corriente* power unit

◇ *alimentador hoja a hoja* cut sheet feeder

◇ *alimentador de papel* paper feeder

alimentar *vt (papel)* to feed

alineación *nf (de caracteres, gráficos)* alignment

alinear *vt (caracteres, gráficos)* to align

almacén de datos *nm* data warehouse

almacenamiento *nm* storage

◇ *almacenamiento de datos* data storage

◇ *almacenamiento de información* information storage

◇ *almacenamiento masivo* mass storage

◇ *almacenamiento permanente* permanent storage

◇ *almacenamiento temporal* temporary storage

almacenar *vt* to store, to hold; **¿cuánta información puede almacenar este disco?** how much data will this disk hold?; **los comandos se almacenan en la memoria** the commands are held in the memory

almohadilla *nf (signo) Br* hash, *US* pound sign

alojamiento *nm* Internet *(de página web)* hosting

◇ *alojamiento de dominios* domain hosting

◇ *alojamiento de páginas web* web hosting

alojar *vt Internet (sitio web)* to host

alquiler *nm Tel* rental

◇ *alquiler de la línea* line rental

alt *nm (tecla)* alt; **para la e con acento hay que presionar alt 130** e acute is alt 130

altavoz *nm* speaker

◇ *altavoz satélite* satellite (speaker)

alto, -a *adj* de alto nivel *(lenguaje)* high-level

◇ *alta densidad* high density

◇ *alta resolución* high resolution

ampersand *nm Am* ampersand

ampliable *adj (memoria)* expandable, upgradable; **98MB ampliables a 392MB** 98MB expandable to 392MB

ampliación *nf (de memoria)* expansion, upgrade

ampliar *vt (memoria)* to expand, to upgrade

análisis *nm inv* analysis

◇ *análisis de datos* data analysis

◇ *análisis de sistemas* systems analysis

analista *nmf* analyst

◊ *analista informático* computer analyst

◊ *analista de sistemas* systems analyst

analógico, -a *adj* analog

ancho de banda *nm* bandwidth

anclaje *nm Internet* anchor

anexo *nm* attachment

anfitrión *nm* host

anillo de webs *nm Internet* web ring

animación *nf* animation

◊ *animación por Esp ordenador* o *Am computadora* computer animation

animar *vt* to animate

antena *nf (para telefonía móvil)* mast

antidentado *nm Autoedición* anti-aliasing

antídoto *nm* antidote

antiestático, -a *adj* anti-static

antivirus *nm inv* antivirus

año 2000 compatible *adj Am* year 2000 compliant

apagado *nm* shutdown

◊ *apagado automático* automatic shutdown

apagar 1 *vt (computadora, impresora)* to switch off, to shut down

2 apagarse *vpr (computadora, impresora)* to switch off, to shut down; **la impresora se apaga automáticamente después de media hora** the printer switches itself off after half an hour

apaisado, -a *adj (formato de papel)* landscape; **imprimir algo en apaisado** to print sth in landscape

aparato *nm (teléfono móvil)* handset

aplicación *nf* application

apodo *nm Internet* nickname, *Br* nick, *US* screen name

apóstrofo *nm* apostrophe

apoyamuñecas *nm inv* wrist rest

applet *nm Internet* applet

apretar *vt (tecla, botón)* to press; **mantener apretado** *(tecla, botón)* to hold down

apuntador *nm (en Macintosh)* scrapbook

araña *nf Internet* spider

árbol *nm (de datos)* tree

◊ *árbol de directorios* directory tree

Archie *n Internet* Archie

archivar *vt* to archive

archivo *nm* file; **no se encuentra el archivo** *(mensaje)* file not found

◊ *archivo activo* active file

◊ *archivo adjunto* attached file

◊ *archivo AIFF* AIFF file

◊ *archivo ASCII* ASCII file

◊ *archivo autodescomprimible* self-extracting file

◊ *archivo binario* binary file

◊ *archivo de comandos* command file

◊ *Internet archivo cookie* cookie (file)

◊ *archivo de direcciones* address file

⋄ *archivo ejecutable* executable file

⋄ *Internet* *archivo de firma* signature file

⋄ *archivo sin formato* flat file

⋄ *archivo GIF* GIF file

⋄ *archivo invisible* invisible file

⋄ *archivo JPEG* JPEG file

⋄ *archivo maestro* master file

⋄ *archivo MP3* MP3 file

⋄ *archivo oculto* hidden file

⋄ *archivo PDF* PDF file

⋄ *archivo RTF* RTF file

⋄ *archivo del sistema* system file

⋄ *archivo temporal* temporary file

⋄ *archivo de texto* text file

⋄ *archivo TIFF* TIFF file

⋄ *archivo WAV* WAV file

⋄ *archivo zip* zip file

área *nf* area

⋄ *área (de escritura) de Graffiti* Graffiti area

⋄ *área de trabajo* work area

⋄ *área visible* viewable area

⋄ *área de visualización* display area

arrancar **1** *vt* to start up, to boot (up)
2 *vi* to start up, to boot up

arranque *nm* start-up

⋄ *arranque automático* autostart

⋄ *arranque en caliente* warm boot *o* start

⋄ *arranque en frío* cold boot *o* start

arrastrar **1** *vt* to drag
2 *vi* **arrastrar y soltar** to drag and drop

array *nm Am* array

arroba *nf Internet (en dirección de correo)* at, *@* sign; **"juan, arroba mundonet, punto, es"** "juan, at mundonet, dot, es"

artículo *nm Internet (en grupo de noticias)* article

ASCII *nm (abrev de* **American Standard Code for Information Interchange***)* ASCII

asignación *nf (de memoria)* allocation

asignar *vt (memoria)* to allocate

asíncrono, -a *adj* asynchronous

asistencia *nf*

⋄ *asistencia por línea directa* hotline support

⋄ *asistencia técnica* technical assistance

asistente *nm (programa)* assistant; *(en Windows)* wizard

⋄ *Internet* *asistente de compras* buy wizard

⋄ *asistente personal (hardware)* personal digital assistant, PDA, handheld (computer)

asistido, -a *adj* asistido por *Esp* ordenador *o Am* computadora computer-assisted, computer-aided

assembler *nm Am* assembler

asterisco *nm* asterisk

asunto *nm* **(a)** *(de correo electrónico)* subject
(b) *(de discusión)* topic

atajo *nm* shortcut

⋄ *atajo de teclado* keyboard shortcut

atasco de papel *nm* paper jam

ATM *nm* (*abrev de* **asynchronous transfer mode**) ATM

atributo *nm* attribute

aumentar *vt* (*en pantalla*) to magnify

auricular *nm* (*de teléfono*) receiver, handset

autenticación *nf* authentication

autenticar *vt* to authenticate

autentificación *nf* authentication

autentificar *vt* to authenticate

autoarranque *nm* autostart

autodiagnóstico *nm* autodiagnosis

autoedición *nf* desktop publishing, DTP

autoeditar *vt* to produce using DTP

autoeditor, -ora *nm,f* desktop publishing operator, DTP operator

autoguardado *nm* autosave

automático, -a *adj* automatic

automatización *nf* automation

autonomía *nf* (*de portátil, teléfono móvil*) battery life

◊ **autonomía en espera** (*de teléfono móvil*) standby (time)

◊ **autonomía en llamada** (*de teléfono móvil*) talktime

autopista de la información *nf* Internet information highway

autoridad de certificación *nf* Internet certification authority

autorización *nf* authorization

◊ **autorización de acceso** access authorization

autorizado, -a *adj* authorized; **no autorizado** unauthorized

autorrecorte *nm* Autoedición autocropping

autorretorno *nm* word wrap

autotest *nm* self-test; **efectuar un autotest** to self-test

avance *nm*

◊ **avance de línea** line feed

◊ **avance de página** form feed

◊ **avance del papel** paper advance

◊ **avance de papel por fricción** friction feed

avatar *nm* Internet avatar

ayuda *nf* help

◊ **ayuda contextual** context-sensitive help

◊ **ayuda en línea** on-line *o* online help

◊ **ayuda on-line** on-line *o* online help

◊ **ayuda en pantalla** on-screen *o* onscreen help

bahía *nf* bay

bajar *Fam Internet* **1** *vt* to download; **bajar un archivo** to download a file

2 bajarse *vpr* to download; **me bajé un juego estupendo** I downloaded an excellent game

bajo, -a *adj*

◇ *baja densidad* low density

◇ *baja resolución* low resolution

balance de blancos *nm Autoedición* white balance

banca *nf*

◇ *banca electrónica* electronic banking

◇ *banca por Internet* Internet banking

◇ *banca telefónica* telephone banking

banco *nm* bank

◇ *banco de datos* data bank, databank

◇ *banco de imágenes* image bank

◇ *banco de memoria* memory bank

banda *nf Tel* **de banda dual** dual-band; *Tel* **de triple banda** tri-band, triple-band; *Tel* **de banda única** single mode

◇ *banda ancha* broadband

◇ *banda magnética (en tarjeta)* magnetic strip

bandeja *nf* tray

◇ *bandeja motorizada* motorized tray

◇ *bandeja de papel* paper tray

banner *nm Internet* banner

◇ *banner de impresiones* impression banner

◇ *banner publicitario* banner ad, advertising banner

barra *nf* (**a**) *(signo gráfico)* slash, oblique; **"www, punto, bbc, punto, com, barra, news"** "www, dot, bbc, dot, com, forward slash, news" (**b**) *(en ventana)* bar

◇ *barra de desplazamiento* scroll bar

◇ *barra espaciadora* space bar

◇ *barra de estado* status bar

◇ *barra de estilos* style bar

◇ *barra de herramientas* tool bar, toolbar

◇ *barra de iconos* icon bar

◇ *barra inclinada* forward slash

◇ *barra invertida* backslash

◇ *barra de menús* menu bar

◇ *barra de navegación* navigation bar

◇ *barra oblicua* oblique

◇ *barra oblicua invertida* backslash

◇ *barra de tareas* taskbar

◇ *barra de título* title bar

◇ *barra vertical* hash

base *nf*

◇ *base de conocimientos* knowledge base

◇ *base de datos* database; **introducir algo en una base de datos** to enter sth into a database

◇ *base de datos cliente/servidor* client-server database

◇ *base de datos distribuida* distributed database

◇ *base de datos documental* documentary database

◇ *base de datos relacional* relational database

BASIC *nm* BASIC

batería *nf* battery

◇ *batería de litio-ión* lithium-ion *o* Li-Ion battery

baudio *nm* baud; **a 58.600 baudios** at 58,600 baud

BBS *nf Internet (abrev de* **bulletin board system***)* BBS

beta *nf* beta

biblioteca *nf (de programas)* library

◇ *biblioteca de programas* program library

bidireccional *adj* bidirectional

bifurcación *nf (de red)* branch

billetera digital *nf Internet* digital wallet

binario, -a *adj* binary

BinHex *(abrev de* **Binary Hexadecimal***)* BinHex

BIOS *nm o nf (abrev de* **Basic Input/Output System***)* BIOS

bisíncrono, -a *adj* bisynchronous, bisync

bit *nm* bit; **bits por segundo** bits per second

◇ *bit de paridad* parity bit

bloc de notas *nm (programa)* notepad, *US* scratchpad

bloque *nm (de texto)* block; **seleccionar un bloque de texto** to block text

◇ *bloque de texto* text block

bloqueado, -a *adj (sistema, pantalla)* frozen

bloquear 1 *vt* **(a)** *(archivo, disquete)* to lock **(b)** *(teléfono móvil)* to lock **2 bloquearse** *vpr (sistema)* to crash; *(sistema, pantalla)* to freeze

bloqueo *nm (de sistema)* crash

◇ *Tel* **bloqueo de llamadas** call barring

◇ *bloqueo numérico* numbers lock, num lock

Bluetooth *nm Tel* Bluetooth

BMP *(abrev de* **bitmap***)* BMP

bomba *nf*

◇ *Internet* **bomba de correo electrónico** e-mail bomb

◇ *bomba lógica* logic bomb

booleano, -a *adj* Boolean

borde *nm (de párrafos, celda)* border

borrado *nm* deletion

borrador *nm* draft (version)

borrar 1 *vt (archivo, datos)* to clear, to delete; *(pantalla)* to clear; *(disco duro)* to erase **2** *vi* to delete

botón *nm (en ratón, pantalla)* button

◇ **botón adelante** *(en navegador)* forward button

◇ **botón atrás** *(en navegador)* back button

◇ **botón de ayuda** help button

◇ **botón de cancelar** cancel button

◇ **botón cambiente** rollover button

◇ **botón de detener** *(en navegador)* stop button

◇ **botón dinámico** rollover button

◇ **botón de expulsión** eject button

◇ **botón de inicio** *(en Windows)* start button

◇ *Tel* **botón inteligente** *(en móvil)* soft button

◇ *Am* **botón del mouse** mouse button

◇ *Esp* **botón del ratón** mouse button

◇ *Andes, RP Tel* **botón de rediscado** recall *o* redial button

◇ **botón de reinicio** reset button *o* switch

◇ *Tel* **botón de rellamada** recall *o* redial button

◇ **botón de tipo radio** radio button

bpp *(abrev de* **bits por pulgada***)* bpi

bps *(abrev de* **bits por segundo***)* bps

brillo *nm* brightness

bruto, -a *adj* en bruto *(datos, estadísticas)* raw

bucle *nm* loop

buffer, búfer *nm* buffer;

saturación del buffer *(mensaje)* buffer underrun

◇ **buffer de impresión** print buffer

bus *nm* bus

◇ **bus de datos** data bus

◇ **bus de direccionamiento** *o* **direcciones** address bus

busca *nm Esp (buscapersonas)* pager, beeper

buscapersonas *nm inv* pager, beeper

buscar 1 *vt* to find, to search; **buscar y reemplazar algo** to search and replace sth
2 *vi* to search; **buscar y reemplazar** to search and replace

búsqueda *nf* search; **hacer una búsqueda** to do a search

◇ **búsqueda hacia adelante** forward search

◇ **búsqueda hacia atrás** backward search

◇ **búsqueda binaria** binary search

◇ **búsqueda booleana** Boolean search

◇ **búsqueda global** global search

buzón *nm Internet* mailbox

◇ **buzón de correo electrónico** electronic mailbox

◇ **buzón electrónico** electronic mailbox

◇ **buzón de entrada** in box, in-box

◇ **buzón múltiple** multiple mailboxes

◇ **buzón de salida** out box, outbox

◇ **buzón de voz** voice mailbox

byte *nm* byte

C++ *nm* C++

cabeza lectora/grabado-ra *nf* read-write head

cabezal *nm* *(en impresora)* head

◇ *cabezal de impresión* print head

cable *nm*

◇ *cable coaxial* co-ax(ial) cable
◇ *cable de impresora* printer cable
◇ *cable de serie* serial cable
◇ *cable USB* USB cable

cableado *nm* cabling

caché *nf* **(memoria) caché** cache (memory); **meter algo en la caché** to cache sth

CAD *nm* *(abrev de* **computer-assisted design)** CAD

CAD/CAM *nm* *(abrev de* **computer-assisted design/computer-assisted manufacture)** CAD/CAM

cadena *nf* string

◇ *cadena de caracteres* character string
◇ *cadena SCSI* SCSI chain

caerse *vpr* *(red, servidor)* to go down, to crash; **la red se ha caído** the network is down

caída *nf (de sistema)* crash

caja *nf (para gráfico)* box

◇ *caja de disquetes* diskette box
◇ *caja en forma de disco* disk box
◇ *caja de herramientas* tool-box

calculadora *nf* calculator

◇ *calculadora de escritorio* desktop calculator

calidad *nf* quality

◇ *calidad borrador (de impresión)* draft quality
◇ *calidad de carta (de impresión)* letter quality
◇ *calidad de imagen* image quality
◇ *calidad de impresión* print quality

CAM *nf (abrev de* **computer-assisted manufacture)** CAM

cámara *nf* camera

◇ *cámara digital* digital camera
◇ *cámara de Esp vídeo o Am video digital* digital video camera
◇ *Internet* **cámara web** webcam

camino *nm (localización)* path

campo *nm (en base de datos)* field

◇ *campo alfanumérico* alphanumeric field

◇ *campo numérico* numeric field

◇ *campo de texto* text field

canal *nm (de comunicaciones, datos, para IRC)* channel

◇ *Internet* **canal IRC** IRC channel

cancelación *nf (de programa)* abort

cancelar 1 *vt (archivo, rutina)* to cancel, to abandon; **cancelar entrada** *(comando)* cancel entry

2 *vi* to cancel, to abandon; **presione 'esc' para cancelar** press 'esc' to cancel

capa *nf Autoedición* layer

capacidad *nf* capacity

◇ *capacidad de almacenamiento* storage capacity

◇ *capacidad del disco* disk capacity

◇ *capacidad de memoria* memory capacity

captura *nf (de datos)* capture

◇ *captura de pantalla* screen capture *o* dump *o* shot

capturar *vt (datos)* to capture

carácter *nm* character; **caracteres por pulgada** characters per inch; **caracteres por segundo** characters per second; **caracteres por minuto/hora** *(al mecanografiar)* keystrokes per minute/hour

◇ *carácter comodín* wildcard character

◇ *carácter de control* control character

◇ *carácter de interrupción* break character

característica *nf Am Tel Br* dialling code, *US* area code

carcasa *nf (de computadora)* casing; *(de teléfono móvil)* fascia

carga *nf Internet (de archivo)* upload

◇ *carga automática (de páginas)* automatic feed

◇ *Am* **carga fría** cold boot

cargador *nm* loader

cargar 1 *vt (disco, programa)* to load; *Internet (archivo)* to upload; **cargar un programa en la memoria** to load a program into the memory

2 cargarse *vpr (programa)* to load

carpeta *nf (directorio)* folder

◇ *carpeta del sistema* system folder

carrito de la compra *nm Internet* shopping basket, *US* shopping cart

carro de la impresora *nm* printer carriage

cartucho *nm* cartridge

◇ *cartucho DAT* DAT cartridge

◇ *cartucho de tinta* ink cartridge

◇ *cartucho de tóner* toner cartridge

◇ *cartucho Zip®* Zip® disk

casilla *nf*

◇ *Am* **casilla de correo** mailbox

◇ *Am* **casilla de correo electrónico** electronic mailbox

◇ *Am* **casilla de correo de entrada** in box, inbox

◇ *Am* **casillas de correo múltiples** multiple mailboxes

◇ *Am* **casilla de correo de salida** out box, outbox

◇ **casilla de verificación** check box

catálogo electrónico *nm* electronic catalogue *o US* catalog

Cco *Internet (abrev de* **con copia***)* Bcc

CD *nm (abrev de* **compact disc***)* CD

◇ *CD* **interactivo** interactive CD

CD-I, CDI *nm (abrev de* **compact disc interactive***)* CD-I

CD-R *nm* (**a**) *(abrev de* **compact disc recorder***)* CD-R
(**b**) *(abrev de* **compact disc recordable***)* CD-R

CD-ROM *nm (abrev de* **compact disc-read only memory***)* CD-ROM

◇ *CD-ROM* **de instalación** setup CD-ROM

◇ *CD-ROM* **interactivo** interactive CD-ROM

CD-RW *nm (abrev de* **compact disc rewritable***)* CD-RW

cederrón *nm* CD-ROM

cedilla *nf* cedilla

celda *nf (en hoja de cálculo)* cell

celular *Am* **1** *adj* **teléfono celular** *Br* mobile phone, *US* cellphone
2 *nm Br* mobile, *US* cell(phone)

central telefónica *nf* telephone exchange

centralita *nf Tel (panel)* switchboard

◇ *centralita* **telefónica** *(edificio)*

telephone exchange

centrar *vt (texto) Br* to centre, *US* to center

centro *nm*

◇ *centro* **de cálculo** computer *Br* centre *o US* center

◇ *Internet* **centro comercial electrónico** electronic mall

◇ *Am* **centro de cómputos** computer *Br* centre *o US* center

cerrado, -a *adj (archivo)* closed

cerrar *vt (archivo)* to close

certificado *nm* certificate

◇ *Internet* **certificado de autenticación** authentication certificate

◇ *Internet* **certificado digital** digital certificate

◇ **certificado de garantía** guarantee *o* warranty certificate

◇ *Internet* **certificado de seguridad** security certificate

cesta de la compra *nf Internet* shopping basket, *US* shopping cart

CGA *nm (abrev de* **colour graphics adaptor***)* CGA

charla *nf Internet* chat

◇ **charla interactiva por Internet** Internet relay chat

◇ **charla en tiempo real** real-time chat

charlar *vi Internet* to chat

chat *nm Internet* chat

chatear *vi Internet* to chat

chatiqueta *nf Internet* chatiquette

chip *nm* chip

◇ *chip CCD* CCD chip

◇ *chip de memoria* memory chip

◇ *chip móvil* mobile chip

chipset *nm* chipset

cibercafé *nm* Internet café, cybercafe

cibercrimen *nm* cybercrime

cibercultura *nf* cyberculture

ciberdelito *nm* cybercrime

ciberdinero *nm* cybermoney

ciberespacio *nm* cyberspace; **en el ciberespacio** in cyberspace

cibernauta *nmf* cybernaut

cibernética *nf* cybernetics

cibernético, -a *adj* cybernetic

ciberokupa *nmf Esp* cybersquatter

ciberokupación *nf Esp* cybersquatting

ciberporno *nm* cyberporn

ciberpunk *nm* cyberpunk

cibersexo *nm* cybersex

ciberterrorismo *nm* cyberterrorism

ciclo *nm* cycle

cifrado, -a 1 *adj* encrypted **2** *nm* encryption

cifrar *vt* to encrypt

cine en casa *nm* home cinema

cinta *nf* (a) *(casete)* tape (b) *(debajo de barra de menús)* ribbon

◇ *cinta digital* digital tape

◇ *cinta digital de audio* digital audio tape

◇ *cinta de impresora* printer ribbon

◇ *cinta magnética* magnetic tape

circuitería *nf* circuitry

circuito *nm* circuit

◇ *circuito lógico* logic circuit

cita *nf (en correo electrónico)* quote

citar *vt (en correo electrónico)* to quote

clasificación *nf* sort

◇ *clasificación por orden ascendente* ascending sort

◇ *clasificación por orden descendente* descending sort

clave *nf* password; **protegido por clave** password-protected

clic, click *nm* click; **hacer clic en algo** to click (on) sth; **hacer clic con el botón izquierdo/derecho en algo** to left-click/right-click on sth; **hacer clic y arrastrar** to click and drag

◇ *Am clic del mouse* mouse click

◇ *Esp clic del ratón* mouse click

clicar 1 *vt* to click on **2** *vi* to click

cliente *nm* client

◇ *Internet cliente de correo electrónico* e-mail client

clip art *nm* clip art

clon *nm Am* clone

clónico *nm* clone

cluster *nm* cluster

◇ *cluster perdido* lost cluster

CMYK *Autoedición (abrev de* **cyan, magenta, yellow, black)** CMYK

cobertura *nf Tel* **no tengo cobertura** I can't get a signal; **mi teléfono móvil no tiene cobertura aquí** my *Br* mobile *o US* cellular network doesn't cover this area; **aquí hay poca cobertura** the reception is poor here

COBOL *nm (abrev de* **Common Business-Oriented Language)** COBOL

codificación *nf* coding, encoding

codificado, -a *adj* coded, encoded

codificador *nm* encoder

codificar *vt* to code, to encode

código *nm* code; **códigos** *(sistema)* coding

◇ *código de acceso* access code

◇ *código alfanumérico* alphanumeric code

◇ *código ASCII* ASCII code

◇ *código binario* binary code

◇ *código de carácter* character code

◇ *código de comando* command code

◇ *código de error* error code

◇ *código fuente* source code

◇ *códigos de fusión* merge codes

◇ *código máquina* machine code

◇ *Internet código de país (en URL)* country code

cola *nf* queue; **poner algo en cola** to queue sth

◇ *cola de impresión* print queue

colgar 1 *vi (al teléfono)* to hang up; **no cuelgue, por favor** hold the line, please

2 colgarse *vpr Fam (sistema)* to crash; **se me ha colgado** *Esp* **el ordenador** *o Am* **la computadora** my computer has crashed

colistero, -a *nm,f Fam Internet* list member

color *nm Br* colour, *US* color; *Autoedición* **de color verdadero** *(imagen) Br* true-colour, *US* true-color

◇ *Autoedición* **color aditivo** additive *Br* colour *o US* color

◇ *Autoedición* **color directo** spot *Br* colour *o US* color

◇ *Autoedición* **color plano** spot *Br* colour *o US* color

columna *nf (en tabla, hoja de cálculo)* column

coma *nf (signo)* comma

◇ *coma flotante* floating point

comando *nm* command

◇ *comando binario* bit command

◇ *comando de búsqueda* find command

◇ *comando DOS* DOS command

◇ *comando erróneo* bad command

◇ *comando externo* external command

◇ *comando de voz (en teléfono móvil)* voice tag

combinación de teclas *nf* key combination

comercio *nm*
◇ *comercio electrónico* e-business, electronic business, e-commerce, electronic commerce
◇ *comercio móvil* m-commerce

comillas *nfpl*
◇ *comillas tipográficas* curly *o* smart quotes

comodín *nm* wildcard

compactación *nf* compression
◇ *compactación de archivos* file compression
◇ *compactación de ficheros* file compression

compactado, -a *adj (archivo)* compacted

compactar *vt (archivo)* to compact

compatibilidad *nf* compatibility

compatible *adj* compatible (con with); **compatible IBM** IBM-compatible; **compatible con (el) Mac** Mac-compatible; **compatible con (el) PC** PC-compatible; **compatible con versiones anteriores** backward-compatible, downward-compatible

compensación de la exposición *nf Autoedición* exposure compensation

compilador *nm* compiler

compilar *vt* to compile

componente *nm* component

compresión *nf (de archivo)* compression
◇ *compresión de archivos* file compression

◇ *compresión de datos* data compression
◇ *compresión de ficheros* file compression

compresor descompresor *nm* compressor/decompressor

comprimido, -a *adj (archivo)* compressed

comprimir *vt (archivo)* to compress

comprobación antivirus *nf* antivirus check

computación *nf Am* computing; **trabaja en computación** she works in computing

computacional *adj* computational, computer

computadora *nf,* **computador** *nm Am* computer; **meter algo en la computadora** to put sth on computer; **tener algo en la computadora** to have sth on computer
◇ *computadora de bolsillo* hand-held computer, PDA
◇ *computadora central* mainframe (computer)
◇ *computadora compatible* compatible computer
◇ *computadora doméstica* home computer, PC
◇ *computadora frontal* front-end computer
◇ *computadora de gama baja* entry-level computer
◇ *computadora multimedia* multimedia computer
◇ *computadora personal* personal computer, PC
◇ *computadora portátil* laptop

(computer), notebook (computer)

◊ *computadora de sobremesa* desktop computer

computadorización *nf Am (de organización, registros)* computerization

computadorizado, -a *adj Am (organización, registros)* computerized

computadorizar *vt Am (organización, registros)* to computerize

computarización *nf Am (de organización, registros)* computerization

computarizado, -a *adj Am (organización, registros)* computerized

computarizar *vt Am (organización, registros)* to computerize

comunicaciones *nfpl* communications, comms

comunicar *vi Esp (teléfono) (estar ocupado) Br* to be engaged, *US* to be busy; **está comunicando, comunica** the line's *Br* engaged *o US* busy

concadenado, -a *adj* concatenated

concatenación *nf* concatenation

condensado, -a *adj Autoedición (tipo de letra)* condensed

conectar 1 *vt (cable, componente)* to conect (**a** to); **conectar algo en bloque** to daisy-chain sth

2 *vi* **conectar y funcionar** plug and play

3 conectarse *vpr (cable, componente)* to connect (**a** to); **conectarse a Internet** *(por primera vez)* to get connected to the Internet, to go on-line *o* online; *(regularmente)* to go on the Internet, to go on-line *o* online; **el disco contiene todo lo necesario para conectarse** the disk contains all you need to get on-line *o* online

conectividad *nf* connectivity

conector *nm* connector

conexión *nf* (a) *(de dos elementos)* connection

(b) *Tel* connection; **teníamos una conexión muy mala** we had a very bad connection

(c) *(a Internet)* connection; *(a servidor remoto)* login; **un hogar con conexión a Internet** a home with an Internet connection, a home connected to the Internet; **establecer una conexión** to establish a connection; **tener una conexión rápida/lenta** to have a fast/slow connection

◊ *Internet* **conexión a Internet** Internet connection

◊ *Internet* **conexión remota** remote login

◊ *Internet* **conexión con tarifa plana** flat-rate connection

conferencia *nf* (a) *Internet (en grupo de noticias)* conference

(b) *Esp (por teléfono)* long-distance call; **poner una conferencia** to make a long-distance call, to telephone *o* call long-distance

◇ **conferencia a cobro revertido** *Br* reverse-charge call, *US* collect call

confidencialidad de los datos *nf* data privacy

config.sys *nm* config.sys

configurable *adj* configurable

configuración *nf* configuration, settings

◇ **configuración de página** page setup

configurar *vt* to configure, to set (up)

confirmar *vt* to confirm

conflicto *nm* conflict

congestión *nf* Internet congestion

conjunto *nm* set

◇ **conjunto de datos** data set

conmutación de paquetes *nm* Internet packet switching

conmutador *nm* Am Tel (centralita) switchboard

◇ **conmutador basculante** rocker switch

consola *nf* (a) (terminal) console
(b) Internet console

construido, -a *adj* construido a medida o a la carta built-to-order

consulta *nf* query

consultar *vt* (base de datos) to query

consumibles *nmpl* consumables

contador *nm* (en página web) counter

contenido *nm* Internet content

contestador (automático) *nm* Tel answering machine, answerphone

continuar *vi* (en ventana de diálogo) to proceed, to resume

contorneo de texto *nm* text wrap

contraer *vt* (subdirectorios) to collapse

contraseña *nf* password

contraste *nm* contrast

control *nm* (tecla) control

◇ **control de acceso** access control

◇ **control del cursor** cursor control

◇ Tel **control de flujo** flow control

controlador *nm* controller, driver

◇ **controlador del bus** bus controller

◇ **controlador del disco** disk controller

◇ **controlador de dispositivos** device driver

◇ **controlador de impresora** printer driver

◇ Am **controlador del mouse** mouse driver

◇ **controlador de periféricos** device driver

◇ Esp **controlador del ratón** mouse driver

◇ **controlador de red** network controller o driver

El viaje de un correo electrónico

1 Tu ordenador
El viaje por Internet comienza en tu ordenador. Para escribir y enviar mensajes utilizas un **cliente de correo electrónico**. El mensaje que has escrito viaja entre tu ordenador y el servidor de tu **Proveedor de Acceso a Internet** a través de una línea telefónica, con la ayuda de un **módem**, una **línea ADSL** o una conexión **ISDN**.

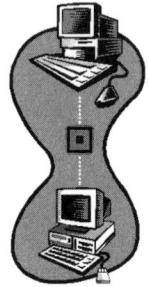

2 Tu proveedor de acceso a Internet (ISP)
Tu proveedor de acceso actúa de intermediario entre tú e Internet. Cuando un mensaje tuyo llega a tu proveedor de acceso, un **router** se encarga de encaminarlo hacia una de las **redes troncales** de Internet - la auténtica autopista de la información-.

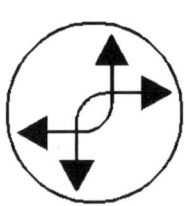

3 En Internet
La información viaja por la Red de un router a otro. Cada vez que tu mensaje llega a un router es reencaminado a otro router, acercándose cada vez más a su destino. Cuanto mayor es la distancia que la información tiene que cubrir, mayor es el número de routers por los que tendrá que pasar.

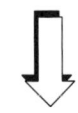

4 El final del viaje
Al final del proceso, tu mensaje llega al router del proveedor de acceso del destinatario, de donde va a poder recogerlo. Dependiendo de cómo esté el tráfico en Internet, y de la distancia cubierta, el viaje puede durar unos pocos segundos o varias horas.

conversacional *adj (modo)* conversational

conversión *nf* conversion

◇ *conversión de archivos* file conversion

◇ *conversión de ficheros* file conversion

convertidor analógico digital *nm* digital analog(ue) converter

convertir *vt (archivo, documento)* to convert (**en** to/into)

cookie *nm o nf Internet* cookie

copia *nf* copy; **hacer una copia de algo** to make a copy of sth

◇ *copia de archivo* archive file

◇ *copia de bloque* copy block

◇ *copia de disco a disco* disk-to-disk copy

◇ *copia impresa* printout

◇ *Autoedición* **copia lista para ser filmada** camera-ready copy

◇ *copia de seguridad* backup; **hacer una copia de seguridad de algo** to back up sth; **hacer copias de seguridad** to back up; **hacer la copia de seguridad** to do the backup; **ha fallado la copia de seguridad** the backup has failed

◇ *copia de seguridad en cinta* tape backup

◇ *copia de seguridad incremental* incremental backup

copiar 1 *vt (documento, carta)* to copy; **copiar algo a un disco** to copy sth to disk; **copiar y pegar algo** to copy and paste sth

2 *vi* **copiar y pegar** to copy and paste

coprocesador *nm* co-processor, coprocessor

◇ *coprocesador matemático* *Br* maths *o US* math co-processor *o* coprocessor

corrección de gamma *nf* *Autoedición* gamma correction

corrector *nm*

◇ *corrector de estilo* style-checker

◇ *corrector de gramática* grammar check

◇ *corrector ortográfico* spell-checker, spelling checker; **pasar el corrector ortográfico a un documento** to do *o* run a spellcheck on a document, to spellcheck a document

corregir *vt* to correct; **corregir automáticamente** to auto-correct

correo *nm (electrónico)* mail

◇ *correo basura* junk e-mail, spam

◇ *Fam* *correo caracol* snail mail

◇ *correo electrónico* e-mail, electronic mail; **ponerse en contacto con alguien por correo electrónico** to contact sb by e-mail; **contacte con nosotros por correo electrónico en la siguiente dirección...** e-mail us at...; **enviar algo por correo electrónico** to send sth by e-mail; **me envió un correo electrónico** *(un mensaje)* she e-mailed me, she sent me an e-mail

◇ *Fam* *correo tortuga* snail mail

◇ *correo tradicional* snail mail

◇ *correo de voz* voice mail

◇ *correo en la web* webmail

correr *Fam* **1** *vi* to run; **el nuevo sistema operativo no correrá en modelos antiguos** the new operating system won't run on older models

2 *vt (programa, aplicación)* to run; **no consigo correr este programa** I can't get this program to run properly

corromper *vt (disco, archivo)* to corrupt

corrompido, -a *adj (disco, archivo)* corrupt

corrupción *nf (de disco, archivo)* corruption

cortafuegos *nm inv Internet* firewall

cortar 1 *vt* to cut; **cortar y pegar algo** to cut and paste sth
2 *vi* **cortar y pegar** to cut and paste

coste por mil *nm Internet (de banner)* cost per thousand

cpp *(abrev de* **caracteres por pulgada)** cpi

cps *(abrev de* **caracteres por segundo)** cps

CPU *nf (abrev de* **central processing unit)** CPU

crack *nm (programa)* crack

cracker *nmf (pirata)* cracker

creación de páginas web *nf* web authoring

criptografía *nf* cryptography

cuadrícula *nf* grid, gridline

cuadro *nm Internet (en página web)* frame

◇ *cuadro de cierre* close box

◇ *cuadro de diálogo* dialogue *o US* dialog box

◇ *cuadro de zoom* zoom box

cuatricromía *nf Autoedición Br* four-colour *o US* four-color process

cuelgue *nm Fam* crash

cuenta *nf (con proveedor de acceso)* account; **abrir una cuenta con alguien** to set up an account with sb

◇ *Internet cuenta de correo* mail account

◇ *Internet cuenta de correo electrónico* e-mail account

◇ *Internet cuenta de Internet* Internet account

◇ *Internet cuenta por línea conmutada* dial-up account

◇ *cuenta de palabras* word count

◇ *Internet cuenta telefónica* dial-up account

◇ *cuenta de usuario (en Windows)* user account

cuerpo *nm (de documento, correo electrónico)* body

cuota de conexión *nf Internet* setup charge *o* fee

cursiva 1 *adj (letra)* italic
2 *nf* italics; **en cursiva** in italics

cursor *nm* cursor; **mover el cursor a la derecha/izquierda** move the cursor to right/left; **la palabra en la que se encuentra el cursor** the word where the cursor is

curva de Bézier *nf Autoedición* Bézier curve

DAT *nf (abrev de* **digital audio tape**) DAT

datagrama *nm Internet* datagram

dato *nm* **un dato** an item of data; **datos** data; **reunir datos sobre alguien/algo** to collect data on sb/sth

debugger *nm Am (programa)* debugger

debugging *nm Am (de programa)* debugging

decodificación *nf* decoding

decodificador *nm* decoder

decodificar *vt* to decode; **el archivo se decodifica automáticamente al recibirse** the file is automatically decoded when it is received

dedicado, -a *adj (terminal, línea)* dedicated

defecto *nm* **por defecto** *(automáticamente)* by default; **la letra que te sale por defecto es Arial** the default typface is Arial; **seleccionar algo por defecto** to default to sth

definición *nf* definition

definir *vt (valor)* to define

degradado *nm Autoedición* blend

◊ **degradado lineal** gradient o graduated fill

delimitador *nm (de campo)* delimiter

delimitar *vt (campo)* to delimit

delito *nm*

◊ **delito electrónico** electronic crime

◊ **delito informático** computer crime

demo *nf (abrev de* **demostración**) demo; **hemos recibido una demo del nuevo software** we have received a demo of the new software

demodulador *nm* demodulator

demostración *nf* demonstration; **hemos recibido una versión de demostración del nuevo software** we have received a demo version of the new software

densidad *nf* density; **de alta densidad** *(disco, impresión)* high-density

dentado *nm Autoedición* aliasing

depuración *nf (de programa)* debugging

depurador *nm (programa)* debugger

depurar *vt (programa)* to debug

desactivado, -a *adj (opción)* disabled

desactivar *vt* to disable, to deactivate

desarrollador, -ora *nm,f* developer

◊ **desarrollador de software** software developer

◊ **desarrollador de terceras partes** third-party developer

desarrollar *vt* to develop

desbloquear *vt* (a) *(archivo, disquete)* to unlock (b) *(teléfono móvil)* to unlock

desbordamiento *nm* overflow

descarga *nf* Internet download

descargable *adj* Internet downloadable

descargar 1 *vt* Internet to download; **descargar un programa de la Red** to download a program from the Net 2 **descargarse** *vpr* to download; **los gráficos tardan mucho en descargarse** graphic files take a long time to download

descifrado *nm* decryption

descifrar *vt* to decrypt

descodificación *nf* decoding

descodificador *nm* decoder

descodificar *vt* to decode; **el** archivo se descodifica automáticamente al recibirse the file is automatically decoded when it is received

descolgar 1 *vt (teléfono) (para hablar)* to pick up; **descolgamos el teléfono para que no nos molestara nadie** we left the phone off the hook so nobody would disturb us 2 *vi (para hablar por teléfono)* to pick up; **para efectuar una llamada descuelgue y espere tono** to make a call, lift the receiver and wait for the dial tone

descompresión *nf* decompression

descomprimido, -a *adj (archivo)* decompressed, unzipped

descomprimir *vt (archivo)* to decompress, to unzip

desconectado, -a *adj (del enchufe)* unplugged

desconectar 1 *vt (máquina)* to disconnect 2 **desconectarse** *vpr (de Internet)* to go off-line *o* offline

desconexión *nf (de sesión)* logoff; *(de línea telefónica)* disconnection

descriptor *nm* descriptor

deseleccionar *vt* to deselect

desfragmentación *nf* defragmentation

desfragmentador *nm* defragmenter

desfragmentar *vt* to defragment

deshacer *vt (comando)* to undo; **deshacer cambios** *(mensaje)* undo changes; **deshacer el último cambio** *(mensaje)* undo last

desinstalación *nf* deinstallation

desinstalador *nm* deinstaller

desinstalar *vt* to deinstall, to uninstall

desmagnetización *nf* degaussing

desplegable *adj (menú)* pop-up

desplegar *vt (menú)* to pull down

desproteger *vt (ilegalmente)* to crack

destinatario, -a *nm,f (de correo electrónico)* recipient

destino *nm* destination

desvío de llamada *nm Tel* call diversion *o* forwarding

detector de virus *nm* virus detector

devorar *vt (números, datos)* to crunch

diagnóstico *nm* diagnostic

diagrama *nm*
◇ **diagrama en árbol** tree diagram
◇ **diagrama de flujo** flowchart

diálogo *nm* dialogue, *US* dialog
◇ *Tel* **diálogo de establecimiento de comunicación** handshake

diccionario de sinónimos *nm* thesaurus

dictáfono *nm* Dictaphone®

dientes de sierra *nmpl Autoedición* aliasing

difuminado *nm Autoedición* dithering

difusión *nf* broadcast

digital *adj* digital

digitalización *nf* digitizing

digitalizador *nm* digitizer

digitalizar *vt* to digitalize

digitalmente *adv* digitally

digitar *vt Am* to key, to type

dígito *nm* digit
◇ *dígito binario* binary digit

DIMM *nm (abrev de dual in-line memory module)* DIMM

dinámico, -a *adj* dynamic

dinero *nm*
◇ *dinero digital* digital cash
◇ *dinero electrónico* electronic money *o* cash

dingbat *nm Autoedición (carácter)* dingbat

diodo emisor de luz *nm* light-emitting diode, LED

dirección *nf* address
◇ *Internet* **dirección de correo electrónico** e-mail address
◇ *Internet* **dirección electrónica** *(de correo)* e-mail address; *(de página)* web page address
◇ *dirección de host* host address
◇ *dirección de Internet* Internet address
◇ *Internet* **dirección IP** IP address
◇ *dirección de memoria* memory address

◇ *Internet* **dirección del remitente** return address

◇ **dirección SCSI** SCSI address

◇ *Internet* **dirección web** web address

direccionable *adj* addressable

direccionador *nm* router

direccionamiento *nm* addressing

direccionar *vt* to address

directorio *nm (de archivos)* directory

◇ **directorio raíz** root directory

◇ *Am* **directorio de teléfonos** telephone directory *o* book, phone book

dirigir *vt* to address

discado *nm Andes, RP Tel Br* dialling, *US* dialing

◇ **discado abreviado** shortcode *Br* dialling *o US* dialing

◇ **discado múltiple** group *Br* dialling *o US* dialing

discar *vt Andes, RP (número de teléfono)* to dial; **discar un número** to dial a number; **volver a discar un número** to redial a number

disco *nm* disk; **poner algo en un disco** to put sth on a disk

◇ **disco de alta densidad** high-density disk

◇ **disco de arranque** start-up *o* boot disk

◇ **disco Bernoulli**® Bernoulli® disk

◇ **disco compacto** compact disc

◇ **disco compacto grabable** recordable CD

◇ **disco compacto interactivo** interactive CD

◇ **disco compacto regrabable** rewritable CD

◇ **disco de copia** copy disk

◇ **disco demo** demo disk

◇ **disco de destino** destination *o* target disk

◇ **disco de diagnóstico** diagnostic disk

◇ **disco de doble densidad** double-density disk

◇ **disco duro** hard disk

◇ **disco duro externo** external hard disk

◇ **disco duro interno** internal hard drive

◇ **disco fijo** fixed disk

◇ **disco de instalación** installation disk

◇ **disco Jaz**® Jaz® disk

◇ **disco de Mac** Mac disk

◇ **disco maestro** master disk

◇ **disco magnético** magnetic disk

◇ **disco multisesión** multi-session disc

◇ **disco óptico** optical disk

◇ **disco de PC** PC disk

◇ **disco de programa** program disk

◇ **disco de sistema** system disk

◇ **disco versátil digital** digital versatile disk

◇ **disco de** *Esp* **vídeo** *o Am* **video digital** digital video disk

◇ **disco Zip**® Zip® disk

diseñador, -ora *nm,f* designer

◇ **diseñador gráfico** graphic designer

◇ **diseñador de páginas web** web designer

diseño *nm (formato de página)* layout

◇ *diseño asistido por Esp* **ordenador** *o Am* **computadora** computer-assisted *o* computer-aided design

◇ *diseño de página* page design

disponible *adj (producto)* available; *(ranura de expansión)* free; **disponible en CD-ROM** available on CD-ROM; **disponible en DVD, disponible en formato DVD** available on DVD, available in DVD format; **disponible para (el) Mac / PC** available for the Mac / PC

disposición del teclado *nf* keyboard layout

dispositivo *nm* device

◇ *dispositivo de almacenamiento* storage device

◇ *dispositivo para copias de seguridad* backup device

◇ *dispositivo de entrada* input device

◇ *dispositivo de entrada y salida* input/output device

◇ *dispositivo periférico* peripheral device

◇ *dispositivo de salida* output device

disquete *nm* diskette, floppy disk; **en disquete** on diskette *o* floppy disk

disquetera *nf* floppy (disk) drive

dividir *vt (archivo, imagen)* to split

DNS *nm Internet (abrev de* **Domain Name System**) DNS

doble *adj*

◇ *doble clic* double click; **hacer doble clic** to double-click; **hacer doble clic en algo** to double-click (on) sth

◇ *doble densidad* double density

documentación *nf (manuales)* documentation

documento *nm* document; **guárdalo en Mis documentos** *(en Windows)* save it in My documents

◇ *documento léeme* read-me file

dominio *nm Internet* domain

◇ *Internet* **dominio de alto nivel** top-level domain

◇ *dominio público* public domain

dormir *vi (portátil)* to sleep; **poner un portátil a dormir** to put a notebook to sleep

DOS *nm (abrev de* **disk operating system**) DOS

DRAM *nf (abrev de* **dynamic random access memory**) DRAM

driver *nm* driver

duotono *nm Autoedición* duotone

dúplex *nm Tel* duplex

◇ *dúplex pleno* full duplex

DVD *nm (abrev de* **Digital Video Disk, Digital Versatile Disk**) DVD

◇ *DVD reescribible* rewritable DVD

◇ *DVD regrabable* recordable DVD

DVD-R *nm (abrev de* **digital**

video disk-recordable) DVD-R

DVD-RAM *nf* (*abrev de* **digital video disk-random access memory**) DVD-RAM

DVD-ROM *nf* (*abrev de* **digital video disk-read only memory**) DVD-ROM

DVD-RW *nm* (*abrev de* **digital video disk-rewritable**) DVD-RW

eco *nm* echo

economía de conocimientos *nf* knowledge economy

EDI *nm* Internet (*abrev de* **electronic data interchange**) EDI

edición *nf* (*menú*) edit; (*acción*) editing

◇ *edición electrónica* electronic publishing

◇ *edición de imágenes* image editing

◇ *edición de textos* text editing

editar *vt* to edit

editor *nm* (*software*) editor

◇ Internet *editor de HTML* HTML editor

◇ *editor de iconos* icon editor

◇ *editor de imágenes* image editor

◇ *editor de textos* text editor

EDO RAM *nf* (*abrev de* **extended data-out random access memory**) EDO RAM

efecto *nm*

◇ *efecto 2000* millennium bug

◇ Autoedición *efecto de filtro* filter effect

◇ Autoedición *efecto de ojos rojos* red-eye effect

◇ *efecto de tachado* (*en texto*) strike-through mode

eficacia *nf* (*de máquina*) efficiency

eficaz *adj* (*máquina*) efficient

EGA (*abrev de* **enhanced graphics adaptor**) EGA

ejecución *nf* (*de comando, programa*) execution

ejecutable *nm* (*archivo*) executable file

ejecutar *vt* (*comando, programa*) to execute; **con** *Esp* **este ordenador** *o Am* **esta computadora se puede ejecutar la mayoría del software** this computer runs most software; **no interrumpa el programa mientras se esté ejecutando** do not interrupt the program while it is running

electrónica *nf* electronics

electrónico, -a *adj* electronic

e-mail *nm* e-mail; **ponerse en contacto con alguien por e-mail** to contact sb by e-mail; **contacte con nosotros por e-mail en la siguiente dirección...** e-mail us at...; **enviar algo por e-mail** to send sth by e-mail; **me envió un e-mail** (*un mensaje*) she e-mailed me, she sent me an e-mail

emilio *nm Esp Fam* e-mail; **mandar un emilio a alguien** to send sb an e-mail, to e-mail sb

emisión *nf* broadcast; **emisión por la web** webcast

emitir *vt* to broadcast; **emitir por la web** to webcast

emoticono, emoticón *nm Internet* emoticon

empresa punto com *nf Internet* dot com company

EMS *nm Tel* (*abbrev de* **enhanced messaging service**) EMS

emulación *nf* emulation
◇ *emulación de terminal* terminal emulation

emulador *nm* emulator
◇ *emulador de terminal* terminal emulator

emular *vt* to emulate

encabezado *nm* header, heading

encabezamiento *nm* header, heading

encaminador *nm* router

encender 1 *vt* (*computadora, impresora*) to switch on
2 **encenderse** *vpr* (*computadora, impresora*) to switch on; **se enciende solo** it switches itself on

encriptación *nf* encryption
◇ *encriptación de datos* data encryption

encriptar *vt* to encrypt

enlace *nm Internet* link (**a** to)
◇ *Internet* **enlace hipertextual** hypertext link

◇ *Internet* **enlace roto** broken link
◇ *enlace para la transmisión de datos* data link

ensamblador *nm* assembler

ensamblar *vt* to assemble

enseñanza *nf*
◇ *enseñanza asistida por Esp ordenador o Am computadora* computer-aided learning

entorno *nm* environment

entrada *nf* input; **entrada/salida** input/output
◇ *entrada de datos* data input

entrar *vi* **entrar en un archivo/programa** to go into a file/program; **entrar en un sistema** to log onto a system

entrelazado, -a *adj* (*monitor*) interlaced; **no entrelazado** non-interlaced

enviar *vt Internet* (*correo electrónico*) to send; (*mensaje a grupo de noticias*) to post; **te enviaré la información por correo electrónico** I'll e-mail the information to you, I'll send you the information by e-mail

EPS *nm* (*abrev de* **encapsulated PostScript**) EPS

ergonomía *nf* ergonomics

ergonómico, -a *adj* ergonomic

erróneo, -a *adj* (*en mensajes de error*) bad

error *nm* (*en software*) bug; **sin errores** bug-free; **plagado de errores** bug-ridden

◇ *error de codificación* coding error

◇ *error fatal* fatal error

◇ *error de programación* programming error

◇ *error de sintaxis* syntax error

◇ *error del sistema* system error

◇ *error de software* software error

E/S *(abrev de* **entrada/salida)** I/O

escala de grises *nf Br* greyscale, *US* grayscale

escalabilidad *nf* scalability

escanear *vt* to scan

escaneo *nm* scan

◇ *escaneo por lotes* batch scanning

escáner *nm* scanner

◇ *escáner de mano* handheld scanner

◇ *escáner de negativos* negative scanner

◇ *escáner óptico* optical scanner

◇ *escáner de páginas* page scanner

◇ *escáner de película* film scanner

◇ *escáner plano* flatbed scanner

◇ *escáner de sobremesa* flatbed scanner

◇ *escáner de tambor* drum scanner

escape *nm (tecla)* escape

escribir **1** *vt (CD-ROM)* to write; **escribir algo a máquina** to type sth; **escribir algo en el** disco to write sth to disk
2 *vi* to write; **escribir a máquina** to type

escritorio *nm* desktop; **el icono aparece en el escritorio** you will find the icon on your desktop

◇ *escritorio activo (en Windows)* active desktop

escritura de paquetes *nf (en CD-RW)* packet writing

espaciado *nm* spacing

◇ *espaciado de caracteres* character spacing

◇ *Autoedición espaciado proporcional* proportional spacing

espacio *nm* space

◇ *espacio en disco* disk space

◇ *Autoedición espacio indivisible* hard space

◇ *Internet espacio web* web space

espera *nf* **poner a alguien en espera** *(en teléfono)* to put sb on hold

esperar *vt* **espere un momento, por favor** *(al teléfono)* hold the line, please; **está ocupado, ¿le importaría esperar?** the line's *Br* engaged *o US* busy, will you hold?

estabilizador *nm RP* uninterruptible power supply, UPS

establecimiento *nm*

◇ *Tel establecimiento de comunicación* handshaking

◇ *Tel establecimiento de llamada o Am llamado* call connection

estación *nf*
◇ *estación base* *(para portátil)* docking station
◇ *estación de trabajo* workstation

estampadora de CD-ROM *nf* CD-ROM burner

estampar *vt* *(CD-ROM)* to burn

estilo *nm* style

estructura *nf* structure
◇ *estructura del archivo* file structure
◇ *estructura de directorio* directory structure
◇ *estructura del fichero* file structure

Ethernet® *nf* Ethernet®

etiqueta *nf* tag
◇ *etiqueta de apertura* opening tag
◇ *etiqueta de cierre* closing tag

etiquetar *vt* to tag

expandible *adj* *(memoria)* expandable; **98MB expandibles a 392MB** 98MB expandable to 392MB

expandir *vt* *(memoria)* to expand

expansión *nf* *(de memoria)* expansion

explorador de Windows® *nm* Windows Explorer®

exportar *vt* *(archivo, datos)* to export (**a** to)

exposición *nf* *Autoedición* exposure

extensión *nf* (a) *(de teléfono)* extension; **¿me puede comunicar** *o Esp* **poner con la extensión 946?** can I have extension 946? (b) *(de archivo)* extension
◇ *extensión del nombre del archivo* file name extension

externo, -a *adj* external

extraer *vt* *(archivo comprimido)* to extract

extraíble *adj* *(disco)* removable

extranet *nf* *Internet* extranet

fabricación *nf*
◇ *fabricación asistida por Esp* **ordenador** *o Am* **computadora** computer-aided *o* computer-assisted *o* computer-integrated manufacturing

fácil *adj* **fácil de manejar** user-friendly

facilidad de manejo *nf* user-friendliness

facturación electrónica *nf Internet* electronic billing, e-billing

falta de convergencia *nf (de monitor)* misconvergence

favorito *nm Internet (de página web)* bookmark, favorite

fax *nm (máquina, mensaje)* fax; **enviar un fax a alguien** to send sb a fax, to fax sb; **enviar algo por fax** to send sth by fax, to fax sth

fibra óptica *nf Br* fibre *o US* fiber optics, optical *Br* fibre *o US* fiber; **de fibra óptica** *(cable) Br* fibre *o US* fiber optic

fichero *nm* file
◇ *fichero activo* active file
◇ *fichero por lotes* batch file
◇ *fichero oculto* hidden file

fila *nf (en tabla, hoja de cálculo)* row

filmadora *nf Autoedición* imagesetter, typesetter

filtrado de llamadas *nm Tel* call screening

filtro *nm (software)* filter
◇ *filtro de pantalla* (anti-)glare filter *o* screen

fin de línea *nm* line end

finger *nm Internet* finger

firewall *nm Am Internet* firewall

FireWire® *nm* FireWire®

firma *nf* signature
◇ *firma digital* digital signature
◇ *firma electrónica* electronic signature

firmware *nm* firmware

flecha *nf* arrow
◇ *flecha abajo* down arrow
◇ *flecha arriba* up arrow
◇ *flecha derecha* right arrow
◇ *flecha de desplazamiento* scroll arrow
◇ *flecha izquierda* left arrow

formateado *nm (de disco, página, texto)* formatting

formatear *vt (disco, página, texto)* to format; **un disco sin**

formatear an unformatted disk

formato nm (de página, texto) format

◇ **formato apaisado** landscape

◇ **formato de archivo** file format

◇ **formato de fichero** file format

◇ **formato de imagen** image format

◇ **formato de impresión** print format

◇ **formato de página** page format

◇ **formato de párrafo** paragraph format

◇ **formato de retrato** portrait

◇ **formato de texto** text format

formulario nm Internet form

foro nm Internet forum

FORTRAN nm FORTRAN

foto CD nm photo CD

fotocomposición nf Autoedición photocomposition

fotocopia nf photocopy

fotocopiadora nf photocopier, photocopying machine

fotocopiar vt to photocopy

fotografía digital nf digital photography

fotorrealismo nm photorealism

fotorrealista adj photorealistic

fragmentación nf (de disco) fragmentation

◇ **fragmentación del disco** disk fragmentation

fragmentado, -a adj (disco) fragmented

fragmentar 1 vt (disco) to fragment
2 **fragmentarse** vpr (disco) to become fragmented

freeware nm freeware

frontal 1 adj front; (sistema) front-end
2 nm front end

FTP nm Internet (abrev de **File Transfer Protocol**) FTP; **enviar algo por FTP** to FTP sth

◇ **FTP anónimo** anonymous FTP

fuente nf (tipo de letra) font

◇ **fuente de alimentación** power supply

◇ **fuente por defecto** default font

◇ **fuente descargable** downloadable font

◇ **fuente escalable** scalable font

◇ **fuente Postscript®** PostScript® font

◇ **fuente predeterminada** default font

◇ **fuente TrueType®** TrueType® font

funcionar vi (software) to run; **este software funciona en DOS** this software runs on DOS; **funciona con 56K** 56K supported

fusión nf (de archivos) merge

fusionar vt (archivos) to merge

gama *nf* **de gama alta** high-end; **de gama baja** low-end; **de gama media** mid-range

garantía *nf (documento, compromiso)* guarantee, warranty; **esta impresora tiene cinco años de garantía** *o* **viene con una garantía de cinco años** this printer has a five-year guarantee *o* warranty, this printer is guaranteed for five years; **estar en garantía** to be under guarantee *o* warranty

◇ **garantía ampliada** extended guarantee *o* warranty

◇ **garantía con devolución al distribuidor** return-to-base guarantee *o* warranty

◇ **garantía in situ** on-site guarantee *o* warranty

◇ **garantía de por vida** lifetime guarantee *o* warranty

garantizar *vt (producto)* to guarantee

GB *nm (abrev de* **gigabyte***)* GB

generación *nf (modelo)* generation; *Esp* **un ordenador** *o* *Am* **una computadora de tercera/cuarta generación** a third-generation/fourth-generation computer

generado, -a *adj* **generado por** *Esp* **ordenador** *o* *Am* **computadora** computer-generated

generador de caracteres *nm* character generator

generar *vt* to generate

gestión *nf* management

◇ **gestión de archivos** file management

◇ **gestión de bases de datos** database management

◇ **gestión de datos** data management

◇ **gestión de ficheros** file management

◇ **gestión de memoria** memory management

◇ **gestión de sistemas** systems management

gestor *nm*

◇ **gestor de memoria** memory manager

GHz *(abrev de* **gigahercio***)* GHz

GIF *nm (abrev de* **Graphics Interchange Format***)* GIF

◇ **GIF animado** animated GIF

gigabyte *nm* gigabyte

gigahercio *nm* gigahertz

GIS *nm inv (abrev de* **geographical information system***)* GIS

global *adj (búsqueda)* global

globos de ayuda *nmpl* balloon help

gopher *nm Internet* gopher

GPRS *nm Tel* (*abrev de* **General Packet Radio Service**) GPRS

GPS *nm Tel* (*abrev de* **Global Positioning System**) GPS

grabadora *nf* recorder, writer
◇ *grabadora de CD-ROM* CD-ROM recorder *o* writer
◇ *grabadora de discos compactos* compact disc recorder *o* writer
◇ *grabadora de DVD* DVD recorder *o* writer

grabar *vt* (*documento*) to save; (*CD-ROM*) to record

grado de inclinación *nm* pitch

Graffiti® *nm* (**escritura de**) Graffiti (*para PDA*) Graffiti®

gráfico *nm* (*ilustración*) graphic; (*con cifras*) chart
◇ *gráfico de barras* bar chart
◇ *gráfico circular* pie chart
◇ *gráficos en color* *Br* colour *o* US color graphics
◇ *gráfico de columnas* column chart
◇ *gráficos informáticos* computer graphics
◇ *gráficos para presentaciones* presentation *o* business graphics
◇ *gráficos rasterizados* raster graphics
◇ *gráficos de sectores* pie chart

◇ *Autoedición gráficos vectoriales* vector graphics

grupo *nm* group
◇ *Internet grupo de discusión* discussion group
◇ *Internet grupo de noticias* newsgroup
◇ *grupo de usuarios* user group

GSM *nm Tel* (*abrev de* **global system for mobile communication**) GSM

guante de datos *nm* dataglove

guardar *vt* to save; **guardar algo en el disco** to save sth to disk; **¿desea guardar cambios?** do you want to save changes?; **guardar como...** save as...; **guardar automáticamente** to autosave

guía *nf* (**a**) (*regla*) guide (**b**) (*telefónica*) telephone directory *o* book, phone book

guión *nm* (**a**) (*símbolo*) (*corto*) hyphen; (*más largo*) dash (**b**) (*programa*) script
◇ *Autoedición guión corto* soft hyphen
◇ *Autoedición guión de final de renglón* soft hyphen
◇ *Autoedición guión indivisible* hard hyphen
◇ *Autoedición guión m* em-dash
◇ *Autoedición guión n* en-dash

gusano *nm* (*programa*) worm

hacker *nmf* hacker

hardware *nm* hardware

herramienta *nf* tool
- ◇ *herramienta de autor* authoring tool
- ◇ *Internet herramienta para la creación de páginas web* web authoring tool
- ◇ *Autoedición herramienta lazo* lasso tool
- ◇ *herramienta de software* software tool
- ◇ *Autoedición herramienta de vectores* vector tool

hexadecimal *adj* hexadecimal

híbrido, -a *adj* (CD-ROM) hybrid

hiperenlace *nm* *Internet* hyperlink

hipermedia *nf* hypermedia

hipertexto *nm* hypertext

hipertextual *adj* hypertext; **enlace hipertextual** hypertext link

historial *nm* *Internet* history list

hoja *nf*
- ◇ *hoja de cálculo* spreadsheet
- ◇ *hoja de cálculo con gráficos* graphics spreadsheet

- ◇ *Internet hoja de estilo en cascada* cascade style sheet
- ◇ *hoja de estilos* style sheet

hospedaje *nm* *Internet (de página web)* hosting
- ◇ *hospedaje de dominios* domain hosting
- ◇ *hospedaje de páginas web* web hosting

hospedar *vt* *Internet (sitio web)* to host

host *nm* host

HSCSD *nm* *Tel* (abrev de **High Speed Circuit Switched Data**) HSCSD

HTML *nm* *Internet* (abrev de **Hyper Text Markup Language**) HTML
- ◇ *HTML dinámico* dynamic HTML

HTTP *nm* *Internet* (abrev de **Hyper Text Transfer Protocol**) HTTP
- ◇ *HTTP seguro* secure HTTP

hub *nm* hub

hueco *nm* (para disco duro) bay

huérfana *nf* *Autoedición (línea)* orphan

huevo de Pascua *nm* (programa) Easter Egg

icono *nm* icon

IDE *nm (abrev de* **integrated drive electronics**) IDE

identidad *nf (en programa de correo)* identity

identificador *nm* identifier

◇ *Tel* **identificador de llamada** caller display, caller ID

igual *nm (signo)* equal(s) sign

ilegal *adj (carácter, instrucción)* illegal

ilegible *adj (archivo, datos)* unreadable

ilustración *nf* illustration; *Autoedición* **ilustraciones** artwork

◇ *ilustraciones en ASCII* ASCII art

imagen *nf* image

◇ *imágenes generadas por Esp* **ordenador** *o Am* **computadora** computer-generated images

◇ *Internet* **imagen integrada** inline image

◇ *Internet* **imagen interactiva** clickable image

IMAP *nm Internet (abrev de* **Internet Message Access Protocol**) IMAP

IMEI *nm Tel (abrev de* **International Mobile Equipment Identity**) IMEI

importar *vt (archivo, datos)* to export (**de** from)

impresión *nf*

◇ *impresión en borrador* draft printing

◇ *impresión en calidad borrador* draft quality printing

◇ *impresión en color Br* colour *o US* color printing

◇ *impresión de pantalla* print screen

◇ *impresión en segundo plano* background printing

◇ *impresión subordinada* background printing

impresora *nf* printer

◇ *impresora de agujas* dot-matrix printer

◇ *impresora de chorro de tinta* inkjet printer

◇ *Am* **impresora color** *Br* colour *o US* color printer

◇ *impresora en color Br* colour *o US* color printer

◇ *impresora de impacto* impact printer

◇ *impresora de inyección* bubble-jet printer

◇ *impresora láser* laser printer

◇ *impresora de margarita* daisy-wheel printer

Diferentes tipos de impresoras

Impresora matricial

▷ utiliza una cinta con tinta para dejar una impresión en el papel
▷ puede imprimir copias múltiples y en papel continuo
▷ costo por página impresa bajo
▷ nivel de ruido alto
▷ calidad de impresión baja

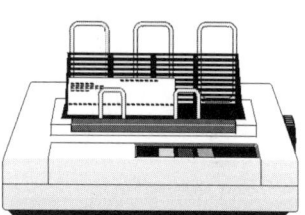

Impresora de chorro de tinta

▷ utiliza un fino chorro de tinta para formar los caracteres en el papel
▷ impresión en color a un precio asequible
▷ costo por página impresa más alto
▷ impresión silenciosa

Impresora láser

▷ utiliza el láser para imprimir el texto en la página
▷ costo por página impresa más barato
▷ impresión silenciosa
▷ rápida
▷ las impresoras láser en color son caras

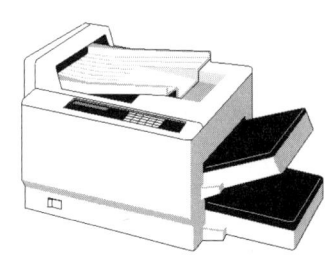

◇ *impresora matricial* dot-matrix printer

◇ *Am* *impresora de matriz de puntos* dot-matrix printer

◇ *impresora en paralelo* parallel printer

◇ *impresora en serie* serial printer

◇ *impresora térmica* thermal printer

imprimir 1 *vt* to print
2 *vi* to print

inactivo, -a *adj (máquina)* idle

inalámbrico, -a *adj (ratón, teléfono)* cordless, wireless

incompatibilidad *nf* incompatibility (**con** with)

incompatible *adj* incompatible (**con** with)

incorporado, -a *adj* built-in

incremental *adj* incremental

incrustado, -a *adj* embedded

incrustar *vt* to embed

indentado *nm Am* indentation

indentar *vt Am* to indent

indexación *nf* indexing

indexar *vt* to index

indicativo *nm Tel Br* dialling code, *US* area code

◇ *indicativo internacional* country code, *Br* international dialling code

índice *nm* index

◇ *índice de compresión (de archivo)* compression ratio

indizar *vt (base de datos)* to index

infectar *vt (archivo, disco)* to infect

infoadicto, -a *nm,f Internet* infoaddict

infografía *nf* computer graphics

infografista *nmf* computer graphics artist

infopista *nf Internet* infohighway

información *nf* (a) *(datos)* information
(b) *(telefónica)* information; *Am* **informaciones** information

◇ *información telefónica* directory *Br* enquiries o *US* assistance

informática *nf (tecnología)* computing, information technology, IT; *(ciencia)* computer science; **trabaja en informática** she works in computing; **el departamento de informática de una empresa** the IT department of a company; **la empresa va a invertir más en informática** the company is going to invest more in IT; **no sé nada de informática** I don't know anything about computers; **se requieren conocimientos de informática** candidates should be computer-literate; **curso de informática** computing course; **experto en informática** computer expert

◇ *informática de gestión* business computing

◇ *informática personal* personal computing

informáticamente *adv* by computer

informático, -a 1 *adj* computer; **equipo informático** computer equipment; **experto informático** computer expert; **red informática** computer network

2 *nm,f (experto)* computer expert; *(técnico)* computer technician

informatización *nf (de organización, registros)* computerization

informatizado, -a *adj (organización, registros)* computerized

informatizar 1 *vt (organización, registros)* to computerize **2 informatizarse** *vpr* to become computerized; **empresas que todavía no se han informatizado** companies which have yet to computerize their operations

informe *nm (de base de datos)* report

Infovía® (Plus) *nf* = Spanish computer network providing access to Internet servers

infrarrojo *nm* infrared

ingeniería *nf*
◇ **ingeniería asistida por** *Esp* **ordenador** *o Am* **computadora** computer-aided *o* computer-assisted engineering
◇ **ingeniería de sistemas asistida por** *Esp* **ordenador** *o Am* **computadora** computer-aided *o* computer-assisted software engineering

ingeniero, -a *nm,f*
◇ **ingeniero informático** computer engineer
◇ **ingeniero de sistemas** systems engineer
◇ **ingeniero de software** software engineer

inicialización *nf (de computadora, módem, impresora)* initialization

inicializar *vt (computador, módem, impresora)* to initialize; **un disco sin inicializar** an unformatted disk

inserción *nf* insert

insertar *vt* to insert

in situ 1 *adj (garantía)* on-site **2** *adv (reparar)* on site

instalador *nm (programa)* installer

instalar *vt (equipo, programa)* to install

instantáneo, -a *adj* instant

instrucción *nf* instruction; **instrucciones** *(de programa)* instructions

integración de bases de datos *nf* database integration

integrado, -a *adj (fax, módem)* integrated

inteligencia artificial *nf* artificial intelligence

inteligente *adj (sistema, edificio)* intelligent; *(tarjeta)* smart

interactivo, -a *adj* interactive

interactuar *vi* to interact (**con** with)

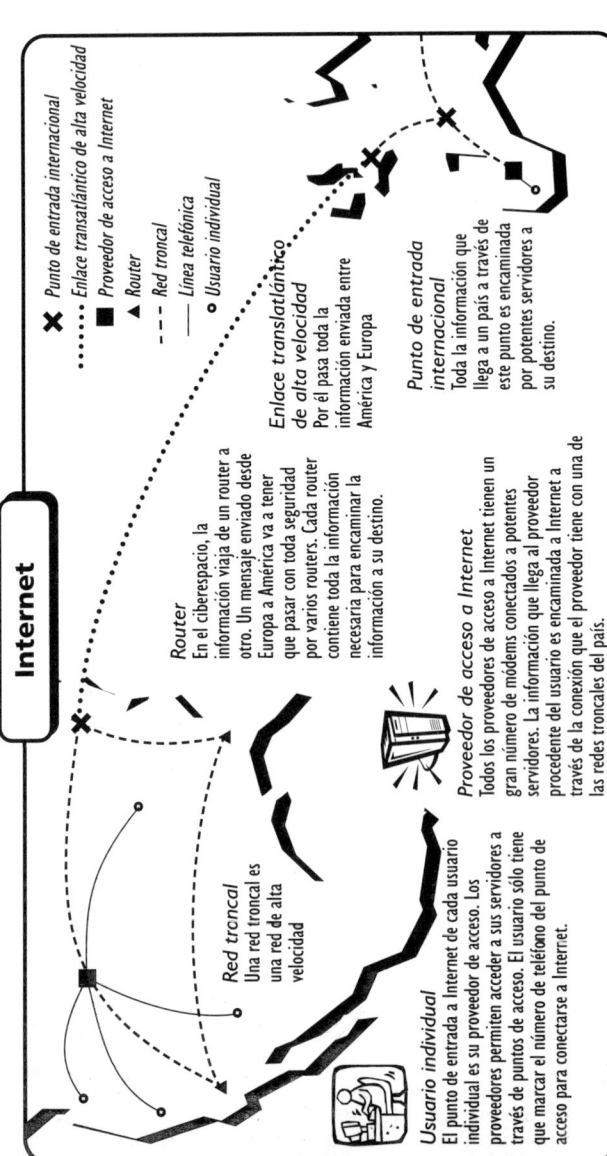

Internet

Leyenda:
- ✕ Punto de entrada internacional
- ••••• Enlace transatlántico de alta velocidad
- ■ Proveedor de acceso a Internet
- ▲ Router
- - - - Red troncal
- —— Línea telefónica
- ○ Usuario individual

Router
En el ciberespacio, la información viaja de un router a otro. Un mensaje enviado desde Europa a América va a tener que pasar con toda seguridad por varios routers. Cada router contiene toda la información necesaria para encaminar la información a su destino.

Enlace translántico de alta velocidad
Por él pasa toda la información enviada entre América y Europa

Punto de entrada internacional
Toda la información que llega a un país a través de este punto es encaminada por potentes servidores a su destino.

Proveedor de acceso a Internet
Todos los proveedores de acceso a Internet tienen un gran número de módems conectados a potentes servidores. La información que llega al proveedor procedente del usuario es encaminada a Internet a través de la conexión que el proveedor tiene con una de las redes troncales del país.

Red troncal
Una red troncal es una red de alta velocidad

Usuario individual
El punto de entrada a Internet de cada usuario individual es su proveedor de acceso. Los proveedores permiten acceder a sus servidores a través de puntos de acceso. El usuario sólo tiene que marcar el número de teléfono del punto de acceso para conectarse a Internet.

intercambio *nm* exchange

◇ *intercambio de datos* data exchange

◇ *intercambio dinámico de datos* dynamic data exchange

◇ *intercambio electrónico de datos* electronic data exchange

interface, interfaz *nm o nf* interface

◇ *Internet* **interface común de pasarela** common gateway interface

◇ *interface gráfico* graphical interface

◇ *interface gráfico de usuario* graphical user interface

◇ *interface paralelo* parallel interface

◇ *interface de programación de aplicaciones* application programming interface

◇ *interface de serie* serial interface

◇ *interface de usuario* user interface

interferencia *nf Tel* interference

interletraje *nm Autoedición* kerning

interlineado *nm Autoedición* leading, line spacing

internauta *nmf* Net user, internaut

Internet *nf* Internet; **navegar por Internet** to surf the Internet; **está en Internet** it's on the Internet; **listo para Internet** Internet-ready

◇ *Internet 2* Internet 2

interno, -a 1 *adj* internal **2** *nm RP (de teléfono)* extension; **¿me puede dar con el interno 946?** can I have extension 946?

interoperabilidad *nf* interoperability

interpolación *nf* interpolation

intérprete *nm (software)* interpreter

◇ *intérprete de comandos* cornmand interpreter

◇ *intérprete de procesos* command processor

interruptor *nm* switch

◇ *interruptor DIP* DIP switch

◇ *interruptor de encendido/apagado* on/off switch

intranet *nf* intranet

introducción *nf* entry

In Spanish, should one write **Internet**, **la Internet** or **el Internet**? Although "Internet" is most commonly used as a proper noun in Spanish and therefore doesn't take a definite article, you may sometimes see or hear **la Internet** or even **el Internet**. Nevertheless, it is much more common to see it used without an article, and that is how we have presented it in this dictionary.

⋄ *introducción de datos* data entry

introducir *vt (datos)* to enter

inválido, -a *adj (nombre de archivo)* invalid

invitado, -a *nm,f* guest

IP *nm Internet (abrev de* **Internet protocol)** IP

IRC *nm Internet (abrev de* **Internet Relay Chat)** IRC

ítem *nm (en menú)* item

itinerancia *nf Tel (de teléfono móvil)* roaming

Java® *nm Internet* Java®

JavaScript® *nm Internet* Java-Script®

jefe(a) de correo *nm,f Internet* postmaster

jerárquico, -a *adj* hierarchical

joystick *nm* joystick

JPEG *nm (abrev de* **Joint Photographic Experts Group***)* JPEG

juego *nm* (a) *(programa)* game (b) *(de caracteres)* set

◇ *juego de caracteres* character set

◇ *juego de Esp ordenador o Am computadora* computer game

justificación *nf (de texto)* justification

◇ *justificación a la derecha* right justification

◇ *justificación horizontal* horizontal justification

◇ *justificación a la izquierda* left justification

◇ *justificación vertical* vertical justification

justificado, -a *adj (texto)* justified; **justificado a la derecha/izquierda** right/left justified; **justificado horizontalmente/verticalmente** horizontally/vertically justified

justificar *vt (texto)* to justify

K *nm* (*abrev de* **kilobyte**) K; **¿cuántos K quedan?** how many K are left?

KB *nm* (*abrev de* **kilobyte**) KB

Kb *nm* (*abrev de* **kilobit**) Kb

Kbps (*abrev de* **kilobits por segundo**) kbps

kilobit *nm* kilobit

kilobyte *nm* kilobyte

kit *nm* kit

◇ **kit de actualización** upgrade kit

◇ *Internet* **kit de conexión** connection kit

LAN *nf* (*abrev de* **local area network**) LAN

lápiz óptico *nm* light pen

laptop *nm* laptop (computer)

láser *nm* laser

latencia *nf* latency

LCD (*abrev de* **liquid crystal display**) LCD

lector *nm* reader
- ◇ *lector de CD-ROM* CD-ROM reader
- ◇ *Internet lector de correo* mail reader
- ◇ *lector de disco compacto* compact disc reader
- ◇ *lector de documentos* document reader
- ◇ *Internet lector fuera de línea* off-line *o* offline reader
- ◇ *Internet lector de noticias* news reader
- ◇ *Internet lector off-line* off-line *o* offline reader
- ◇ *lector óptico de caracteres* optical character reader
- ◇ *lector de tarjetas magnéticas* magnetic card reader

lectura *nf* **ese archivo es de sólo lectura** that file is read-only; **hacer que un archivo sea de sólo lectura** to make a file read-only

LED *nm* (*abrev de* **light-emitting diode**) LED

leer *vt* to write

lenguaje *nm* language
- ◇ *lenguaje de alto nivel* high-level language
- ◇ *Am lenguaje assembler* assembly language
- ◇ *lenguaje de autor* authoring language
- ◇ *lenguaje de bajo nivel* low-level language
- ◇ *lenguaje comando o de comandos* command language
- ◇ *lenguaje ensamblador* assembly language
- ◇ *lenguaje extensible de marcado* extensible markup language
- ◇ *lenguaje macro* macro language
- ◇ *lenguaje máquina* machine language
- ◇ *lenguaje de programación* program *o* programming language
- ◇ *lenguaje de usuario* user language

letra *nf* letter; *Autoedición* type; **en letra grande/pequeña** in large/small type
- ◇ *letra bastardilla* italic type, italics

◇ *letra capitular* drop cap
◇ *letra cursiva* italic type, italics
◇ *letra gótica* Gothic
◇ *letra itálica* italic type, italics
◇ *letra mayúscula* capital letter, upper-case letter; **en letra(s) mayúscula(s)** in capitals *o* capital letters, in upper case
◇ *letra minúscula* small letter, lower-case letter; **en letra(s) minúscula(s)** in small letters, in lower case
◇ *letra negrita* bold (face)
◇ *letra redonda o redondilla* roman type
◇ *letra versalita* small capital

leyenda urbana *nf Internet* urban legend

liberalizar *vt Tel* to unlock

librería *nf (de programas)* library
◇ *librería de programas* program library

libro *nm*
◇ *libro electrónico* e-book, electronic book
◇ *libro de visitas (de página web)* guestbook

licencia *nf (para software) Br* licence, *US* license
◇ *licencia para un único usuario* single-user *Br* licence *o US* license

línea *nf* **(a)** *(telefónica)* line; **no hay línea** the line is dead, the lines are down **(b)** *(de texto)* line **(c)** *Internet* **en línea** *(conectado)* on-line, online; **comprar/hacer pedidos en línea** to buy/order on-line; **trabajar en línea** to work on-line; **fuera de línea** off-line, offline
◇ *Tel* *línea abierta* open line
◇ *línea ADSL* ADSL line
◇ *Tel* *línea alquilada* leased line
◇ *Tel* *línea arrendada* leased line
◇ *línea de asistencia técnica* support line
◇ *Autoedición* *línea de base* baseline
◇ *línea de comando* command line
◇ *Tel* *línea conmutada:* **acceso por línea conmutada** dial-up access; **cuenta por línea conmutada** dial-up account
◇ *Tel* *línea dedicada* dedicated line
◇ *línea digital por suscripción* digital subscriber line
◇ *Tel* *línea directa* direct line
◇ *línea de estado* status line
◇ *Tel* *línea exterior* outside line
◇ *línea con la firma (en correo electrónico)* signature line
◇ *Tel* *línea privada* private line
◇ *líneas por pulgada* lines per inch
◇ *línea RDSI* ISDN line
◇ *línea de suscripción asimétrica digital* asymmetrical digital subscriber line
◇ *línea de teléfono* telephone line
◇ *Tel* *línea terrestre* land line

Linux *nm* Linux

lista *nf* list
◇ *lista de control de accesos* access control list
◇ *Internet* *lista de correo* mailing list

⋄ *Internet* **lista de discusión** discussion list

⋄ *Internet* **lista de distribución** distribution list

⋄ *Internet* **lista de marcadores** bookmark list, favorites list

⋄ *Internet* **lista moderada** moderated list

⋄ *Autoedición* **lista con topos** o **viñetas** bulleted list

listar *vt* to list

listero, -a *nm,f Fam Internet* list member

listín *nm (telefónico)* telephone directory o book, phone book

llamada *nf, Am* **llamado** *nm* call; **contestar una llamada** to take a call; **hacer una llamada** to make a call; **recibir una llamada** to receive a call; **te llamaron** there was a call for you; **no me pase ninguna llamada** hold all my calls; **tienes dos llamadas en el contestador** you have two messages on your answering machine

⋄ **llamada a cobro revertido** *Br* reverse-charge call, *US* collect call

⋄ **llamada en espera** call waiting

⋄ **llamada internacional** international call

⋄ **llamada interurbana** long-distance call

⋄ **llamada de larga distancia** long-distance call

⋄ **llamada nacional** national call

⋄ **llamada telefónica** telephone call

⋄ **llamada urbana** local call

llamar *vt* to call; **llamar a alguien** to call sb; **¿quién lo/la llama, por favor?** who's calling, please?; **te ha llamado Luis** Luis phoned (for you), there was a call from Luis for you; **llamar a cobro revertido** *Br* to reverse the charges, *US* to call collect

llamarada *nf Internet* flame

llave *nf* key

⋄ *Internet* **llave de autenticación** authentication key

⋄ *Internet* **llave de cifrado** encryption key

⋄ *Internet* **llave criptográfica** cryptographic key

⋄ *Internet* **llave de encriptación** encryption key

⋄ **llave de hardware** *(protección)* dongle

local *adj* local

localización *nf* localization

localizador *nm Méx (buscapersonas)* pager, beeper

lógica *nf* logic

⋄ *lógica* **booleana** Boolean logic

⋄ *lógica* **borrosa** fuzzy logic

⋄ *lógica* **difusa** fuzzy logic

lógico, -a *adj* logical, logic

Mac *nm* Mac; **disponible para el Mac** available for the Mac

macro *nf* macro

macroinstrucción *nf* macro(instruction)

magnético, -a *adj* magnetic

magneto-óptico, -a *adj* magneto-optical

mail *(pl mails) nm* e-mail (message); **enviar un mail a alguien** to send sb an e-mail, to mail sb; **ponerse en contacto con alguien por mail** to contact sb by e-mail

manejador *nm Autoedición* handle

manipulación de imágenes *nf* image manipulation

mano *nm* **de manos libres** *(teléfono, marcado)* hands-free; **teléfono con (opción de) manos libres** phone with a hands-free facility

mantenimiento *nm* maintenance

manual *nm* manual

◊ **manual de instrucciones** instruction manual

◊ **manual del usuario** user manual

mapa *nm* map

◊ *mapa de bits* bitmap; **una imagen en mapa de bits** a bitmap *o* bit-mapped *o* bit-mapped image

◊ *mapa de caracteres* character *o* keyboard map

◊ *Internet* **mapa interactivo** (clickable) image map

◊ *Internet* **mapa del sitio** site map

maquetación *nf* page layout

maquetador, -ora *nm,f* layout editor

maquetar *vt* to do the layout for

marca *nf* mark

◊ *Autoedición* **marca de corte** crop mark

◊ *marca de párrafo* paragraph mark

◊ *Autoedición* **marca de recorte** crop mark

marcado *nm*, **marcación** *nf Br* dialling, *US* dialing

◊ *Tel* **marcado abreviado** shortcode *Br* dialling *o US* dialing

◊ *Tel* **marcado automático** automatic *Br* dialling *o US* dialing

◊ *Tel* **marcado rápido** speed dial

◊ *Tel* **marcado por voz** voice *Br*

dialling o *US* dialing

marcador *nm Internet (de página web)* bookmark, favorite

marcar *vt (número de teléfono)* to dial; **marcar un número** to dial a number; **el número marcado no existe** *(mensaje)* the number you have *Br* dialled o *US* dialed has not been recognized; **volver a marcar un número** to redial a number

marco *nm Internet (en página web)* frame

◊ *Autoedición* **marco rectangular** marquee

margen *nm* margin; **fijar los márgenes** to set the margins

◊ *Autoedición* **margen interior** gutter

márketing, marketing *nm*

◊ *Internet* **márketing boca a boca** viral marketing

◊ *Internet* **márketing electrónico** electronic marketing, e-marketing

◊ *Internet* **márketing viral** viral marketing

máscara *nf* (**a**) *Autoedición* mask

(**b**) *(de programa)* skin

material fungible *nm (cartuchos, disquetes)* consumables

matricial *adj (impresora)* dot-matrix

matriz *nf* matrix; *(de datos)* array

◊ *matriz activa (de monitor)* active matrix

maximizar *vt* to maximize

mayúsculas *nfpl* (**a**) *(letras)* upper case; **en mayúsculas** upper-case; **esta URL no distingue entre mayúsculas y minúsculas** this URL is case-insensitive; **esta dirección de correo distingue entre mayúsculas y minúsculas** this e-mail address is case-sensitive

(**b**) *(tecla)* shift; **para el asterisco hay que presionar mayúsculas y 8** an asterisk is shift 8;

◊ *mayúsculas fijas* caps lock

MB *nm (abrev de* **megabyte***)* MB

Mb *nm (abrev de* **megabit***)* Mb

Mbps *(abrev de* **megabytes por segundo***)* Mbps

Mbps *(abrev de* **megabits per second***)* Mbps

mega *nm Fam* meg

megabit *nm* megabit

megabyte *nm* megabyte; **128 megabytes de memoria** 128-megabyte memory

megaflop *nm* megaflop

megahercio *nm* megahertz; **500 megahercios** 500 megahertz

megapíxel *nm* megapixel

mejora *nf (de imagen, calidad)* enhancement

mejorado, -a *adj (imagen, calidad)* enhanced

mejorar *vt (imagen, calidad)* to enhance

melodía *nf (en teléfono móvil)* ringtone

memoria *nf* memory; **un programa que requiere mucha**

memoria a memory-intensive program; **un programa residente en memoria** a memory-resident program

◊ *memoria de acceso aleatorio* random access memory

◊ *memoria alta* high memory

◊ *memoria buffer* buffer memory

◊ *memoria de burbuja* bubble memory

◊ *memoria convencional* conventional memory

◊ *memoria de disco* disk memory

◊ *memoria disponible* available memory

◊ *memoria estándar* standard memory

◊ *memoria expandida* expanded memory

◊ *memoria extendida* extended memory

◊ *memoria flash* flash memory

◊ *memoria principal* main memory

◊ *memoria RAM* RAM

◊ *memoria ROM* ROM

◊ *memoria SDRAM* SDRAM

◊ *memoria de sólo lectura* read-only memory

◊ *memoria de Esp vídeo o Am video* video memory

◊ *memoria virtual* virtual memory

mensaje *nm* message

◊ *mensaje de alerta* alert message

◊ *mensaje de bienvenida* welcome message

◊ *mensaje de error* error message

◊ *mensaje instantáneo* instant message

◊ *Internet mensaje rebotado* bounce(d) message

◊ *Tel mensaje SMS* SMS message

◊ *mensaje telefónico* telephone message

◊ *Tel mensaje de texto* text message

mensajería *nf Tel* messaging

◊ *mensajería instantánea* instant messaging

menú *nm* menú; **un programa a base de menús** a menu-driven program

◊ *menú Apple (en Macintosh)* Apple menu

◊ *menú de ayuda* help menu

◊ *menú en cascada* cascading menu

◊ *menú despegable* drop-down menu, pop-up menu, pull-down menu

◊ *menú flotante* tear-off menu

◊ *menú de impresión* print menu

◊ *menú de inicio (en Windows)* start menu

◊ *menú jerárquico* hierarchical menu

MHz *(abrev de* **megahercio***)* MHz

microchip *nm* microchip

microcomputadora *nf*, **microcomputador** *nm Am* microcomputer, micro

microinformática *nf* microcomputing

micronavegador *nm Tel* microbrowser

microordenador *nm Esp* microcomputer, micro

micropago *nm Internet* micropayment

microprocesador *nm* microprocessor

microprogramación *nf* microprogramming

MIDI (*abrev de* **musical instrument digital interface**) MIDI

milisegundo *nm* millisecond

millón de instrucciones por segundo *nm* million instructions per second

MIME *nm Internet* (*abrev de* **Multipurpose Internet Mail Extensions**) MIME

minería de datos *nf* data mining

miniatura *nf* thumbnail

minicomputadora *nf,* **minicomputador** *nm Am* minicomputer

MiniDisc® *nm* MiniDisc®

minimizar *vt* (*ventana*) to minimize

miniordenador *nm Esp* minicomputer

minitorre *nf* mini tower

minúsculas *nfpl* lower case; **en minúsculas** lower-case

mips (*abrev de* **millón de instrucciones por segundo**) mips

MMM *nf Internet* (*abrev de* **Multimalla Mundial**) WWW

MMS *nm Tel* (*abrev de* **multimedia messaging service**) MMS

MMX *nm* (*abrev de* **multimedia**

extensions) MMX

mochila *nf* (*protección*) dongle

modelado *nm Br* modelling, *US* modeling
- ◇ **modelado de alambres** wireframe *Br* modelling *o US* modeling
- ◇ **modelado de sólidos** solids *Br* modelling *o US* modeling
- ◇ **modelado de superficies** surface *Br* modelling *o US* modeling

modelar *vt* to model

modelo cliente/servidor *nm* client-server model

módem *nm* modem; **enviar algo a alguien por módem** to send sth to sb by modem
- ◇ **módem cable** cable modem
- ◇ **módem externo** external modem
- ◇ **módem fax** fax modem
- ◇ **módem interno** internal modem
- ◇ **módem RDSI** ISDN modem

moderador, -ora *nm,f Internet* moderator

modo *nm* mode; *Tel* **de modo dual** dual-mode
- ◇ **modo de apagado automático** power save mode
- ◇ **modo apaisado** landscape mode
- ◇ **modo asíncrono de transferencia** asynchronous transfer mode
- ◇ **modo borrador** draft mode
- ◇ **modo carácter** character mode
- ◇ **modo sin conexión** off-line *o* offline mode

◇ *modo continuo* continuous mode

◇ *modo diálogo* Br dialogue o US dialog mode

◇ *modo de edición* edit mode

◇ *modo gráfico* graphics mode

◇ *modo de inserción* insert mode

◇ *modo en línea* on-line o on-line mode

◇ *modo multisesión* (en grabadora de CD) multi-session mode

◇ *modo off-line* off-line o off-line mode

◇ *modo on-line* on-line o on-line mode

◇ *modo película* movie mode

◇ *modo preparada* (de impresora) ready mode

◇ *modo de recepción (de llamadas)* (de módem) answering mode

◇ *modo de reposo* (de portátil, impresora) standby mode

◇ *modo de sobreescritura* overwrite mode

◇ *modo de suspensión* (de portátil, impresora) standby mode

◇ *modo (de) texto* text mode

moiré nm Autoedición moire

monedero electrónico nm Internet electronic purse

monitor nm monitor, display unit

◇ Am *monitor color* Br colour o US color display

◇ *monitor en color* Br colour o US color display

◇ *monitor de cristal líquido* LCD monitor

◇ *monitor digital* digital display

◇ *monitor de escala de grises* Br greyscale o US grayscale monitor

◇ *monitor de pantalla completa* full page display

◇ *monitor de pantalla plana* flat monitor, flat panel display

◇ *monitor con tubo de rayos catódicos* cathode ray tube monitor

monocromo, -a adj monochrome

monoespaciado, -a Autoedición **1** adj monospaced
2 nm monospacing, proportional spacing

mostrar vt (archivos, registros) to show

motor de búsqueda nm Internet search engine

mouse nm Am mouse

◇ *mouse de bola* trackball

◇ *mouse inalámbrico* cordless o wireless mouse

◇ *mouse de infrarrojos* infrared mouse

◇ *mouse óptico* optical mouse

◇ *mouse con rueda de desplazamiento* wheelmouse

◇ *mouse táctil* trackpad, touch pad

◇ *mouse de tres botones* three-button mouse

móvil 1 adj teléfono móvil Br mobile phone, US cellphone
2 nm Br mobile, US cell(phone)

movimiento nm movement

◇ *movimiento del cursor* cursor movement

MP3 nm (abrev de **MPEG1 Audio**

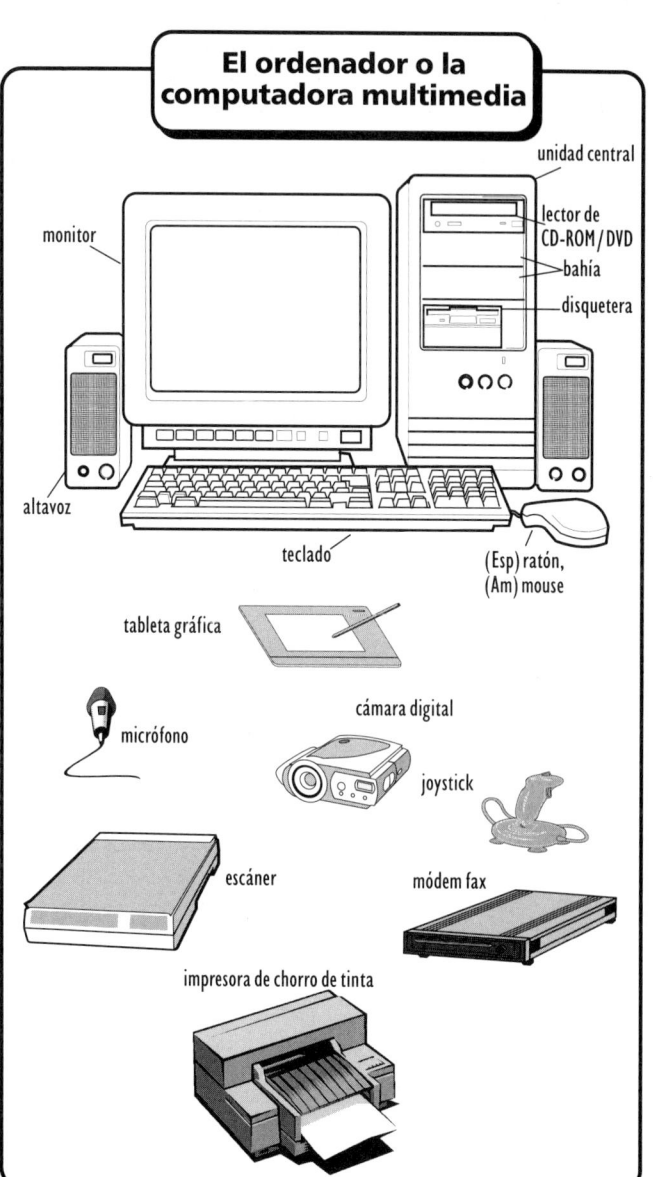

El ordenador o la computadora multimedia

unidad central

lector de CD-ROM / DVD

bahía

disquetera

monitor

altavoz

teclado

(Esp) ratón, (Am) mouse

tableta gráfica

micrófono

cámara digital

joystick

escáner

módem fax

impresora de chorro de tinta

Layer 3) MP3; **archivo MP3**
MP3 file

MPEG *nm* (*abrev de* **Moving Pictures Expert Group**) MPEG; **archivo MPEG** MPEG file

ms (*abrev de* milisegundos) ms

MS-DOS® *nm* (*abrev de* **Microsoft Disk Operating System**) MS-DOS®

muerto, -a *adj RP* **da muerto** (*teléfono*) the line is dead

multiconferencia *nf Tel* conference call

multidifusión *nf Internet* multicast

multifrecuencia *nf* multiscan, multiscanning

multimalla *nf*
◊ *Internet* **la multimalla mundial** the World Wide Web

multimedia 1 *nf* multimedia **2** *adj* multimedia

multiplataforma *adj inv* cross-platform

múltiplex *adj inv* multiplex

multiprocesador *nm* multiprocessor

multiproceso, multiprocesado *nm* multithreading
◊ *Autoedición* **multiproceso de imágenes** multi-image processing

multiprogramación *nf* multiprogramming

multipuesto *adj inv* multistation

multitarea *nf* multitasking
◊ **multitarea preferencial** preemptive multitasking

multitratamiento *nm* multiprocessing

multiusuario *adj inv* multiuser

nanosegundo *nm* nanosecond

nanotecnología *nf* nanotechnology

navegación *nf Internet* browsing; **navegación rápida/segura** fast/secure browsing; **una página de fácil navegación** a page that is easy to navigate

navegador *nm Internet* browser

navegar *vi* navegar por Internet to browse *o* surf the Net; **lleva toda la mañana navegando** he's been surfing the Net all morning, he's been on the Internet all morning

negrita 1 *adj (letra)* bold
2 *nf* bold; **en negrita** in bold (type)

netiqueta *nf Internet* netiquette

news *nfpl Internet* newsgroups

nivel *nm*
◊ **nivel de acceso** access level
◊ **niveles de gris** *Br* grey *o US* gray levels, levels of *Br* grey *o US* gray

nodo *nm* node

nombre *nm* name; **cambiar de nombre un archivo** to rename a file
◊ *nombre de archivo* file name
◊ *nombre de archivo incorrecto* bad file name
◊ *Internet nombre de dominio* domain name
◊ *Internet nombre de dominio totalmente cualificado* fully qualified domain name
◊ *nombre de fichero* file name
◊ *nombre de usuario* user name

nota *nf*
◊ *nota de fin de documento* endnote
◊ *nota a pie de página* footnote

noticias *nfpl Internet* news

novato, -a *nm,f Fam Internet* newbie

numeral *nm Am (en teléfono, canal IRC) Br* hash, *US* pound sign

numérico, -a *adj* numeric

número *nm* number
◊ *número de acceso (a Internet)* access number
◊ *Tel número de extensión* extension number
◊ *número de fax* fax number
◊ *número de Internet* Internet number

◇ *Internet* **número IP** IP number

◇ **número de registro** registration number

◇ **número con tarifa local** local rate number

◇ **número de teléfono** telephone number

◇ **número de teléfono gratuito** *Br* Freefone® number, *US* toll-free number, *US* 1-800 number

objeto *nm* object; **orientado a objeto** object-oriented

obturador *nm Autoedición* shutter

OCR *nm* (a) (*abrev de* **optical character reader**) OCR (b) (*abrev de* **optical character recognition**) OCR

octeto *nm* byte

ocultar *vt (archivos, reglas)* to hide

oculto, -a *adj (archivo)* hidden

ocupación ilegal de dominios *nf Internet* cybersquatting

ocupado, -a *adj* (a) *(teléfono) Br* engaged, *US* busy; **el teléfono da o está ocupado** the number is *Br* engaged *o US* busy (b) *(impresora)* busy

oficina electrónica *nf* electronic office, paperless office

ofimática *nf* office automation, office IT

ofimático, -a *adj* **material ofimático** office computer equipment; **gestión ofimática integrada** integrated office automation

opción del menú *nf* menu option

operación *nf* operation

operador, -ora **1** *nm,f Tel (persona)* telephonist; (switchboard) operator **2** *nm* operator

◇ *operador booleano* Boolean operator

◇ *operador lógico* logic operator

◇ *operador del sistema* systems operator

óptico, -a *adj* optical

optimización *nf* optimization

optimizador *nm* optimizer

optimizar *vt* to optimize

orden *nm* order

◇ *orden ascendente* ascending order

◇ *orden descendente* descending order

ordenación *nf* sort; **el programa va a realizar una ordenación alfabética** the program will do an alphasort

◇ *ordenación alfabética* alphasort

◇ *ordenación a la inversa* reverse sort

ordenador *nm Esp* computer; **meter algo en el ordenador**

to put sth on computer; **pasar algo al ordenador** to type sth into a computer; **tener algo en el ordenador** to have sth on computer

◇ *ordenador de bolsillo* handheld computer

◇ *ordenador central* mainframe (computer)

◇ *ordenador compatible* compatible computer

◇ *ordenador doméstico* home computer

◇ *ordenador frontal* front-end computer

◇ *ordenador de gama alta* high-end computer

◇ *ordenador de gama baja* entry-level computer

◇ *ordenador de gama media* mid-range computer

◇ *ordenador multimedia* multimedia computer

◇ *ordenador personal* personal computer, PC

◇ *ordenador portátil* laptop (computer), notebook (computer)

◇ *ordenador de sobremesa* desktop computer

ordenar *nf* to sort; **ordenar algo alfabéticamente** to sort sth alphabetically, to do an alphasort on sth

ordenata *nm Esp Fam* computer

organigrama *nm* flowchart

organizador *nm* organizer

◇ *organizador personal* personal organizer, PDA, handheld (computer)

orientación *nf* orientation

◇ *orientación horizontal* horizontal orientation

◇ *orientación vertical* vertical orientation

orientado, -a *adj* **orientado a objeto** object-oriented; **orientado a usuario** user-oriented

página *nf* page
◇ *las páginas amarillas* the Yellow Pages
◇ *Internet* **página de búsqueda** search engine
◇ *Autoedición* **páginas enfrentadas** facing pages
◇ *Internet* **página inicial** *(de sitio web)* home page
◇ *Internet* **página de inicio** home page
◇ *Internet* **página personal** (personal) home page
◇ **página de portada** *(de fax)* cover page *o* sheet
◇ *Internet* **página web** web page

paginación *nf* pagination
◇ **paginación automática** automatic pagination

paginar *vt* to paginate

palabra *nf* word
◇ **palabra clave** keyword

paleta *nf* palette
◇ **paleta flotante** floating palette
◇ **paleta de herramientas** tool palette

palm, palmtop *nm o nf* palmtop

pancarta publicitaria *nf* *Internet* banner (ad)

panel *nm* panel
◇ **panel de control** control panel
◇ **panel frontal** front panel

pantalla *nf* screen; **trabajar en pantalla** to work on screen; **visualizar la siguiente pantalla** to bring up the next screen
◇ **pantalla de arranque** start-up screen
◇ **pantalla de ayuda** help screen
◇ **pantalla completa** full screen; **a pantalla completa** full-screen
◇ **pantalla de cristal líquido** liquid crystal display, LCD screen
◇ **pantalla de matriz activa** active matrix screen
◇ **pantalla plana** flat screen
◇ **pantalla táctil** touch screen
◇ **pantalla TFT** TFT screen

pantallazo *nm* *Fam* screen capture *o* dump

papel *nm* paper
◇ **papel continuo** continuous *o* stationery paper
◇ **papel couché** *o* **cuché** coated paper
◇ **papel fotográfico** photographic paper
◇ **papel de impresora** printer paper

◇ *papel perforado* perforated paper

◇ *papel tapiz (en Windows)* wallpaper

◇ *papel térmico* thermal paper

papelera *nf (en Windows)* recycle bin; *(en Macintosh) Br* wastebasket, *US* trash can

◇ *papelera de reciclaje* recycle bin

paquete *nm* (a) *(software)* package
(b) *Tel (de datos)* packet

◇ *paquete integrado* integrated package

◇ *paquete de software* software package

paralelo, -a *adj* parallel

parámetro *nm* parameter

parche *nm (corrección)* patch

paréntesis *nm inv* bracket

◇ *paréntesis angulares* angle brackets

paridad *nf* parity

parpadear *vi (pantalla)* to flicker

parpadeo *nm (de pantalla)* flicker

párrafo *nm* paragraph

partición *nf (en disco)* partition; **crear particiones en un disco** to partition a disk

◇ *partición de palabras* hyphenation

◇ *partición silábica* hyphenation

par trenzado *nm Tel* twisted pair

pasarela *nf Internet* gateway

◇ *pasarela de correo* mail gateway

◇ *pasarela de pago* payment gateway

PASCAL *nm* PASCAL

patch *nm Am (corrección)* patch

patilla *nf (de enchufe)* pin

pausa *nf* pause

PC *nm (abrev de* **personal computer***)* PC; **disponible para (el) PC** available for the PC

PCI *nm (abrev de* **peripheral component interface***)* PCI

PCMCIA *(abrev de* **PC memory card international association***)* PCMCIA

PDA *nm (abrev de* **personal digital assistant***)* PDA

PDF *nm (abrev de* **portable document format***)* PDF

pegar *vt (texto)* to paste (**en** into/onto)

Pentium® *nm* Pentium®

pérdida *nf* **con pérdidas** *(compresión)* lossy; **sin pérdidas** *(compresión)* lossless

◇ *pérdida de datos* data loss

◇ *Internet* **pérdida de paquetes** packet loss

periférico *nm* peripheral

◇ *periférico de entrada* input device

◇ *periférico externo* external device

◇ *periférico de salida* output device

◇ *periférico en serie* serial device

periódico electrónico *nm* electronic journal

Perl nm (abrev de **practical extraction and report language**) Perl

permanente adj (conexión a Internet) permanent, always-on

personalizable adj (menú, programa) customizable

personalizado, -a adj (programa, computadora) customized

personalizar vt (programa, computadora) to customize

photo CD nm photo CD

pie de página nm footer

pin nm pin

pinchar 1 vt to click on **2** vi to click

ping nm Internet ping

pirata nmf **pirata (informático)** cracker, hacker

piratear vt **piratear un programa** (desproteger) to hack o crack into a program; (hacer copia ilegal) to pirate a program

piratería nf, **pirateo** nm **piratería informática** (copias ilegales) software piracy; (acceso no autorizado) cracking, hacking

pista nf (de disco) track

pitch nm pitch

píxel nm pixel

pixelación nf (de imagen) pixellation

pixelado, -a adj (imagen) pixellated

placa nf board

◊ **placa aceleradora** accelerator board

◊ **placa base** circuit board

◊ **placa de circuitos** circuit board

◊ **placa lógica** logic board

◊ **placa madre** motherboard

◊ **placa de** Esp **vídeo** o Am **vídeo** video board

plano nm **primer plano** foreground; **segundo plano** background; **el programa se ejecuta en segundo plano** the program works in the background

plantilla nf template

plataforma nf (de hardware) platform; **un programa que funciona en cualquier plataforma** a platform-independent program

◊ **plataforma de software** software platform

pleca nf pipe

plóter, plotter nm plotter

◊ **plóter incremental** incremental plotter

plug-in nm plug-in

POP nm Internet (abrev de **post office protocol**) POP

portabilidad nf (de programa) portability

portada nf Internet (de sitio web) home page

portadora nf Tel carrier; **no hay portadora** (mensaje) no carrier

portal nm Internet portal

portapapeles nm inv clipboard

portátil 1 *nm (computadora)* laptop, portable
   2 *adj (computadora)* portable

posición del cursor *nf* cursor position

posterización *nf Autoedición* posterization

posterizar *vt Autoedición* to posterize

PostScript® *nm* PostScript®

ppm *(abrev de* **páginas por minuto)** ppm

PPP *nm Internet (abrev de* **point-to-point protocol)** PPP

ppp *(abrev de* **puntos por pulgada)** dpi

predeterminado, -a *adj (valor, tipo de letra)* by default

preferencias *nfpl* preferences

prefijo *nm Tel Br* dialling *o* dial code, *US* area code

preformateado, -a *adj (disco)* preformatted

preimpresión *nf Autoedición* prepress

preinstalado, -a *adj (programa)* preinstalled

preinstalar *vt (programa)* to preinstall

prender *Am* 1 *vt (computadora, impresora)* to switch on
   2 **prenderse** *vpr (computadora, impresora)* to switch on; **se prende solo** it switches itself on

preprogramado, -a *adj* preprogrammed

preprogramar *vt* to preprogram

presentación preliminar *nf* preview

previsualización *nf* (print) preview

prioridad *nf* priority
◇ *Autoedición* **prioridad a la abertura** aperture priority
◇ *Autoedición* **prioridad a la obturación** shutter priority

privacidad *nf* privacy

privilegio *nm (para entrar a red, base de datos)* privilege
◇ **privilegios de acceso** access privileges

problema *nm* problem; **problema de hardware/software** hardware/software problem

procesado *nm* processing

procesador *nm* processor
◇ **procesador de coma flotante** floating point processor
◇ **procesador de datos** data processor
◇ **procesador digital de señales** digital signal processor
◇ **procesador RISC** RISC processor
◇ **procesador de textos** text processor

procesar *vt (datos)* to process

proceso *nm* processing
◇ **proceso automático de datos** automatic data processing
◇ **proceso de datos** data processing
◇ **proceso digital de señales** digital signal processing
◇ **proceso por lotes** batch processing

◇ *proceso en paralelo* parallel processing

◇ *proceso secuencial* sequential processing

◇ *proceso de textos* word processing

profundidad *nf* depth

◇ *profundidad de bits* (de escáner, cámara digital) bit depth

◇ *Autoedición* *profundidad de campo* depth of field

◇ *Autoedición* *profundidad de color* Br colour o US color depth

programa *nm* program

◇ *programa activo* active program

◇ *programa antivirus* antivirus program

◇ *programa de aplicación* application program

◇ *programa de autoedición* desktop publishing program

◇ *programa de configuración* setup program

◇ *programa de contabilidad* accounting program

◇ *programa de conversión* conversion program

◇ *Internet* *programa de correo electrónico* e-mail program

◇ *Internet* *programa para la creación de páginas web* web authoring program

◇ *programa de diagnóstico* diagnostic program

◇ *programa de dibujo* draw program, paint program

◇ *programa de edición de imágenes* image editing program

◇ *programa informático* computer program

◇ *programa de instalación* install program

◇ *programa en lenguaje ensamblador* o *Am* *assembler* assembly language program

◇ *programa de maquetación* desktop publishing program

◇ *programa de presentaciones* presentation graphics program

◇ *programa virus* virus program

programación *nf* (computer) programming

◇ *programación lineal* linear programming

programador, -ora *nm,f* (computer) programmer

programar 1 *vt* to program; **programar** *Esp* **un ordenador** o *Am* **una computadora para que haga algo** to program a computer to do sth

2 *vi* to program; **programar en lenguaje ensamblador** to program in assembly language

propiedades *nfpl* (de archivo, unidad) properties

protección *nf* protection

◇ *protección de archivos* file protection

◇ *protección por clave* password protection

◇ *protección por contraseña* password protection

◇ *protección contra copia* copy protection

◇ *protección de datos* data protection

◇ *protección contra escritura* write protection

◇ *protección de ficheros* file protection

protector *nm*

◇ *protector de pantalla* screen-saver

◇ *protector de sobrecarga* surge protector

proteger *vt* to protect; **proteger contra copia** to copy-protect; **proteger contra escritura** to write-protect

protegido, -a *adj* protected; **protegido contra copia** copy-protected; **protegido contra escritura** write-protected; **protegido por contraseña** password-protected

protocolo *nm* protocol

◇ *protocolo de comunicaciones* communication protocol

◇ *Internet* *protocolo de configuración de anfitriones dinámicos* dynamic host configuration protocol

◇ *protocolo de Internet* Internet protocol

◇ *Internet* *protocolo punto a punto* point-to-point protocol

◇ *Internet* *protocolo de transferencia de ficheros* file transfer protocol

proveedor *nm Internet* provider

◇ *proveedor de acceso* access provider

◇ *proveedor de acceso a Internet* Internet access provider, ISP

◇ *proveedor de contenidos* content provider

◇ *proveedor de presencia* presence provider

◇ *proveedor de servicios* service provider

proxy *nm Internet* proxy

proyección de diapositivas *nf* slideshow

prueba *nf Autoedición* proof; **corregir pruebas, hacer corrección de pruebas** to proofread

◇ *prueba de paridad* parity check

pseudónimo *nm Internet* nickname, *Br* nick, *US* screen name

PSI *nm Internet* (*abrev de* **Proveedor de Servicio Internet**) ISP

publicar *vt* (*página web*) to publish

puente *nm* (*en red*) bridge; (*jumper*) jumper

puerto *nm* port

◇ *puerto para auriculares* headphones socket

◇ *puerto de comunicaciones* communications port

◇ *puerto FireWire*® FireWire® port

◇ *puerto de gráficos acelerado* accelerated graphics port

◇ *puerto de la impresora* printer port

◇ *puerto de infrarrojos* IrDA port

◇ *puerto de juegos* game port

◇ *puerto del módem* modem port

◇ *Am* *puerto del mouse* mouse port

◇ *puerto paralelo* parallel port

◇ *Esp* *puerto del ratón* mouse port

◇ ***puerto (de) serie*** serial port

◇ ***puerto USB*** USB port

pulsación *nf* keystroke

pulsar *vt (tecla)* to press

pulso *nm Tel* pulse

puntero *nm* pointer

punto *nm* (**a**) *(signo) (al final de frase) Br* full stop, *US* period; *(sobre i, j, en dirección de correo electrónico)* dot; **punto y coma** *(signo de puntuación)* semicolon; **dos puntos** *(signo de puntuación)* colon; **"juan, arroba mundonet, punto, es"** "juan, at mundonet, dot, es"

(**b**) *Autoedición (tamaño de letra)* point; **tamaño en puntos** point size

◇ *Internet* **punto de acceso** point of presence

◇ *Internet* **punto de conexión** point of presence

◇ ***punto de inserción*** insertion point

◇ ***puntos por pulgada*** dots per inch

◇ ***punto de referencia*** benchmark

◇ ***punto de venta electrónico*** electronic point of sale

punto com *nf Internet* dot com (company)

radiomensaje *nm RP (buscapersonas)* pager, beeper

RAM *nf (abrev de random access memory)* RAM

◇ *RAM caché* cache RAM

◇ *RAM DDR* DDR RAM

◇ *RAM dinámica* dynamic RAM

ramificación *nf (de red)* branch

ranura *nf* slot

◇ *ranura de expansión* expansion slot

◇ *ranura para tarjeta* card slot

rasterizado *nm* rasterizing

rasterizar *vt* to rasterize

rastreador *nm Internet* crawler

ratón *nm Esp* mouse

◇ *ratón de bola* trackball

◇ *ratón inalámbrico* cordless *o* wireless mouse

◇ *ratón de infrarrojos* infrared mouse

◇ *ratón óptico* optical mouse

◇ *ratón con rueda de desplazamiento* wheelmouse

◇ *ratón táctil* trackpad, touch pad

◇ *ratón de tres botones* three-button mouse

RDSI *nf (abrev de red digital de servicios integrados)* ISDN

realidad virtual *nf* virtual reality

realzar *vt (texto)* to highlight

rebotar *vi Internet (mensaje)* to bounce

recogida *nf*

◇ *recogida de datos* data collection

reconectar 1 *vt* to reconnect

2 reconectarse *vpr* to reconnect

reconfigurar *vt* to reconfigure

reconocimiento *nm* recognition

◇ *reconocimiento de caracteres* character recognition

◇ *reconocimiento del habla* speech recognition

◇ *reconocimiento óptico de caracteres* optical character recognition

◇ *reconocimiento de voz* voice recognition

recopilar *vt (documentos, datos)* to collate

recortar *vt Autoedición (gráfico)* to crop

recuperación *nf (de documentos, datos)* recovery

◇ *recuperación de datos* data recovery

◇ *recuperación de información* information retrieval

recuperar *vt (archivo, datos)* to recover

recurso *nm* resource

red *nf* (a) *(de terminales)* network; **conectar algo en red** to network sth; **sistemas en red** networked systems; **poderse conectar en red** *(terminal)* to have networking capabilities (b) **la Red** *(Internet)* the Net; **lo encontré en la Red** I found it on the Net; **la Red de redes** the Internet

◇ *red en anillo* ring network

◇ *red de área extensa* wide area network

◇ *red de área local* local area network

◇ *red de comunicaciones* communication network

◇ *Internet* **red ciudadana** freenet

◇ *Internet* **red digital de servicios integrados** integrated services digital network

◇ *red en estrella* star network

◇ *red inalámbrica* wireless network

◇ *red informática* computer network

◇ *red neural* neural network

◇ *Internet* **red troncal** backbone

redactar *vt (correo electrónico)* to write, to compose

redibujar *vt* to redraw

redimensionable *adj* resizable

redireccionador de correo *nm Internet* remailer

redireccionar *vt Internet (correo electrónico)* to readdress, to redirect

rediscado *nm Andes, RP* redial

◇ *rediscado automático* autoredial

redonda, redondilla *nf Autoedición* roman

reemplazar *vt* to replace; **reemplazar todos** *(comando)* replace all

reemplazo en caliente *nm (de periféricos)* hot swap

referencia *nf* reference

◇ *referencia circular* circular reference

◇ *Am* **referencia cruzada** cross-reference

reformatear *vt* to reformat

refrescar *vt* to refresh

refresco *nm* refresh

◇ *refresco de pantalla* screen refresh

RGB *(abrev de* **red, green and blue**) RGB

registrar *vt (programa)* to register

registro *nm (en base de datos)* record; *(de memoria)* register; *(archivo de Windows)* registry

◇ *registro de actividad* log file

◇ *registro en línea (de software)* on-line *o* online registration

◇ *registro on-line (de software)* on-line *o* online registration

Topologías de red

Red centralizada
Una unidad central controla el acceso a la red

Red en estrella
Su configuración recuerda a una estrella. En el centro está el procesador central de la red

estación de trabajo

servidor

Red descentralizada
Cada estación de trabajo puede acceder a la red independientemente y establecer sus propias conexiones con otras estaciones de trabajo

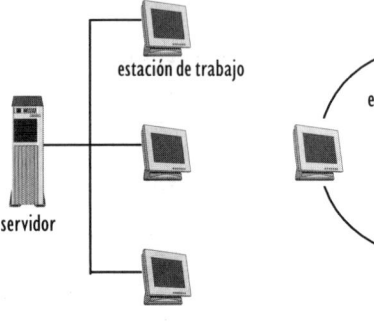

estación de trabajo

servidor

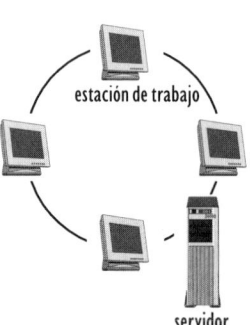

estación de trabajo

servidor

Red en bus
Los nodos, que incluyen estaciones de trabajo e impresoras compartidas, comparten un único cable, el bus.

Red en anillo
Los nodos están dispuestos alrededor de un cable en forma de bucle cerrado

regla *nf* (a) *(en procesador de textos)* ruler
(**b**) *Autoedición* ruler

regrabable *adj* rewritable

regrabadora de CD-ROM *nf* CD-ROM rewriter

regulador *nm Méx* uninterruptible power supply, UPS

reinicializar, reiniciar *vt* *(computadora)* to reboot, to restart; *(impresora)* to reset

reinicio *nm (de sistema)* restart

reinstalar *vt* to reinstall

reloj *nm* clock

◇ **reloj interno** internal clock

remarcado automático *nm Tel* autoredial

remisión *nf* cross-reference

remitir *vt (a otra parte)* to cross-refer; *(mensaje de correo)* to forward

remoto, -a *adj* remote

removible *adj (disco)* removable

remuestrear *vt Autoedición (imagen)* to resample

renderizado *nm Autoedición* rendering

renderizar *vt Autoedición* to render

renombrar *vt (archivo)* to rename

repaginar *vt* to repaginate

repetir *vt (acción)* to redo

reposamuñecas *nm inv* wrist rest

reposar *vi (portátil)* to sleep; **poner un portátil a reposar** to put a notebook to sleep

reproductor *nm* player

◇ **reproductor de CD** CD player

◇ **reproductor de discos compactos** compact disc player, CD player

◇ **reproductor de DVD** DVD player

◇ **reproductor de MP3** MP3 player

reprogramable *adj* reprogrammable

reprogramar *vt* to reprogram

residente *adj* resident

resolución *nf* resolution; **alta/baja resolución** high/low resolution; **de alta resolución** high-resolution; **de baja resolución** low-resolution

restaurar *vt* to restore

restricción de llamadas *nf Tel* call barring

resultado *nm (en búsqueda)* hit

resumen *nm Internet (de grupo de noticias, lista de correo)* digest

retocado, -a *adj* retocado por *Esp* ordenador *o Am* computadora computer-enhanced

retocar *vt (fotografía)* to retouch

retorno *nm* return

◇ **retorno automático** soft return

◇ **retorno de carro** carriage return

◇ **retorno manual** hard return

retroceso *nm* backspace

retroiluminación *nf (de pantalla)* backlight

retroiluminado, -a *adj (pantalla)* backlit

revista electrónica *nf* electronic magazine

robot *nm* robot

◇ *Internet* **robot de compras** shopbot

◇ *Internet* **robot de conocimiento** knowbot

ROM *nf (abrev de* **read only memory***)* ROM

router *nm* router

RTF *(abrev de* **rich text format***)* RTF; **archivo RTF** RTF file

rueda de desplazamiento *nf (en ratón, mouse)* scroll wheel

ruido *nm Tel* noise

◇ **ruido en la línea** line noise

rutina *nf* routine

sacar *vt (datos, información)* to output

SAI *nm (abrev de* **sistema de alimentación ininterrumpida***)* UPS

sala de charla *nf Internet* chat room

salida *nf (de datos, información)* output

saliente *adj (llamada, correo)* outgoing

salir *vi (de programa)* to exit, to quit; *(de servidor remoto)* to log off, to log out; **salir de un programa** to exit *o* quit a program

salto *nm Internet (en red)* hop
◊ *salto de línea* line break
◊ *salto de línea automático* word wrap
◊ *salto de página* page break
◊ *salto de párrafo* paragraph break

salvapantallas *nm inv* screensaver

salvar *vt Am* to save; **salvar algo en el disco** to save sth to disk; **salvar como...** save as...

sangrado *nm Autoedición* indentation

sangrar *vt Autoedición* to indent

sangría *nf Autoedición* indentation
◊ *sangría francesa* hanging indent

saturación *nf Autoedición (de imagen)* saturation
◊ *saturación del buffer* buffer underrun

script *nm* script

SCSI *nm (abrev de* **small computer systems interface***)* SCSI

SDRAM *nf (abrev de* **synchronous dynamic random access memory***)* SDRAM

sector *nm* sector
◊ *sector de arranque* boot sector
◊ *sector dañado* bad sector

secuencia *nf* sequence
◊ *secuencia de comandos* command sequence

secuencial *adj* sequential

seguridad *nf* security
◊ *seguridad de los datos* data security

seguro, -a *adj Internet (servidor, transacción)* secure

selección *nf* selection

seleccionar *vt* to select; **seleccionar una opción** to select an option

selector *nm* chooser

señal *nf Tel* signal

◇ *Tel* **señal de descolgado** off-hook signal

◇ **señal digital** digital signal

◇ **señal de DOS** DOS prompt

◇ *Tel* **señal de llamada** ringtone, ringing tone

◇ *Tel* **señal de portadora** carrier (detect) signal

separación de colores *nf Autoedición Br* colour o *US* color separation

separador *nm* separator

serie *nf* **de serie** *(cable, puerto)* serial; **en serie** *(impresora, interfaz)* serial

serretado *nm Autoedición* aliasing

servicio *nm*

◇ **servicio de asistencia (telefónica)** help desk, helpline

◇ **servicio de asistencia técnica** technical support

◇ *Tel* **servicio de atención de llamadas** o *Am* **llamados** answering service

◇ *Tel* **servicio de desvío de llamadas** o *Am* **llamados** call forwarding service

◇ *Autoedición* **servicio de filmación** service bureau

◇ **servicio en línea** on-line o online service

◇ *Tel* **servicio de llamada** o *Am* **llamado en espera** call waiting service

◇ **servicio on-line** on-line o online service

◇ **servicio in situ** on-site service

servidor *nm* server

◇ **servidor de archivos** file server

◇ *Internet* **servidor de comercio electrónico** e-commerce server

◇ *Internet* **servidor de correo** mail server

◇ **servidor doméstico** home server

◇ **servidor de ficheros** file server

◇ *Internet* **servidor FTP** FTP server

◇ *Internet* **servidor de grupos de noticias** news server

◇ *Internet* **servidor de HTTP** HTTP server

◇ *Internet* **servidor de listas** list server

◇ *Internet* **servidor de nombres** name server

◇ *Internet* **servidor proxy** proxy server

◇ **servidor de red** network server

◇ **servidor remoto** remote server

◇ *Internet* **servidor seguro** secure server

◇ **servidor de terminales** terminal server

◇ *Internet* **servidor web** web server

sesión *nf* (a) *Internet* session; **abrir una sesión** *(en servidor remoto)* to log in (b) *(al escribir un CD-R)* session

SGML *nm* *(abrev de* **Standard Generalized Markup Language***)* SGML

shareware *nm* shareware

SIG *nm* (*abrev de* **sistema de información geográfica**) GIS

siglas *nfpl* acronym

signo *nm*

◇ **signo de admiración** exclamation mark *o US* point
◇ **signo del dólar** dollar sign
◇ **signo de exclamación** exclamation mark *o US* point
◇ **signo de igual** equal(s) sign
◇ **signo de intercalación** caret
◇ **signo de interrogación** question mark
◇ **signo de la libra** pound sign
◇ **signo más** plus sign
◇ **signo menos** minus sign

símbolo *nm* symbol

◇ **símbolo del dólar** dollar sign
◇ **símbolo de la libra** pound sign

SIMM *nm* (*abrev de* **single in-line memory module**) SIMM

simulación *nf* simulation

◇ **simulación por** *Esp* **ordenador** *o* *Am* **computadora** computer simulation

simulador *nm* simulator

◇ **simulador de realidad virtual** virtual reality simulator

simular *vt* to simulate

síncrono, -a *adj* synchronous

síndrome del túnel carpiano *nm* carpal tunnel syndrome

sintaxis *nf* syntax

sintetizador de voz *nm* voice synthesizer

sistema *nm* system

◇ **sistema de alimentación ininterrumpida** uninterruptible power supply, UPS
◇ **sistema de archivos jerárquicos** hierarchical file system
◇ **sistema auxiliar** backup system
◇ **sistema de copias de seguridad** backup system
◇ **sistema de copias de seguridad en cinta** tape backup system
◇ **sistema experto** expert system
◇ **sistema de gestión de archivos** file management system
◇ **sistema de gestión de bases de datos** database management system
◇ **sistema de gestión de bases de datos relacionales** relational database management system
◇ *Internet* **sistema de gestión de contenidos** content management system
◇ **sistema de gestión de ficheros** file management system
◇ **sistema de gestión de la información** information management system
◇ **sistema informático** computer system
◇ **sistema multiusuario** multiuser system
◇ *Internet* **sistema de nombres de dominio** domain name system
◇ **sistema operativo** operating system

◇ *sistema operativo de disco* disk operating system

◇ *Internet* *sistema de pago electrónico* electronic payment system

sitio *nm Internet* site

◇ *sitio de archivos* archive site

◇ *sitio de comercio electrónico* e-commerce site

◇ *sitio espejo* mirror site

◇ *sitio fantasma* ghost site

◇ *sitio FTP* FTP site

◇ *sitio réplica* mirror site

◇ *sitio web* web site

slot *nm Am* slot

SMS *nm Tel* (*abrev de* **short message service**) SMS

SMTP *nm Internet* (*abrev de* **Simple Mail Transfer Protocol**) SMTP

sobreescribir *vt* (*archivo*) to overwrite

sobremuestreo *nm* oversampling

sociedad *nf*

◇ *sociedad de la información* information society

◇ *Sociedad Internet* Internet Society

socket *nm Internet* socket

software *nm* software; **paquete de software** software package

◇ *software de aplicación* application software

◇ *software de autoedición* desktop publishing software

◇ *software de autor* authoring software

◇ *Internet* *software de charla o de chat* chat software

◇ *software de comunicaciones* communications software

◇ *Internet* *software de control* blocking software

◇ *software de conversión* conversion software

◇ *Internet* *software de correo electrónico* e-mail software

◇ *software de diseño gráfico* illustration software

◇ *software de dominio público* public domain software

◇ *Internet* *software espía* spyware

◇ *Internet* *software de filtrado* filtering software

◇ *software de gráficos* graphics software

◇ *software integrado* integrated software

◇ *software multiusuario* multi-user *o* multiuser software

◇ *software de OCR* OCR software

◇ *software de red* network software

◇ *software de sistema* system software

◇ *software de terceras partes* third-party software

◇ *software de usuario* user software

soltar *vt* (*icono*) to drop

sombreado *nm* shade

sonido *nm* sound

◇ *sonido envolvente* surround sound

soporte *nm* (**a**) (*para teléfono*) cradle
(**b**) (*formato*) **el documento se facilita en soporte informático**

the document is available in electronic form; **una edición en soporte electrónico** an electronic edition

◇ *soporte físico* hardware

◇ *soporte lógico* software

◇ *soporte técnico* *(a usuario)* technical support

SQL *nm* (*abrev de* **structured query language**) SQL

SSL *nm Internet* (*abrev de* **secure sockets layer**) SSL

suavizado *nm Autoedición* feathering

◇ *suavizado de caracteres* character smoothing

◇ *suavizado de contornos* anti-aliasing

subdirectorio *nm* subdirectory

subíndice *nm* subscript; **"a" escrita como subíndice** subscript "a"

submenú *nm* submenu

subred *nf* subnet

subrutina *nf* subroutine

suma *nf* sum

◇ *suma de comprobación* checksum

◇ *suma de control* checksum

sumidero térmico *nm* heat sink

superautopista de la información *nf Internet* information superhighway

supercomputador *nm Am* supercomputer

superíndice *nm* superscript; **"a" escrita como superíndice** superscript "a"

superordenador *nm Esp* supercomputer

supletorio *nm Tel* extension

surfear *Fam* **1** *vt* to surf **2** *vi* to surf

SVGA (*abrev de* **Super Video Graphics Array**) SVGA

tabla *nf* table

◇ *tabla de referencia* look-up table

tableta *nf* tablet

◇ *tableta gráfica* graphics tablet

tablón de anuncios (electrónico) *nm Internet* bulletin board service

tabulador *nm* tabulator, tab; **separado por tabuladores** tab-delimited

tabular *vt (texto)* to tabulate, to tab

táctil *adj* touch-sensitive

tamaño *nm* size

◇ *tamaño de la letra* type size

tarea *nf* task

◇ *tarea en segundo plano* background job *o* task

tarifa *nf*

◇ *Internet* **tarifa de alta** joining fee

◇ *Internet* **tarifa plana** flat rate

◇ *Internet* **tarifa plana mensual** flat-rate monthly charge

tarjeta *nf* card

◇ *tarjeta aceleradora* accelerator card

◇ *tarjeta aceleradora gráfica* graphics accelerator card

◇ *tarjeta adaptadora* adapter card

◇ *tarjeta de ampliación* expansion card

◇ *tarjeta CompactFlash®* CompactFlash® card

◇ *tarjeta controladora del disco* disk controller card

◇ *tarjeta de fax* fax card

◇ *tarjeta gráfica* graphics card

◇ *tarjeta inteligente* smart card

◇ *tarjeta lógica* logic card

◇ *tarjeta magnética* magnetic card

◇ *tarjeta de memoria* memory card

◇ *tarjeta de módem* modem card

◇ *tarjeta de monitor* display card

◇ *Tel* **tarjeta (de) prepago** prepaid card

◇ *tarjeta RDSI* ISDN card

◇ *Tel* **tarjeta de recarga** *Br* top-up card, *US* replenishment *o* refill card

◇ *tarjeta de red* network card

◇ *tarjeta de registro* registration card

◇ *tarjeta SmartMedia®* SmartMedia® card

◇ *tarjeta SCSI* SCSI card

◇ *Tel* **tarjeta SIM** SIM card

◊ *tarjeta sintonizadora de TV* TV tuner card
◊ *tarjeta de sonido* sound card
◊ *tarjeta telefónica* phonecard
◊ *tarjeta de* Esp *vídeo* o Am *video* video card

TCP/IP *nm* Internet (*abrev de* **transmission control protocol/Internet protocol**) TCP/IP

tecla *nf* key

◊ *tecla alt* alt key
◊ *tecla de avance de página* page down key
◊ *tecla de ayuda* help key
◊ *tecla de bloqueo de desplazamiento* scroll lock key
◊ *tecla de bloqueo numérico* numbers lock key, num lock key
◊ *tecla de comando* command key
◊ *tecla de control* control key
◊ *tecla de cursor* cursor key
◊ *tecla de dirección* arrow key
◊ *teclas de edición* edit keys
◊ *tecla de encendido* power-on key
◊ *tecla esc* esc key
◊ *tecla de escape* escape key
◊ *tecla fin* end key
◊ *tecla de flecha abajo* down arrow key
◊ *tecla de flecha arriba* up arrow key
◊ *tecla de flecha derecha* right arrow key
◊ *tecla de flecha izquierda* left arrow key
◊ *tecla de función* function key
◊ *tecla de impresión de pantalla* print screen key

◊ *tecla de inserción* insert key
◊ *tecla de interrupción* break key
◊ *tecla intro* enter key
◊ *tecla de mayúsculas* shift key
◊ *tecla de mayúsculas fijas* caps lock key
◊ *tecla modificadora* modifier key
◊ *tecla de movimiento del cursor* arrow key
◊ *tecla multifuncional* multifuntional key
◊ *tecla numérica* number key
◊ *tecla de opción* option key
◊ *tecla de pausa* pause key
◊ *tecla de retorno* return key
◊ *tecla de retroceso* backspace key
◊ *tecla de retroceso de página* page up key
◊ *tecla de suprimir* delete key
◊ *tecla de tabular* tabulator key, tab key

teclado *nm* keyboard

◊ *teclado alfanumérico* alphanumeric keypad
◊ *teclado expandido* enhanced o expanded keyboard
◊ *teclado extendido* extended keyboard
◊ *teclado inalámbrico* cordless o wireless keyboard
◊ *teclado numérico* (numeric) keypad
◊ *teclado QWERTY* QWERTY keyboard

teclear *vt* (*datos, texto*) to key (in)

teclista *nmf* keyboarder

técnico, -a *nm,f* tehnician

La disposición del teclado inglés

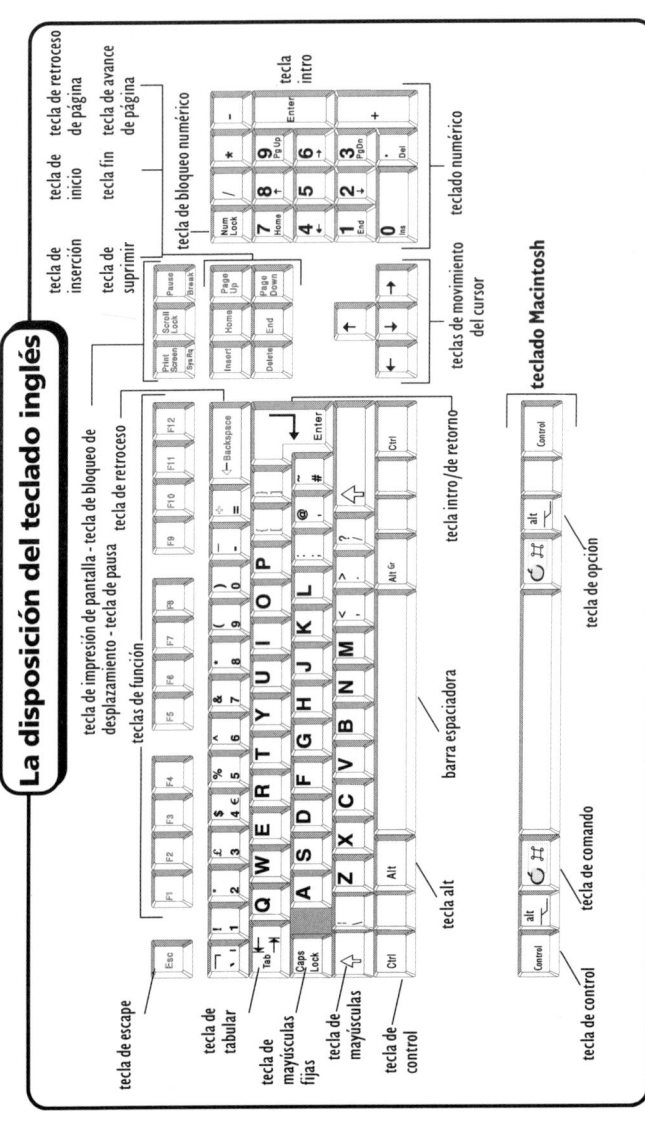

tecla de impresión de pantalla - tecla de bloqueo de
desplazamiento - tecla de pausa

teclas de función

tecla de retroceso

tecla de escape

tecla de tabular

tecla de mayúsculas fijas

tecla de mayúsculas

tecla de control

tecla alt

barra espaciadora

tecla intro/de retorno

tecla de inserción

tecla de suprimir

teclas de movimiento del cursor

tecla de bloqueo numérico

tecla de retroceso de página

tecla de inicio

tecla de avance de página

tecla fin

tecla intro

teclado numérico

teclado Macintosh

tecla de control

tecla de comando

tecla de opción

◇ *técnico informático* computer technician

tecnologías de la información *nfpl* information technology

tel (*abrev de* **teléfono**) tel

telaraña mundial *nf Internet* World Wide Web

telebanca *nf* telephone banking

telebanco *nm* telephone banking

telecompra *nf* home shopping

teleconferencia *nf* teleconference

teléf. (*abrev de* **teléfono**) tel

telefonear 1 *vt* to telephone **2** *vi* to telephone; **telefonear a Nueva York** to telephone New York

telefonía *nf* telephony

◇ *telefonía básica* basic telephony

◇ *Am telefonía celular Br* mobile phones, *US* cellphones, mobile telephony; **el mercado de la telefonía celular** the *Br* mobile phone *o US* cellphone market

◇ *telefonía fija* fixed telephony

◇ *telefonía por Internet* Internet telephony

◇ *telefonía móvil* mobile telephony; **el mercado de la telefonía móvil** the *Br* mobile phone *o US* cellphone market

Telefónica *nf* (*empresa*) = main Spanish telecommunications company, formerly a state-owned monopoly

telefonista *nmf* telephonist, (switchboard) operator

teléfono *nm* telephone

◇ *Esp teléfono 900 Br* ≃ Freefone® number, *US* ≃ 1-800 number

◇ *Am teléfono celular* cellular phone, *Br* mobile phone, *US* cellphone

◇ *teléfono gratuito Br* Freefone number, *US* toll-free number

◇ *teléfono inalámbrico* cordless telephone

◇ *teléfono por Internet* Internet telephone

◇ *teléfono de marcado por tonos* touch-tone telephone

◇ *teléfono sin SIM* SIM-free phone

◇ *teléfono de tonos* touch-tone telephone

◇ *teléfono WAP* WAP phone

◇ *teléfono web* web phone

telemática *nf* telematics

teleproceso *nm* teleprocessing

teletexto *nm* teletext

Telnet *nm Internet* Telnet

tema *nm Internet* topic

temperatura del color *nf Autoedición Br* colour *o US* color temperature

terabyte *nm* terabyte

terminador *nm* (*de cadena*) terminator

terminal *nm* terminal

◇ *Am terminal de computadora* computer terminal

◇ *terminal inteligente* intelligent terminal

◇ *Esp terminal de ordenador* computer terminal

◇ *terminal remoto* remote terminal

texto *nm* texto; **enviar un mensaje de texto a alguien** *(con teléfono)* to text sb

◇ *texto en ASCII* ASCII text

◇ *texto oculto* hidden text

◇ *Autoedición texto simulado* Greek text

textura *nf Autoedición* texture

tfno. *(abrev de* **teléfono**) tel

TFT *nm (abrev de* **thin film transistor**) TFT

TI *nfpl (abrev de* **tecnologías de la información**) IT

tiempo *nm* time

◇ *tiempo de acceso* access time

◇ *tiempo de acceso al disco* disk access time

◇ *Tel tiempo de antena* airtime

◇ *tiempo de búsqueda* search o seek time

◇ *tiempo de conexión* connection time, on-line o online time

◇ *Tel tiempo de conversación* talktime

◇ *Tel tiempo en espera* standby time

◇ *tiempo de procesamiento* processing time

◇ *tiempo real* real time; **en tiempo real** real-time

◇ *tiempo de respuesta* response time

TIFF *nm (abrev de* **Tagged Image File Format**) TIFF; **archivo TIFF** TIFF file

tilde *nf* (a) *(acento gráfico)* accent

(b) *(de la ñ)* tilde

(c) *(en URL)* swung dash

tipear *vt Am (datos, texto)* to key (in)

tipo *nm* type

◇ *tipo de letra* typeface

tipografía *nf* typography

tóner *nm* toner

tono *nm* (a) *Tel* tone

(b) *Autoedición (de color)* tone; **medio tono** half-tone

◇ *Autoedición tono continuo* continuous tone

◇ *Andes, RP Tel tono de discado o de discar* Br dialling o US dial tone

◇ *Autoedición tonos de gris* shades of Br grey o US gray

◇ *Tel tono de llamada* Br dialling o US dial tone

◇ *Tel tono de marcado o de marcar* Br dialling o US dial tone

◇ *Tel tono de ocupado* Br engaged tone, US busy signal

◇ *Tel tono de portadora* carrier tone

topo *nm Autoedición* bullet

torre *nf (computadora)* tower

tostar *vt Fam (CD-ROM)* to burn

trabajo *nm* job

◇ *trabajo de impresión* print job

traducción *nf* translation

◇ *traducción asistida por Esp*

ordenador *o Am* **computadora** computer-assisted *o* computer-aided translation
◇ **traducción automática** machine translation

traducir *vt (software)* to translate

traductor, -ora *nm,f (de software)* translator

tráfico *nm Internet (de sitio web)* traffic
◇ **tráfico de datos** data traffic
◇ **tráfico de red** network traffic

transacción electrónica segura *nf Internet* secure electronic transaction

transceptor *nm* transceiver

transferencia *nf* transfer
◇ **transferencia de archivos** file transfer
◇ **transferencia de datos** data transfer
◇ **transferencia electrónica de fondos** electronic funds transfer
◇ **transferencia electrónica de fondos en el punto de venta** electronic funds transfer at point of sale
◇ **transferencia de ficheros** file transfer
◇ *Tel* **transferencia de llamadas** call transfer

transferir *vt* (**a**) *Tel (llamada)* to transfer
(**b**) *(datos)* to transfer

transmisión *nf* transmission

tratamiento *nm* processing
◇ **tratamiento electrónico de datos** electronic data processing
◇ **tratamiento de imagen** image processing
◇ **tratamiento de textos** *(programa)* word processor; *(actividad)* word processing

3G *Tel (abrev* **third generation***)* 3G

troyano *nm (virus)* Trojan Horse

tubo *nm RP, Ven (de teléfono)* receiver, handset
◇ **tubo de rayos catódicos** cathode ray tube

tunelado *nm* tunneling

tutorial *nm* tutorial

UAL *nf* (*abrev de* **unidad aritmético-lógica**) ALU

UCP *nf* (*abrev de* **unidad central de proceso**) CPU

UMTS *nm Tel* (*abrev de* **Universal Mobile Telecommunications Services**) UMTS

unidad *nf* (*de disco*) drive; **unidad a:/c:** a:/c: drive

◊ *unidad aritmético-lógica* arithmetic logic unit

◊ *unidad Bernoulli*® Bernoulli® drive

◊ *unidad de CD-ROM* CD-ROM drive

◊ *unidad de CD-RW* CD-RW drive

◊ *unidad central de proceso* central processing unit

◊ *unidad de cinta* tape unit

◊ *unidad de coma flotante* floating point unit

◊ *unidad para copias de seguridad* backup unit

◊ *unidad para copias de seguridad en cinta* tape backup unit

◊ *unidad DAT* DAT drive

◊ *unidad por defecto* default drive

◊ *unidad de destino* destination drive

◊ *unidad de disco* disk drive

◊ *unidad de disco duro* hard drive

◊ *unidad de disco externa* external disk drive

◊ *unidad de disco interna* internal disk drive

◊ *unidad de DVD* DVD drive

◊ *unidad de DVD-RAM* DVD-RAM drive

◊ *unidad de DVD-ROM* DVD-ROM drive

◊ *unidad externa* external drive

◊ *unidad interna* internal drive

◊ *unidad Jaz*® Jaz® drive

◊ *unidad predeterminada* default drive

◊ *unidad de procesamiento de gráficos* graphics processing unit

◊ *unidad RAID* RAID drive

◊ *unidad Zip*® Zip® drive

unir *vt* (*archivos*) to merge

Unix *nm* Unix; **basado en Unix** Unix-based

URL *nf Internet* (*abrev de* **uniform resource locator**) URL

USB *nm* (*abrev de* **universal serial bus**) USB

Usenet *nf Internet* Usenet

usuario, -a *nm,f* user

◊ *usuario final* end user

◇ *usuario* *registrado* regis-   **utilidad** *nf* utility
tered user

vaciar *vt (papelera)* to empty

vacío, -a *adj (papelera)* empty

validación *nf* validation

validar *vt* to validate

valor *nm* value
- ◇ *valor ASCII* ASCII value
- ◇ *valor por defecto* default value
- ◇ *valor predeterminado* default value

variable *nf* variable

velocidad *nf* speed; **un CD-ROM de velocidad 32x** a 32 speed CD-ROM; **de alta velocidad** high-speed
- ◇ *velocidad de acceso* access speed
- ◇ *velocidad de escritura* write speed
- ◇ *velocidad de impresión* print speed
- ◇ *velocidad de la impresora* printer speed
- ◇ *velocidad de parpadeo* blink rate
- ◇ *velocidad de parpadeo del cursor* cursor blink rate
- ◇ *velocidad del procesador* processor speed
- ◇ *velocidad de proceso* processing speed
- ◇ *velocidad de refresco* refresh speed
- ◇ *velocidad de reloj* clock speed
- ◇ *velocidad de transferencia* transfer rate
- ◇ *velocidad de transferencia de datos* data transfer rate

ventana *nf* window
- ◇ *ventana activa* active window
- ◇ *ventana de ayuda* help screen
- ◇ *ventana dividida* split screen
- ◇ *ventana flotante* floating window

ventilador *nm* fan

versalita *nf Autoedición* small caps

versión *nf (de software)* version, release
- ◇ *versión alfa* alpha version
- ◇ *versión beta* beta version
- ◇ *versión completa* full version
- ◇ *versión demo* demo version
- ◇ *versión limitada* lite version
- ◇ *versión de prueba* trial version

VGA *(abrev de* **Video Graphics Array***)* VGA; **Super VGA** Super VGA

vibración de llamada *nf (en teléfono móvil)* vibrating alert

vídeo *nm Esp* video

◇ *vídeo a la carta* video-on-demand

◇ *vídeo digital* digital video

◇ *vídeo interactivo* interactive video

video *nm Am* video

◇ *video a la carta* video-on-demand

◇ *video digital* digital video

◇ *video interactivo* interactive video

videoconferencia *nf* video-conference

vínculo *nm Internet* link (**a** to)

viñeta *nf Autoedición* bullet

virgen *adj (disquete)* blank

virgulilla *nf* (**a**) *(de la ñ)* tilde (**b**) *(en URL)* swung dash

virtual *adj* virtual

virus *nm inv* virus; **desactivar un virus** to disable a virus; **sin virus** virus-free

◇ *virus informático* computer virus

◇ *virus de macro* macro virus

visita *nf Internet (a sitio web)* hit, visit; **esta página web registró 20.000 visitas durante la semana pasada** this web site counted 20,000 hits last week

visitante único *nm Internet* unique visitor

visor electrónico *nm* electronic viewfinder

vista preliminar *nf* print preview

visualizador *nm* viewer

◇ *visualizador de archivos* file viewer

◇ *visualizador de ficheros* file viewer

visualizar *vt* to display, to view

viuda *nf Autoedición* widow

volcado de memoria *nm* memory dump

volcar *vt (memoria)* to dump

volumen *nm* volume

VRAM *nf (abrev de* **video random access memory***)* VRAM

VRML *nm (abrev de* **virtual reality modelling language***)* VRML

WAN *nf* (*abrev de* **wide area network**) WAN

WAP *nm* (*abrev de* **Wireless Application Protocol**) WAP

Web, web 1 *nf* (*World Wide Web*) **la Web** the Web
2 *nm o nf* (*página web*) web site

webcam *nf* webcam

webmail *nm* webmail

Word *nm* Word; **está en Word** it's in Word; **un documento/archivo de Word** a Word document/file

World Wide Web *nf* World Wide Web

WORM (*abrev de* **write once read many times**) WORM

WWW *nf* (*abrev de* **World Wide Web**) WWW

XML *nm* (*abrev de* **Extensible Markup Language**) XML

zócalo *nm* socket

zoom *nm* zoom
◇ *zoom **digital*** digital zoom
◇ *zoom **óptico*** optical zoom